Wild Man

Wild Man

BY TOBIAS SCHNEEBAUM

With Illustrations by the Author

New foreword by David Bergman

The University of Wisconsin Press

The University of Wisconsin Press
1930 Monroe Street
Madison, Wisconsin 53711

www.wisc.edu/wisconsinpress/

3 Henrietta Street
London WC2E 8LU, England

1   3   5   4   2

Printed in the United States of America

Library of Congress Cataloging-in-Publication Data
Schneebaum, Tobias.
Wild man / by Tobias Schneebaum, with illustrations by
the author ;
with a new foreword by David Bergman.
p. cm.
Originally published: New York: Viking Press, 1979.
ISBN 0-299-19344-6 (pbk. alk. paper)
1. Schneebaum, Tobias—Journeys. 2. Voyages and travels.
I. Title.
G465.S36   2003
910'.92—dc21   2003050129
[B]

To Floriano and Andrew

The trouble with life isn't that there is no answer, it's that there are so many answers. There's the answer of Christ and of Buddha, of Thomas à Kempis and of Elbert Hubbard, of Browning, Keats, and of Roosevelt. By turns their answers fit my needs. And yet, because I am I and not any one of them, they can none of them be completely mine.

RUTH BENEDICT, *An Anthropologist at Work:
Writings of Ruth Benedict,* edited by Margaret Mead

The more enlightened lamas teach that man—or any other being—by his thoughts and actions, creates affinities which, quite naturally, lead him to a kind of existence in keeping with the nature of these affinities.

ALEXANDRA DAVID-NEEL
Magic and Mystery in Tibet

Acknowledgments

I wish to thank warmly Berenice Cortelle, Claire Brook, and Richard Selzer, who read the manuscript and made valuable suggestions. I am grateful to Richard Seaver and Jeannette Seaver, who suggested the book and saw it through many phases. And I am deeply indebted to the work of Father Gerard A. Zegwaard, the first white man to settle in Asmat.

I also wish to thank the Corporation of Yaddo and the Ossabaw Island Project for giving me the opportunity of working without distractions, as well as Belle Notkin Burke and David Burke for their extraordinary generosity.

Foreword

David Bergman

Tobias Schneebaum is the author of four remarkable autobiographical works: *Keep the River On Your Right* (1969), *Where the Spirits Dwell* (1988), *Secret Places* (2000), and *Wild Man*, which was originally published in 1979. Of these, *Wild Man* has for many years been the hardest of the books to lay hands on. In part, its scarcity comes from never having been published in paperback. But there has been another problem. *Wild Man* was published at a time when Viking Press was experimenting with new binding techniques, and the result is that the books break easily apart. Of the three copies I have had, only one is together, and this is because I rarely open it. To read *Wild Man* is to hold a volume that separates page by page. In some ways this is a wonderful metaphor for the book, which is about self-destruction as a form of self-renewal and about the search for a way to escape the materialism and brittleness of American culture, but it has made finding and reading *Wild Man* difficult and frustrating. Although briefly available from an electronic publisher, this is the first time in nearly a quarter century that *Wild Man* has been in print. And this is also a metaphor for Schneebaum's life and work—his continual renewal and transformation. Now in his eighties and suffering from Parkinson's disease, Schneebaum still travels—albeit not to remote places—and has met his first live-in lover, the sort of relationship he has always wanted and thought he would never have.

Schneebaum did not become an author until relatively late in life; he was forty-eight. Up until then, he devoted himself to the visual arts. But in 1969, the year of the Stonewall riots, Tobias Schneebaum published *Keep the River on Your Right,* his account of living a decade earlier among the Harakhambuts, a cannibal community in the jungle headwaters of the Amazon. During his time with them, he was presumed dead, since no outsider had survived an encounter with these war-like people.

Keep the River on Your Right soon developed a cult following, and like so many books of this sort, it was surrounded by controversy. Its explicitly homosexual content was revolutionary at the time, for Schneebaum wrote not only unapologetically about being gay, but also rapturously about his sex with the men. Then there was Schneebaum's report of participating in a cannibal raid. Although not accused of murder, he was attacked for depicting aborigines as man-eaters. Anthropologist friends of mine—who are expert in the area—claim there are no cannibals in that region; indeed, some scholars claim that cannibalism is a myth created by early explorers and missionaries to justify their brutal oppression of supposedly "primitive" people. The book's beautiful prose and extraordinary narrative structure suggested to others that *Keep the River on Your Right* was a work, if not entirely of fiction, at least dependent on a certain amount of poetic license. Some people even doubted that Schneebaum had made contact with the Harakhambuts at all since he could not account for the fact that he alone, of all the foreigners they encountered, had not been killed but was instead adopted into their ranks.

The recent documentary about Tobias Schneebaum does not answer all of these questions, but it does show Schneebaum returning after nearly fifty years and meeting several of the Harakhambuts with whom he lived. But anyone who had met Schneebaum did not have to wait for the film to know that he was telling the truth as he knew it. He is a man of such child-like simplicity that he could not have sustained such a lie. Indeed, it's this very quality that probably saved him from being killed by the Harakhambuts and why they made an exception for him. For Schneebaum is exceptional. You feel it immediately. It is not that he is physically imposing or particularly good-looking (I first met Schneebaum in his seventies, but photos of him as a young man show a person who, while not as ugly as he claims to have been, was never a beauty). But he is surrounded by an aura of permanent wonder and a saintly lack of pretension.

This aura of simplicity, openness, and wonder has protected him time and time again from a world whose complexity, violence, and misunderstanding he not only accepts, but also welcomes. As he writes in *Wild Man,* the idea that the wild men whom he sought "might kill and cannibalize me . . . occurred as a hope, a suggestion that always underlay the strength and virileness that I expected of him." In such a passage Schneebaum does not shy away from the expression of masochistic desire, nor does he try to dramatize it. He acknowledges the hope that he might be consumed by his very experience, since for him all true communion is self-destructive as well as self-constructing.

A decade after *Keep the River on Your Right* appeared, Schneebaum published *Wild Man*. It was not clear to him that he would ever write another book after *Keep the River on Your Right*. After all, he was a painter, not a writer, and there was so much more to do, so many more journeys to take, so many places yet to see. Still it must have occurred to him that his first book told merely an episode in a much, much longer story, and that just as he needed to continue to explore and paint, he also needed to continue writing the account of what he was becoming. Moreover, he had finally found the people who would consume his interest for the rest of his life— the Asmat of Irian Jaya. *Wild Man* is much more an autobiography than *Keep the River on Your Right*, and it provides a far clearer portrait of Tobias Schneebaum. In addition, *Wild Man* is filled with his wonderful drawings, which are more than illustrations. The best of them continue the story. Quick and precise, suggestive and shaky, they mirror the excitement, curiosity, and eroticism of his prose.

At issue is what the "wild man" means for Schneebaum. Schneebaum is no academic anthropologist, although in his fifties he went back to school to learn how to catalogue the artifacts of indigenous peoples and has become an expert in Asmat art. His journey in search of the wild man is a journey of personal compulsion and enlightenment, and is not entirely separable from the Western fantasy of the primitive. Indeed, as he recounts in the early pages of *Wild Man*, his desire to meet up with people untouched by Western civilization grew out of the sideshow curiosity he encountered as a boy in Brooklyn, when the Wild Man of Borneo was exhibited on the boardwalk of Coney Island. It is a sign of Schneebaum's ruthless honesty that he does not try to hide that his lifelong preoccupation with the wild man began in a Barnum & Bailey–like tawdriness.

Yet if Schneebaum's image of the wild man began in vulgarity, it developed in an environment of brutality, loss, and isolation. One needn't be a psychologist to see the connection between Schneebaum's wild man and his father. Both are brutal, terrifying forces that seem to hover at the edge of extinction. But the wild man can give what the father cannot— love, ecstatic joy, community, and acceptance. Schneebaum is quite aware of the connection. Toward the end of the book, for example, he goes to sleep with Bimanum, the Asmat who has adopted him as a son:

"I huddled up to my father, closer to his warmth. I huddled up to my father in Brooklyn and he moved away. My mother had just died, relatives slept in my bed with my brother, and I was left alone. I put my hand on my father's hip and he turned away. Bimanum pushed himself back into me, clasped my hand and held it against the muscles of his chest."

Quite literally, the wild man possesses a warmth that Schneebaum's biological father lacks, a warmth that American society has taught fathers to avoid, to be fearful of showing, and to be ashamed of possessing. If the wild man is also violent, it is not the ongoing, resentful, uncathartic violence of his biological father, a violence that, because it is never fully expressed, is never expiated. The wild man's violence may end with a blood bath—indeed, it is with such a scene that *Wild Man* concludes—but it is a cleansing act, one that gives peace, rebirth, and joy.

Schneebaum's father lacked more than warmth; he lacked the spirituality that Schneebaum needs. An orthodox Jew, Schneebaum's father initiated his son into his own dry, pinched, calcified form of faith. The father's narrowness is exemplified in the incident when he knocks over the telescope that Schneebaum and his brother Moe, who was to become a NASA physicist, had put together, shattering the lens and mirrors. "No-goods!" the father yells at them. "Wasting time and money on this nothing when I'm busy in the store." The father has no sense of the majesty of finding Arcturus and Betelgeuse. In contrast, the wild man brings a cosmic sense to his daily life; indeed, it is the cosmic importance of even small acts that makes his world so violent.

Schneebaum's wild man, although rooted in Western thinking, is not the same as Rousseau's noble savage. The wild man may live closer to nature than the New Yorker, but he is not a child of nature. In fact, Schneebaum has no illusions about nature's benignity. One of his adopted mothers is a woman ravaged by yaws, and he describes the horrors of the disease with the same painstaking precision he uses to describe everything else. "There was a hole where her nose had been," he writes, "and parts of her lips and ears were gone, leaving scars of dried sores. There were no lids to her round, shining eyes." When he is directed to suckle from her breast as part of the adoption ritual, Schneebaum writes honestly that he "wondered whether yaws was infectious" and that the breast "tasted like cardboard." But the horrors of nature, rather than repelling Schneebaum, excite and attract him. "I envied them their life in wilderness. I envied even their early death, the pain of unset bones, the diseases that ravaged them. I envied them the spirit, the fears, the apparitions that ruled their lives and made them one." Schneebaum does not screen out the pain and suffering of the Asmat. He takes it as part of the whole of their lives. But he does not see it—as so many have—as a way to diminish their existence.

This elaborate ritual of adoption is only one of many that Schnee-baum describes, and his point is not only the beauty of these ceremonies, but that the wild man is as intricately wrought by history, social custom, and religion as the New Yorker; in fact, he is more closely bound by tra-dition. What the wild man has avoided is the commodification and in-ternal isolation of the Westerner.

For Schneebaum, Western society has made a bargain: it has ex-changed community for individuality. Individualism is based on the isola-tion of the person; it erects a barrier even in the most intimate of situa-tions, and it invites tension, competition, and intragroup violence. It also makes possible the remarkable expressions of Western art, the achieve-ments of science and technology. Unlike several of the people Schnee-baum meets in his journey, he never decides to live entirely among the wild men either by settling permanently in a village or by creating a small colonial outpost. He can tolerate the loss of individuality only so much. But, as T. S. Eliot wrote in "Tradition and the Individual Talent," in which he articulates his impersonality theory of art, "only those who have personality and emotion know what it means to want to escape from these things."

Among the Asmat, Schneebaum was able to lose his individuality. It was a bit shocking for me to read about his first encounter with them when he declares: "They were the wild man as I had always envisioned him." I am sensitive to the subtle violence of plurals becoming singular, such as when Jews become The Jew or when women become Woman. Such linguistic slides are often a sign of bigotry. Yet Schneebaum is not entering into this conversion of plural into singular naively; he wants to emphasize the loss of individuality among the Asmat and their unity as a people.

In one passage he describes the houses of one tribe. They live in low two-story dwellings. The first floor is for eating, and the second floor—reached through a narrow hole in the ceiling—is for sleeping. The sec-ond floor is so dark, that when Schneebaum reaches it, he turns on his flashlight. There he discovers the men resting "with their heads to the outer edge of the hut, their feet to the center, lying like spokes of a wheel." When Schneebaum lies down, he too becomes "another spoke of the wheel." It is a mystical moment of feeling a part of a larger whole, and Schneebaum realizes:

Being that spoke should have satisfied me then, satisfied ideas and images and thoughts, I was even coupled with a wild man in a way that might have made us one; I might have dissolved and been absorbed by him, might have absorbed him into myself. But I was wanting then a different closeness, an emotional intimacy, not sex, though that too, not love, though that too, but an absolution from past living, a dissolution of him *through* me that would filter out absurdities, stupidities, my humiliations. I rent my soul and guts, pulled them to pieces. I, a spoke of the wheel, was thinking back to my father, my pain of him, never, almost never, thinking of my mother's love, thinking only of the pain he brought and I accepted.

Even at the threshold of becoming just one more spoke in the turning world, Schneebaum is brought back to his own individual history, his own personal pain, and that most Western of spiritual notions, absolution. It is in this moment—one of many—that, despite himself, Schneebaum learns the wild man cannot give him what he cannot give himself.

But we can be grateful that Schneebaum can never quite content himself with being yet one more spoke on the wheel of the men's house. Had he been satisfied, he would never have written *Wild Man* or drawn the pictures for this volume, he would not have come back to us and told us of his journey. There is another reason, I suppose, that Schneebaum never becomes a mere spoke. It would have meant that his own development would have ended. For the loss of individuality is also a loss of spiritual evolution. Even in his eighties, Schneebaum continues to discover new parts of himself, new possibilities of living. Now that he is closer than ever to his death, he seems as open to the possibility of living as he has ever been. The wild man remains with him and in him, but he is always also looking out—despite the shattered mirror—toward Arcturus and Betelgeuse and the ever expanding universe, trying to grow slowly with it and toward its violent beauty.

Introduction

Return to Peru

When WILD MAN was published in 1979 by Richard Seaver and Viking Press, it was a resounding flop. My first book, KEEP THE RIVER ON YOUR RIGHT, which had come out ten years earlier, had attracted both positive and negative attention, partly because its subject matter dealt (briefly) with same-gender love as well as same-gender sex and (still more briefly) with cannibalism. As the years passed and I reflected on both books time and again, I wondered what it was that attracted some readers to my work and concluded that in revealing my innermost feelings concerning my sexual attitudes, I led some gay men and women to a better understanding of the predicament in which they found themselves. I have always been writing what I think of as truth about myself and, on occasion, I do think I have done just that. I had opened a Pandora's Box of secrets that some readers were eager to unlock for themselves but feared retribution in the workplace and/or at home. I received several phone calls and letters from both men and women who had read KEEP THE RIVER ON YOUR RIGHT, asking whether or not I had copies of WILD MAN for sale. Although they knew it had been published, they could not find it in the bookstores, they said. Hence the republication of WILD MAN in this edition.

Happily, KEEP THE RIVER ON YOUR RIGHT is still in print and has been so for the past thirty years. The climate at the time for books with homosexual themes was not a happy one, although it was better than it had been a few years earlier. Gore Vidal has been lucky enough to have the chance of rewriting parts of THE CITY AND THE PILLAR, the first edition of which had come out in the late 1940s. He rewrote the book some years later in order to return to it the strength, the temperament and the animus that Vidal had wanted in the first place. Fritz Peters, who wrote a fine novel of the same period, called FINISTERE, was asked by his editor to change the ending from a happy one to an ending that was tragic, to conform with contemporary ideas concerning what interested the public and what was obscene. Novels and biographies with homosexual themes were dismissed or were reviewed badly as a matter of principle. Publishers rejected such material almost out of hand. Some satisfying novels have been written on the subject and were published, although authors had to keep in mind the fact that the book's ending had to be a tragic one for the main characters. Few publishers would risk putting into print anything that was sympathetic to homosexuals and had a happy ending. It is not that all books with story lines that dealt with homosexuality were rejected but that publishers were wary of anything that might be thought of as sexually offensive. Of course, "obscene" was the operative word at the time since its interpretation was open to various definitions. Surprisingly, John Rechy's CITY OF NIGHT (1963) fared well in spite of its explicit sexual content between men. In fact, it fared well because of its content, because of its originality and its place in the hierarchy of the history of gay novels. This book is surely destined to be printed year after year.

WILD MAN is a book about myself in various societies. It is a book in which I allow myself to speculate on a number of themes, perhaps most often on sexual matters. But it is also a book on travel, a book on people who live in communities that some call primitive, a book with drawings that show the remarkable beauty of men and women in their own environment, in climates warm enough for them to need no clothing or almost none. They were not aware that their bare bodies revealed more of themselves than would fully clothed beings, how they are part of the forest and part of the gardens of cassava. It is about other ways of living, other ways of thinking. It moves around in time and place, from a brief visit with the Dalai Lama above McCleodganj in northern India to an intoxicating affair with a warrior in Borneo. The scene is set in four continents: in Africa, in South America, in North America and in Asia, in addition to the dream world I created for myself. There is no straight narrative, no story line for the reader to follow from first page to last.

The lands in which I sought comfort filled me with thoughts of erotic love, and of the wonders wrought inside me by Borroughs' Tarzan as he traveled through the trees, yodeling his mournful cry that even now breaks my heart. He was alone in his early life even though he lived with and loved the gorillas that took him in and fed him He was an intriguing version of the wild man, another being who captured my head and heart. Tarzan seemed easier to search out than the original wild man, for he resembled the Caucasians he finally met, who took him out of the green jungle to live in the drab jungle of city life. It did not take long for him to return to his beloved forest and his primate family.

In the Murut village of Pensiangan in North Borneo, population a little under 200, I met Mathurin Daim, the assistant district officer, who taught me more in ten minutes than in all my years of travel. His questions and statements sometimes left me bewildered but he was always sympathetic with me. Mathurin and his wife were Kedazans, a group of people who lived along the coast of North Borneo. When I was there, they were living among the Murut who were noted for having been headhunters. Mathurin had been educated by a Catholic priest in a Catholic school, where he could not bare to be close to the priest who taught there. The horrific aroma that came from his black garments, mixed with his body odor, made Mathurin gag when the priest was close by. The lack of cleanliness among the Caucasians troubled most of the local people. When I asked what the smell came from, Mathurin insisted that it was from the unwashed clothing the priest wore. He often stayed away from class simply because he could not bare that smell. "You do not seem to be troubled by my smell," I said, "unless you are just being polite." "Oh, no," he said." My wife also commented on your lack of foul odors. It must be that you have been eating the same foods that we normally eat, especially the rice."

Mathurin seemed to have a number of gripes to confess. "The way the English blow their noses into a rag and then put that dirty rag back in their pockets, is positively disgusting. Or the way they sit in a bathtub of dirty water and wash themselves with that, is just as revolting. The river is infinitely cleaner."

WILD MAN did not fit into any literary category. It was not particularly well-written and was neither erotic nor offensive (except to extremists) but did verge on the explicit. Soon after its publication and its disappearance from book shelves, a friend suggested that I look for a publisher who might reprint it in a longer version, one that would make for a stronger work. I would concentrate on the section of the book that dealt with my family when I was growing up in Brooklyn. However, I preferred leaving the text as is except for the addition of this Introduction.

Today, pornography is easily found in bookstores in New York. Few novels are written without explicit descriptions of sexual acts and contain an abundance of such words as fuck, shit, cock, cunt and prick, take your pick. Dildos are found in shop windows as are photographs of naked men with hard-on's and naked women sucking one another's tits. TV producers now seem to vie with one another in searching out programs that are more outlandish than anything seen before. Discussions on television of sexual activities are becoming more and more graphic. All can be seen in subway kiosks and on television programs that discuss the most explicit activities. It is difficult to get away from this kind of material. Only a few years ago, this openness would not have been tolerated but now such programs are broadcast all afternoon and late at night. I like this new way of looking at the body in action since it gives both men and women an opportunity to talk freely about their sexual lives, thereby relieving them of the burden of hiding same-sex love from the general public. There is no question but that this new-found freedom is healthier than the repression that was formerly seen in the U.S. Even the hilarious Dr. Ruth struggles to open the minds of those too terrified of frank talk to go to Confession or to the office of a therapist.

Some problems can be inferred from nothing more than a glance at the statistics of the high rate of suicide among gay teenagers, particularly those with homophobic families. The rate of suicide continues to rise. The young have not yet learned to cope with this frightening increase in the death rate of their peers. It is sad that while many are coming out of the closet, there remain hundreds of thousands who are demoralized by the idea of admitting that they are homosexual.

Although in my youth, I never knew what it meant to be queer, I did know what it meant to engage in sexual relations with another male. Such pleasures were too insistent, too tenacious, too urgent to ignore. I did learn to open up in various ways when travelling in distant lands with relatively uncultivated people. I knew that I was sexually attracted only to men but I did not have the experience to know what to do or how to go about making a direct pass at someone who might respond to my approaches. I never knew the ramifications of such gestures. I knew enough to keep my mouth shut but not much else. To be queer, for me, was to accept an appellation that was derogatory. Maybe that was part of the pleasure, that I was doing the forbidden, acting out the worst of my daydreams, the delicious nightmares that left my sheets stained. To be queer was something I learned by keeping my ears as well as my eyes open. It did not happen through anyone telling me what was going on but by my taking part in a sexual performance itself. I was frightened of sexual contact, yet there were encounters that could surely be called satisfactory. Not many, to be sure but when I began to travel (first in Mexico in 1946) I began to expand my horizons. Even in the distant past, I learned that wearing a ring on one's pinkie meant the wearer was queer. The more I traveled, the more I saw men who liked men. Knowing there were others like me unburdened me. So it was in this way that I learned the process of integrating myself into societies that saw nothing wrong in life styles that included men sexually involved with other men. There is no question but that this new-found freedom is healthier than the repression seen in the U.S. in former times.

During my time in Peru on a Fulbright Fellowship, I rarely found opportunities for casual sex-or for sex of any kind, for that matter. It was much simpler for me in the headwaters of the Amazon where the men I met wore nothing but the paint on their bodies. Still, the short stature of the people of the Andes and their bulkiness attracted me almost as much as the people of the jungle who were somewhat taller and had narrower frames. The warmth of those bodies of the mountain people at 10,000 feet above sea level was very pleasant indeed.

The fact is that I regretted leaving the Amazonian jungle where everything was simple for me. The group with whom I slept, huddled together in a darkness that surrounded us like a cloud, enveloping us so that the only sensation we conveyed to one another was one of touch. Nothing could be seen beyond the line of banked fires that ran through the center of the great house. I regretted leaving there, but I could no longer stay.I could no longer escape the dreams that protected me and devastated me. I could not simply cut away those hours we had spent on the raid and hide that time in some corner of my brain. I could no longer live with people who might, at any moment, go off on another raid, to kill, to cannibalize. To think of it pained me, made my body ache. I left my friends then to return to my origins, thousands of miles from the Madre de Dios River, only five hundred feet away from where we slept.

I had had an astonishing time, living with and loving men. True, I had not formed any relationships with women but it was too difficult to talk to them. They were too shy. Too frightened, even after we had lived in the same big house for some months. The men, however, were more than enough for me. They were right there at night, every night. They were right there, sometimes pushing their penises into me, giving and taking pleasure. To leave was to give up a closeness that I felt had turned my world upside down, giving me the appearance of loving and of being loved.

I do not understand what it is to love. Perhaps it is nothing more than an overwhelming moment of deep affection. I know that I have always wanted to feel love; I have always wanted to be fondled, caressed, sucked, fucked. I wanted it all right there in the midst of that great forest of the Amazon, with all the decay beneath my feet, the trees reaching up to openings in the screen of leaves and from the darkness stretching even further upwards to sky. I do not know what I felt, only that it was glorious at times. I who, in my youth, had complained bitterly to myself over and over that I had no one with whom I could share my bed, no one to love. I had found a place where I was accepted, the dream of my adult life, though there were strings attached that were connected with violent death. Even now, so many years later, I cannot articulate what was going on in my head, whether it all was real or whether it was hallucination.

One day, six or seven years ago, I was asked to return to Peru by a pair of film-makers, Laurie Shapiro and her brother David Shapiro, whose roles as Producer and Director were interchangeable. They hoped to make a film based on KEEP THE RIVER ON YOUR RIGHT. They wanted to film me on location in the forest of the Amazon. I was not particularly interested in returning to the region that had been the subject of my first book. I had liked Peru immensely but the year and a half I had spent there was enough. In truth, at age 78, I was not looking for a place that was as strenuous as the formidable Andes and the jungle of the Amazon. I did wonder what it would be like to meet old friends there but there wasn't much chance that anyone would still be alive after forty-five years. I did not want my memories disturbed, did not want them completely changed, for that was certain to happen if we met people who had known me.

We flew from New York, spent two nights in Lima and then went on to Cuzco, which did not to me appear to have changed in the least. We retraced my route to Machu Picchu and then took a strange vehicle, part bus, part truck, that made travel on land relatively simple. There were five of us on that trip down into the vast jungle: the cameraman John Kovel, the sound engineer, John Murphy, the Shapiros, and our guide, Barry Walker. The landscape was spectacular with one mountain range after another. The local people knew what they were doing when they built the city of Machu Picchu in that Sacred Valley of the Incas. It was completely unknown to the Spanish. In fact, it wasn't until 1911 that Hiram Bingham discovered Machu Picchu, which he apparently thought was the lost city of Vilcobamba, famous for its gold and other riches.

It was cold at 14,000 feet, cold during the day and colder still at night. The whole feeling of the valley was one of sanctity. There were terraces everywhere but unlike my first visit when numerous crops were visible, most of the terraces then lie fallow, dried up, partly because of a lack of rain. There were fields of corn and fields of barley, both to be used for making beer. As everywhere in the world, the population was moving to the city.

From Machu Picchu, we went down to Pilcopata, thousands of feet below. It was a comparatively new town, considerably dilapidated in spite of its recent construction. Seeds of the hamlet I had known forty-five years earlier might still be found there. We met a Senor Rivas on the street in front of a small grocery shop and even had a telephone. He had been in the area since 1958. He knew the man I call Fr. Moiseis in the book, who had invited me to stay at the mission back in 1955/56. Senor Rivas seemed to have a phenomenal memory for he almost immediately said he remembered me. I did not recognize him and had no idea who he was. He called over a small group of people who pointed out where the mission had been. Barry, who was determined to find out exactly where I had lived, took up a copy of KEEP THE RIVER ON YOUR RIGHT, and pointed out the contours of the landscape which looked exactly like the photo on the book jacket, almost proving to me that we were at the right spot. It was where I had spent one night with the Harakhambut on the Rio Madre de Dios.

True, it looked like the right place but I remained uncertain. It was where I had first met the Harakhambut, a name the people insisted was their real name, not Amarakaire. I was reluctant to agree that the photo and the actual landscape were one and the same. Senor Rivas' memory was remarkable but he had not arrived in this part of the jungle until after I left. My own memory is faulty but I cannot imagine having met Senor Rivas and then forgetting him completely. There were a few people in Pantiacola who immediately recognized me and although I could not recognize anyone of them, I did trust them. Certainly, Jesus Jesus not only knew me but could remember where the gardens of cassava, the lemon tree and avocado had been. For a while, I kept getting confused about what was real and what was not. The people were ready to show me not only where I had slept but where the pool in the jungle was in which Manolo and I used to swim.

We went to Shintuyu which did look like what my visual memory evoked. We went to the gardens of Alejo and Marta, neither of whom said they knew me until after I took out some enlarged photos I had brought along. After a time, Marta held up a photo and said, "Oh! Oh! This is my father. This is my father!" She jabbed the photos with her forefinger and took them around to show everyone. "This is my father! My father!" Alejo looked at the photo of me taken forty-five years ago and cried out that he recognized me.

Most of the people I might have known were there in San Jose. Some from Shintuyu were also there. A chair was brought out for me. Others sat on the ground. Everyone was exhilarated by my presence and by the photos. I was never certain as to who was telling the truth and who were the ones who really did recognize me. It was like group memory, everyone having one consciousness, all apparently remembering me right after someone else remembered me. Several described with great comic timing the ways in which I tried to learn how to use the bow and arrows. They were very funny and I could not help but laugh at myself. Some described Manolo of KEEP THE RIVER ON YOUR RIGHT perfectly. I too talked of Manolo who was a strong but tragic character in the story of my stay there. No one seemed to know what happened to him. It was thought that Manolo had done something that offended the spirits.

Everyone remembered Fr. Moiseis with great affection. "He was a good man," they said. He was exactly as the people described him, thick white beard, bent back, wearing a filthy white cassock. His humpbacked assistant Hermano, apparently had died through some freak accident during which he was killed by his brother with a spear. Hermano and his brother heard a noise and thought it was some animal close by. Hermano had been in the jungle with Fr. Moiseis for over thirty years.

Our guide, Barry, returned to Cusco; his place was taken over by a young German woman named Jessica Bartrami whom I liked very much from the first. The people seemed to trust her.

We had a dinner party at Pantiacola Lodge with Marta, Alejo, Wancho, Mario, Jesus Jesus, and Guido. David invited them all to the lodge for dinner. It was a marvelous time, a celebration of my life, so to speak, with Jesus Jesus doing most of the talking (in Spanish) He talked of my being remarkable. His praise for me was for a man who had traveled thousands of miles just to see his old friends when he himself was already old and infirm.

He called me a great man, always with my light shining onto people, exuding love and friendship. I spoke, David Shapiro spoke. Tears welled up in the eyes of us all. Jesus Jesus wept openly.

One of the Harakhambut came up to me and asked that I go with him to the house of Ari'ke, in the jungle. He had been bitten in the leg by a snake and could barely walk. I agreed to go the following morning. The house was said to be less than an hour's walk away. Back in 1955, it was said, we had slept together in the big house with four other young men, all now deceased. Although I had agreed to go to Ari'ke's house, I awoke the next morning to find him right there in San Jose. He had been so afraid that he would miss me that he decided it was wisest for him to come to me. He was using two branches as crutches. I stood and watched him, this man whom I did not recognize. I watched him slowly change, shedding the wrinkles of his face, shedding the years until he came to look like someone I had known, someone I had loved, someone handsome and wise. We had been close. Slowly, we began to recognize one another. I could see the tears in his eyes and feel my own tears running down my cheeks. He came over and we hugged one another. I left with the film crew the next day.

Wild Man

Chapter One

I have always lusted after the Wild Man of Borneo, and my earliest memories reach back to him. The picture I see now in my mind is of a caged creature in a sideshow, half man, half ape, human or orangutan I don't remember. I was six or seven at the time. That first sight of him in the cage, his existence there, the context of him, the very presence of him, startled and confused me and filled me with the wildness of his look. He took hold of me, captured me, and turned my insides on end. I was in Coney Island at the time with my two brothers and my mother, she herding us along Surf Avenue into the dark shadows under the boardwalk. I took off my clothes and put on my bathing suit and ran down the beach to the water's edge. The sun was hot, but I was shivering. He'd stayed with me, that creature, rattling around my heart and brain, and visions of him loaded me down with fear and terror, longing and excitement. I sat in the sand and molded shapes of beings with long hair, gorillas and yaks, men with long nails and bent legs, and unknowingly, I was molding a shape of him inside myself, with my body hurting, my mind unthinking, not sensing in any way that I was accepting into myself the eternal presence of pain and pleasure. On occasion, we went to the beach on dark nights, for my mother had skin cancer and had been advised to bathe naked in the salt water of the sea. The wild man could not be seen then, but his image appeared as soon as we neared the ocean and heard the roar of the surf.

It is nowhere known to me that I ever understood who or what the wild man was, what he meant to me, and who I was in his connection; yet something of him insisted on pushing itself into me, moving me on; something was paining me, forcing me into a search, a yearning that had nothing to do with the life I was living then or with the life of later years or with the thought of any future that could come within the range of my imagination.

My youthful years were agonizing. I felt a need to hold the wild man, to touch and taste him, but I never understood my thoughts. Woman was the only object of man's needs, though I shied away from contact with all but my mother and remained frightened and tormented by my inabilities. I was thin and unattractive; I was silent and suppressed. I knew nothing of sex but the pages of Maggie and Jiggs, of Popeye and Olive Oyl that made the rounds from desk to desk at school.

To pass the days and years, I turned the Hebrew alphabet into abstractions, sitting at the kitchen table, teaching myself to draw, learning to hide my fears and depression. I found myself contained in time, a time that enveloped me, enabled me to search out the world and the whole of my interior for the responses that gave me life. Inside there, I could look forward into my future, always the same, for I was always wandering, running, flying through the forest, sparkling, glistening, exuding water from my pores, my skin covered with beads of perspiration, lust welling up, beating its way through my bowels and glowing up my whole interior, lighting up my outer self so that I sometimes lived in marvels of exhilaration. And it was *he* who was the object of it all, the one that I would love.

All through those years, all through my life, sometimes barely beneath the surface, the wild man was with me. I think I'd seen a loneliness in him, a terrifying sameness that I could not identify or recognize; but I knew that he was different as I knew that I was different, never knowing why or in what way. When I thought of him, my face flushed with heat, and mist appeared in front of me. At night there were dreams, as there were always dreams, waking ones and sleeping ones: I run, I run, and the forest is all around me. It nurtures me and fills me with longing for that elemental apparition. Always in the years that pass, I see him in an isolated time, living fierce and strong, his body hewn of ironwood, my own ancestor, my own self, flying through the trees. And when he moved within me and shook me, when he flows along my bloodstream, I ache and yearn to yell out, to yell at the top of my lungs, to release the voices, the forces, the days and nights, the destinies, the terrors and beauties that make up the meaning I give to myself. He flowed and thumped and vibrated and eased and took possession of all of me, so that I saw him everywhere, in everything that meant romance and mystery, in everything that was primitive and distant, strong and violent, everything that was full of love and hate. I summoned him up in shamanistic names like Zululand and Oxiana, Machu Picchu and Sumatra, and I dreamed to find him in the selves I lived in painting, in the selves I lived in future times and places.

I tremble at the thought of the vanished lives and boundless stretches of wilderness that are my futures. From childhood and youth to now, I search; I look for him, the whole of myself, the total man whom I've never satisfied, no matter where I go, no matter what I do. Is it then a dream I want, or is it reality? Was fulfillment no more than an illusion in South America? Does rest or satisfaction never come? Oh, yes! I tell myself. Oh, yes! My goal, my wildest self, is always there ahead of me, another step, one more step to take me there beyond the dream, to where, I dare not even think.

My parents had arrived in New York as immigrants from Eastern Poland. They lived, unknown to one another, on the Lower East Side, where my father sold eggs from a pushcart on Avenue B, and my mother was janitor for the buildings on her block, carrying up the cans of ash and garbage. A matchmaker arranged a meeting, and they married for the sake of marriage, I suppose, certainly not for love. My older brother and I were born without a doctor in a fifth-floor railroad flat, and on both occasions my mother was shoveling coal the day after giving birth. By the time I was four, my father had saved enough money to buy a small grocery store in Brooklyn, and we moved to Third Avenue, to a neighborhood of Scandinavians and a hospital, in which my younger brother was born. We lived in three small rooms behind the store: my mother, my father, my brothers, and myself. My mother's brother came from Europe to live with us, and when he married, his wife moved in as well. They had a baby that lived six months, and when it died my uncle bought a store for himself, with help from my father, and moved away. He was replaced by another uncle and other relatives, all of whom arrived secretly, stowaways who managed to legalize their presence with money in the right hands and trips to Canada.

My father was obsessed with religion and discipline, demanding to the point of irrationality, I thought, and full of unrelenting cruelty. He was not a pious man but believed in the anger and vengeance of the Lord. He never smiled at us or showed a single sign of affection. Yet in the afternoon he would sit at the kitchen table, read the story in the *Jewish Daily Forward,* and weep in sympathy with the characters. He often said his father used to beat him every day and it was therefore only right that he should do the same to us. Those early years, and even later ones, as I remember them, were full of never-ending battles—arguments between my mother and my father that even now I can hear with anguish. I listened, always fearful, always cringing in some corner, hiding inside some secret place, until I discovered that I could draw and paint and live inside that world as well. We grew up, my brothers and I, frightened of my father, even hating him, and loving my mother for her gentleness. She died of cancer at the age of thirty-seven; my father, twenty-five years later. He was lonely at the end of his life. Having alienated his children with his brusque and violent ways, he lived alone until cancer attacked his bowels. My younger brother took him into his home, but my father preferred his own bed. I stayed with him until he went into the hospital and felt nothing for him when he died.

They say, my relatives, that my mother was never so beautiful and gentle as my memory demands, and that my father was often kind and generous to his friends. He was certainly more than a series of isolated incidents; but my most vivid memories are these:

On the afternoon of July 4th, in 1929, I turned the corner of Third Avenue and Senator Street in Brooklyn, on my way to deliver groceries to Mrs. Landsen. As I made the turn, I noticed a group of boys scattering and then heard an explosion. My right eye began to itch, and I put my hand up to it. I went on to deliver the order to Mrs. Landsen, but she wasn't home. I left the package on the stoop and went back to Third Avenue. In the middle of the block, Mrs. Izzo was

4

standing outside her husband's shoe parlor, in front of the window in which rows of tagged shoes were displayed. She looked at me, leaned forward, frowned, and said, "Come here! Come here! What have you done to your eye?" She took me through the store into a back room and gently washed my face. I looked into the mirror and saw blood running from one side of the eye. I became frightened at the thought of my father and ran back to the store, holding a handkerchief over the eye. I walked slowly past my father, who was behind the counter waiting on a customer. When I entered the kitchen, my mother was rolling out dough on the table. I uncovered my eye and burst into tears. My mother immediately enveloped me with her small body. I cried out that it wasn't my fault, that I had done nothing but walk around a corner. She took off her apron, smoothed the bun of her hair, and pushed in loose pins. She said something to my father as we went through the store. He rushed out from behind the counter and smacked me in the face. "Didn't I tell you not to play with firecrackers! I hope you're blinded for life!" Dr. Kopp, on Sixty-eighth Street, said it was a minor injury, that the tiny piece of shrapnel from the cherry bomb did not touch the eye itself. I wore a bandage for several weeks and had the discomfort of seeing with only one eye, so that the world was flat.

My older brother and I used to deliver milk and rolls at six every morning. We worked again in the store after school, filling the shelves with needed stock, bringing cases of goods up from the basement, taking down the cartons and boxes that might have been stacked on the sidewalk by the jobber's truckman, delivering whatever orders there were, and sometimes waiting on customers as well. Even in our preteens, we were efficient at cutting slabs of butter from the tub or pieces of gjetost or Gouda to an almost exact weight, and we knew how to cut the bread or smoked salmon in even slices.

My brother received the same unpleasant treatment from my father that I did, but my mind tells me only of myself, of the times I was slapped and shoved and slandered. I have no memories of kindness on my father's part and cannot evoke a single moment of ease between us. It is true that later, in 1946, I worked with him in his store on Eighty-sixth Street and he rarely complained of anything I did, but I choose now to remember only the times of fury.

I admired my brother Moe, was was eighteen months older than I, and I often copied his ways. He was clever and more experienced and he knew how to calm my father's anger. Sometimes he diverted my father's rage from me, taking it onto himself, for I knew only how to sulk and hide within myself. Bernie, my younger brother, seemed to have an easier life, for he was not yet old enough to work. His time would come, but he learned early the value of humor and was able to make my father laugh. I felt myself different from my brothers but could not understand why. When I was older, I used to wonder: Did my father seek me out to punish me? Or did I seek the punishment myself?

There was a garden behind our three rooms in back of the store. With money saved from tips he and I had earned delivering orders, Moe sent away for a telescope kit. We set the disk of glass in pitch on top of an empty pickle barrel we'd filled with rocks to keep it steady, sprinkled it with carborundum, added a few drops of water, and began the precise and tedious movements of rotating the glass on top that would curve the lower one into a reflecting mirror. We were very proud when we finally put the whole thing together and were able to look up and find Arcturus and Betelgeuse. My father came out one afternoon and knocked it down. The tube of the telescope cracked and the mirror broke into several pieces. "Fools!" he yelled at us. "No-goods! Wasting time and money on this nothing when I'm busy in the store and your mother's out shopping for *shabbos*!"

About twice a month, on Monday mornings, I would wake up and find my father at the kitchen table with several of his friends. "Oh!" one of them would say. "The kids are up. It's time to go home." The decks of cards would be gathered up and put away. My mother would serve coffee; the men would stretch and count their winnings or losses and go on their way. These Sunday night pinochle or poker games were one of my father's great pleasures. It was a time when we children felt less uncomfortable, for my father never complained on those nights. We watched the games and sometimes earned a nickle or two by running across the street to the candy store when a new pack of cards was needed or to Vogel's Saloon for a pitcher of beer. My father's one other pleasure was going to the fights and wrestling matches at Fort Hamilton on Tuesday and Thursday nights. He usually came back from those performances angry about the niggers who pushed him and the whites who, like all *goyim,* got drunk and

6

noisy. Moe was sometimes taken along because he was overweight and my father used to talk of what a big man he'd be one day. My father was proud of this and spoke of his becoming a wrestler. Moe never said a word about his future plans, but he laughed at the obvious fakery of the wrestling matches and infuriated my father by mentioning it. My father could not believe that the pain was not real when the contenders grimaced and cried out. Moe wore steel-rimmed glasses from the age of ten and was always at the head of his class. He faced my father's outbursts in 1937 when he enrolled at City College. My father never understood why he chose to study physics and mathematics rather than to train for the ring. When Moe went into the army in 1942, he got the highest mark ever recorded on the IQ test and then was promptly put into the military police as a buck private. His first duty was as guard at a prisoner-of-war camp in Texas. He was "promoted," as he said, into the Signal Corps a couple of years later but was never allowed much use of his brain. In the 1960s, he sent up NASA's first satellite, designed and worked on several others, and finally, shortly before his death from cancer in 1973, saw his Earth Resources Satellite successfully in orbit. Posthumously, awards were heaped on him, but my father had not lived to see this.

Even now, when I think back to the months of my mother's final illness, I become agitated and disturbed. Not from the thought of her cancerous womb or from her death itself, but from my own lack of understanding, my childlike misinterpretation of what I saw and did not understand.

In 1935, the board of health forced us out of our rooms because of overcrowding. We moved above the store to the apartment that was vacant at the time. Not long afterward, my mother went into the hospital. She was going in for tests, she said. I don't remember which hospital it was because we were never allowed to visit her. I know it wasn't Montefiore because I do remember that her brother died there of cancer a few months after her death. Later, we learned (my father, too, for she had told no one but her elder brother) that the surgeon had opened her abdomen and closed it after a look inside. She seemed fine when she came home. Two months later, she fainted, was put to bed, and awoke unable to speak. She could open her eyes and move her arms, but her mouth could make no words. She stared and blinked her eyes. She slept in the front room in the large bed she shared with my father, and my father continued to sleep there with her. A nurse came in during the day, from eight to four. The rest of the time, I took care of her, feeding her and washing her hands and face, trying to understand her talk, trying to teach her the movements of tongue and lips that would form words, and watching her get weaker and weaker. One day, there was a conference in the living room. Two or three male relatives were talking to the doctor. I remember hearing only this: "But if she's dying, why can't you pack her in ice and see what happens? We have nothing to lose, have we?" It was the first time I understood that she was near death, for only weeks before I had read in the newspaper of experiments in freezing cancer to stop its progression.

In the middle of that night, I woke up, got out of bed, and went to the bathroom. I heard moans from my mother's bed. The door to the bedroom was open, as it always was. My mother was on her back and my father was on top of her, being cruel to her, hurting her in some way, for each time he pressed down, she let out an agonizing groan. I wanted to go in and pull him away from her, but instead, I went into the bathroom, strained to empty my bladder, and returned to my bed, still hearing the sounds of pain in my ears.

When my mother died, I did not believe in her death, though I was at her side when it happened. For months I searched for her in the subways, standing and watching strangers come down the stairs, following them from car to car, sometimes from station to station. I don't know why the subway intruded on me in this way, but the roar of the train was like the moans she made that night. A few weeks later, I was assaulted by a headache so painful that I took to bed for the first time since my brothers and I had had measles when I was five. The doctor came, gave me some pills, and said it would pass. Ice packs, the pills, and darkness were not much help during the next twenty hours, but the pain finally went away. It returned two weeks later and visited me regularly twice a month until I left my father's household in 1942.

By then, I'd been at City College almost four years, having followed my brother's footsteps by majoring in math, though I also took courses in art. I had already been at a WPA school for two years, working from nude models. The drawings I'd done there had to be hidden from my father, for he was horrified by nudity and considered it dirty, just as words like "sex" or "penis" were never to be mentioned in front of his children.

Moe and I had continued to work in the store before and after school. When he graduated, he took a job in Pompton Lakes, and I worked on alone. I usually arrived at the store around three in the afternoon and waited on customers while my father candled eggs in the back. Mrs. Eagan telephoned one day and ordered a case of Pabst. I told my father I was delivering the beer and asked the price. "Three dollars and twenty-five cents," he said, or so I thought. I rang the money up on the register when I got back. When my father saw the amount there, he threw up his hands and yelled, "What's the matter with you, you fool! Don't you ever learn anything? I told you three seventy-five, not three twenty-five. Are you deaf or something? Get out of here! I don't want you in the store! Get out!" I went out, got the extra fifty cents from Mrs. Eagan, and put it down in front of my father. He lifted his arm, swung at me, and knocked me down. I walked out of the store, went home, packed a bag, and went to the house of a relative. It was then a few weeks after Pearl Harbor, not a difficult time to decide what to do.

My training in math, unlike Moe's, turned out to be useful during the war, and I became a radar mechanic, receiving instruction at the Philadelphia Signal Depot and then at the Philco School at Rutgers University. I ended up at Baer Field in Fort Wayne, Indiana, where I checked the equipment on the ground and in the air but spent most of my time in the radar shop, changing resistors, capacitors, and tubes. There was a tool crib in which a plump, blonde Wac from a small town in Indiana worked. Whenever any of us in the shop needed equipment or tools, we ordered and signed for them at the crib. I had been there eight or nine months, signing out material at least once a day, when the Wac asked where I came from. I told her I was a New Yorker.

"Then you must be Catholic," she said.

"No, Grace, not Catholic. I'm Jewish, like a lot of other people in New York."

"Jewish?" she squealed out in horror and jumped back. "But I *liked* you!"

Frank Brendel, the sergeant in charge of the tool crib, later said that Grace refused to believe me. I must have been kidding her. After all, she said, I had no horns and looked like everyone else. Even so, she never spoke to me again and avoided looking at me whenever I came up for stock or tools.

I was stationed in Fort Wayne for two years, keeping mostly to myself, as I had always done. Every once in a while Bruno Haake, a chubby, balding Dutchman from Pennsylvania who worked at the bench next to mine in the shop, insisted that we go out double-dating. He always found a girl for me and didn't question my never initiating romantic encounters. He was paying court to Janet, a woman fifteen years older than he was, thin, fast, overly rouged and lipsticked. She usually wore a ruffled petticoat that showed below her skirt. We often went roller-skating at the indoor rink on the edge of town.

One night, a nineteen-year-old girl came along with us. She was fleshy and good-humored and wore her hair in long ringlets. I don't remember her name, but I remember she skated well. Bruno was very taken with her, and after a few beers we exchanged partners. Janet took hold of me as if she were a novice and afraid of falling. During our third or fourth turn around the rink, she pulled or pushed me so that I fell on my back, and she fell on top of me, face down. She lifted her head, smiled down at me, kissed me on the lips, and rubbed her body against mine. She put her hand between us and fondled me through my trousers. I was hot, flushed, embarrassed, scared, repelled by the smell of her perfume. I rolled over, stood up, and pulled her to her feet. She laughed and skated away, turned, came back, and took hold of my elbow. On our way to the base, we stopped for a last drink at Janet's house, a frame building with a railed porch in front and a covered swing in the yard under an elm tree. We went inside and sat at the kitchen table and drank from a bottle of rye. Haake took the nineteen-year-old into the dark living room, and Janet put out the kitchen lights. I wanted to run out of the house, to tell her that I didn't want her, didn't like her, that I had hated the whole evening. I was terrified by her aggressiveness, by my own virginity, by my anxieties of impotence. She unbuttoned my pants and reached inside. The heavy smell of her was making me gag and I feigned dizziness. "Shit!" she said, and then called out, "Hey, Haake! Come and take your buddy home. He's passing out!" It was the closest I ever got to getting laid in all those years.

After the war, I went back to work in my father's store and at night attended the Brooklyn Museum Art School and studied with the Mexican artist Rufino Tamayo, a brilliant painter of the time but not a good teacher. He had, however, an infectious enthusiasm for his country, and under his influence, when I had saved the money, I took a bus down to Mexico City and stayed at Paris Siete, a pension recommended by a cousin of mine. Though I didn't understand the implications when I moved in, because the relative had never indicated his political or emotional attachments, the pension was owned and run by the Arenál family, who had been prime movers in the Mexican revolution and were said to have devised the murder of Trotsky. David Alfaro Siqueiros was married to one of the Arenál daughters and was there for lunch almost every day; he liked my drawings and invited me to join his workshop, but I preferred to work alone. Another daughter had married Pablo Neruda and spent most of her time in Chile. She turned up for a week while I was there and was the center of attention. Diego Rivera and other political painters came to meetings on the ground floor once a week. A third daughter, a dentist who had been enamored of the cousin who had recommended the pension, also attended these meetings. At that time I understood no Spanish and only glanced into the meeting room once or twice.

An elderly woman, a Rumanian osteopath, lived in the penthouse and often asked me up for meals. One day she announced that she was going to visit a former patient in the small village of Ajijic on Lake Chapala and invited me to accompany her. Ajijic was up the lake from the village of Chapala, where D. H. Lawrence had lived and Tennessee Williams had visited.

The patient, Zara Alexeyeva Ayenara, lived on the edge of the beach in Ajijic, in a house whose ceilings were all painted with blue skies full of white clouds. On most of the walls were photographs and paintings of her adopted brother, a Russian who had been a great dancer, they said, and who had recently died. Above the piano was the largest portrait of him, a stunningly beautiful man in the costume of the Specter of the Rose. Señora Ayenara, who was born to a different name and life-style in Pennsylvania, always wore clothes that had been designed for her by her brother: long-sleeved, long-skirted garments covered with embroidery. Her graying hair was worn in long braids that gave her a peasant quality belied by the elegance of her carriage and style. She never left the compound of her house and garden on foot but went everywhere on her huge, brown, well-curried horse. She bathed in the lake, riding into the water on horseback to the level of her horse's flanks, then floating off in sweeping breaststrokes. Once I saw her silhouette in the moonlight, whirling along the beach in wide turns and reaching toward the stars with swaying motions, while her radio played Tchaikovsky's *Pique Dame* at top volume. When Zoe came the following year, she sometimes played Liszt on the piano while the Señora danced at the water's edge. The agreeable character of the village and its people, plus the eccentricity of the señora and the three other foreigners who lived there, fused into an atmosphere that led me to stay on, and I remained almost four years, painting and having occasional exhibitions in Mexico City and Guadalajara.

A young blond painter, born in Guadalajara of German parents, also lived in Ajijic. He was twenty-seven, blue-eyed, four inches over six feet, and very handsome, and was subject to the attentions of both the men and the women who later passed through town. In spite of his height, one never had a feeling of hugeness about him or of being dwarfed by his stature, for he bent himself to the level of his companions. He was engaging and irresistible; he was slender and deeply tanned and had just the right amount of softness to his body and mind so that he threatened no one. His family owned property in Ajijic, fields of corn and beans through which he moved like a country squire. Ajijic was small, with a population of three thousand, barely a third of whom had homes in the village itself, the other two-thirds living on their farms. He knew everyone by name and was adored and respected by old and young alike. He'd changed his Germanic name to Linares, to identify more closely with the country of his birth, and liked to be called Lynn. He painted during the day with bright reds and yellows in wide bands of color, freely brushed and dripped on, a technique he claimed preceded Jackson Pollock, who he insisted had seen his work. He'd had one-man shows in New York and Mexico City. He entertained at night, his guests coming from Chapala, a larger village, or from Guadalajara, sixty miles to the north over a rutted road, or even from distant Mexico City. Two or three times a month, he gave big parties with local mariachis playing throughout the night. I liked his hospitality, his generosity, and his whole manner of living. He was a good cook and rarely served anything but Mexican foods.

There were two other foreigners in Ajijic at that time, Herr Müller and Fräulein Müller, a German brother and sister at whose pension—the only one in town—I stayed for months. Both were misanthropes and kept to themselves, rarely talking even to each other. Each took an evening walk along the beach alone, passing but never acknowledging the other's presence. Both dressed in khaki shorts and shirts, and they resembled each other to some extent, though he was thin and gaunt, while she was heavy with fat. When the Rumanian osteopath returned to Mexico City, I was their only guest. I liked the solitude of the day and painted on the porch of the small house in which I stayed. I walked into the hills every afternoon and on the way home stopped at Lynn's for a glass of tequila or rum.

Nicolas arrived during my third month and stirred the vitals of Ajijic. He was easily as tall as Lynn and was cold, haughty, and grand, an exquisite who moved with conscious suppleness and settled down with the air of one who knew his own charm. He too was a painter and had come down from Black Mountain College, where he was a protégé of Josef Albers, who visited him later that summer with his wife, Anni. Nicolas's paintings were as tight, involuted, and hard-edged as his body, and were somber with browns and dirtied yellows, unlike the clarity, brilliance, and simplicity of the work of his teacher. He talked mysteriously of his Croatian background and hinted at royal blood and family madness. His sister was with him for a few weeks, a pale creature with a delicate, ethereal look about her, and an incestuous love for her brother. When she left, Nicolas and I took a house together for a month, hired a maid, painted, and gave dinner parties.

Nicolas and Lynn were so different from each other it was almost inevitable that they would fall in love. Lynn's casual ways bewitched and irritated Nicolas, just as Nicolas's arrogant, snobbish manner attracted and mortified Lynn. Nicolas moved into Lynn's house and began a frenzied, volcanic affair that lasted two years. Sometimes Lynn woke me at two or three in the morning and asked to spend the night. At other times, it was Nicolas knocking at my door. When life together turned out to be too explosive, Nicolas bought the property on which they lived and forced Lynn to move out. They continued to see each other, spending most of the time in bed, until Nicolas involved himself in the sybaritic crowd of Guadalajara, inviting them to dinner parties with good wines, his own cooking, and imported mariachis. He was captivated with Alfredo, an exceedingly handsome, aristocratic, hedonistic young man with a pencil moustache and black eyes, who drove into Ajijic in a yellow convertible and took Nicolas away for days at a time. Except when he was out of town, Nicolas never allowed his painting to suffer from any emotional crises and was always in his studio by nine in the morning. Lynn stopped working altogether and began his day with large glasses of rum for breakfast, circulated vitriolic stories of Nicolas's satanic soirées, and accepted hordes of strangers into his bed. My own relationship with them varied according to what was happening between them at the moment. Both confided in me, and I regretted only that I hadn't the courage to further our intimacy. I had hoped that when Nicolas and I moved into the same house, we would be more than housemates, but Nicolas was not interested in me physically, only in the comfort and admiration I could give.

I felt outside them both, my allegiance to Lynn having diminished with the arrival of Nicolas, and the immediate closeness between them shutting me out. I was hurt when Nicolas ignored me in the house we shared, and I fell into despair when he moved out. Everything around me was empty—my room, my table, my canvases, my self—and I could do no work. The paintings I had been doing for an exhibition later in the year in Mexico City had been going well, somewhat influenced by Lynn and by his large collection of pre-Columbian art. But my urge to paint evaporated when Nicolas left, and I could only stare at my blank canvases.

I had made no sexual advances to Lynn and had been content with a hug when we met and another when we parted. I had not been able to move into a more intimate alliance except in my fantasies, for I was frightened that any obvious gesture on my part would lead to rejection. It wasn't until Lynn's meeting with Nicolas and the clear attraction between them that I sensed the backwardness of my behavior. Yet, sensing this did not stop me from transferring my affections to Nicolas, even though, or perhaps because, he was already pursuing Lynn. It was as if I had willed myself to choose only those who would not return my desire.

During their first weeks together in what seemed like harmony, an anguish so intense came over me one morning that I took nineteen phenobarbital tablets and went to bed. Nicolas came by two hours later to invite me to lunch and, when he couldn't awaken me, threw a bucket of water in my face and went for Lynn. Nicolas stuck a finger down my throat and I threw up in great pain. He and Lynn then took turns walking me back and forth for hours and forcing black coffee into me, Nicolas screaming all the time, "You shit! You damned self-ish bitch! Why the fuck did you have to put me through this mess!" It wasn't until I had taken the pills and lay upon the bed hating myself that I became aware of the depth of my jealousy of their relationship. It took weeks for me to recover. Though they invited me to meals, I could not face Nicolas or Lynn without shame, and so I stayed in my house alone until I was able to paint again and then gave a big party.

Zoe became a fourth member of our group. Haughty and radiantly beautiful, she had a deep laugh that came from some unknown depths inside her. When she laughed she lifted her chin, closed her eyes, and tossed her straight black hair around her bare shoulders. She wore sheath dresses of black or white and penciled dark lines around her eyes to shape them into almonds and enlarge the black pupils. Her skin was pale, the color of pearls, and against it was the color painted on her lips by Nicolas. She had quickly become ob-sessed with him, and he encouraged her in the extravagance of her appearance. They spent hours together every night while Nicolas ar-ranged her hair in various styles and coated her face with makeup and sequins. After dinner, the voices of Edith Piaf and Charles Trenet would come from the record player, and they would dance with their slender bodies tightly together, moving to slow foxtrots and tangos, dipping deeply, and turning with elegance and grace.

Although it was Nicolas who most attracted Zoe, she had come down to Ajijic because she'd heard of Lynn in Big Sur, where she had lived with Henry Miller. She had earlier given up hope of a career as a concert pianist when her intelligence and good ear told her of her musical limitations. When invited, she would play Señora Ayenara's piano, and Nicolas and Lynn and I would sit on the beach and listen.

Less often, we watched the señora dance along the shore to her music.

The parties that Nicolas and Lynn gave, together or separately, were often huge and always ended with Zoe dancing out into the night with Nacho, the bus driver with whom she had a long affair. Pairs of young men, dazzlers in the most chic garments, would dance with passion and then go off together while I sat in pain and watched them embrace and move into the darkest corners and other rooms. In my silence, my stillness, no emanations went out from my body or voice to cause others to notice me, to pause and look; perhaps the pain released vibrations that screened me from them, for I had not yet dissolved my fear of gratification. In my self-abasement, I was too invisible for anyone to approach me.

Manolocito, brought several times by Alfredo for the pleasure of all, was given to me one night. His comely appearance and his snobbish self-assurance, in contrast to my wretchedness and inexperience, led to failure and humiliation. No sooner had I wrapped my arms around his body and had he touched me with his friendly hands, when I burst forth into them and heard his voice in ugly tones, "For Christ's sake!" And again, he said, "For Christ's sake!" and turned aside and went to sleep. I was mediocre, I was even less than that, no good for anyone, least of all a whore.

Nicolas also dreamed. He was a Croatian prince who dispensed largesse and had only to lift a finger to move a man or mountain. He built a world around himself as I did and was equally vulnerable, though he was up and I was down, he the receiver of adulation, I the receiver of contempt. He was loved and I despised. Yet he too could awaken from his dream.

Alfredo led a fleet of cars from Guadalajara one afternoon, and Nicolas's house became crowded with young men. We drank for hours from the gallons of rum Alfredo had brought, while men and boys sat on the ecru cloth of the living room couches holding hands or looking longingly into one another's eyes, others clinging to each other, stilled in positions of dance by their ecstasy. Zoe was at a moment of pause in a tango with Lynn, her body arched backward, arms stretched out, fingers touching the floor. Her hair shone with sparkles, as did her eyelids, also covered with them. Lynn swung her around and a falsie popped up above the line of Zoe's dress. "Haha!" she laughed, then shouted, "I don't want them! I don't need them!" and took them out and sailed them across the room. She pulled the top of her dress down below her breasts and Lynn bent over her to kiss her nipples.

"How small they are," she said in sadness. She laughed again. "They're just like a boy's! Just like a boy's!" She pushed Lynn away and paraded around the room. *"Mira, chicos!* I'm a boy! I'm a boy!"

A young man wearing a transparent blouse and nothing more grabbed the falsies and cupped them to his breast. *"Mira!"* he shouted. *"Mira, hombres! Mira, mira!"*

In another room, Nicolas sat stiffly on a chair, leaning forward, holding Alfredo's chin in one hand, a thin brush in the other. He was painting purple onto Alfredo's lips and eyelids, gluing sequins to his forehead, painting circles around his nipples. Alfredo was naked; Nicolas wore his white shorts and white shirt. A noise outside signaled new arrivals, and men danced into the bedroom with mariachis playing guitars. Nicolas turned his head and a woman stood there, short, squat, wearing mannish clothes that sat easily around her frame. He was appalled.

"Where's Lynn?" she asked without a sign that what was happening around her was anything but normal.

"Irma!" shouted Lynn. "Irma Jonas! We didn't expect you until tomorrow!" He threw his arms around her and they danced into the living room.

"Wow!" she said after swallowing a glass of rum offered her by Zoe.

By then Nicolas had leaped over the high wall to the street. "What happened to that handsome young man?" Irma wanted to know.

"That's Nicolas," said Lynn. "He'll be around later. He's a bit of a prude in front of strangers."

I went to my house, where Nicolas lay upon the bed crying. "Oh, how could she do this to me! I'm ashamed! Humiliated! What am I going to do? I've planned an elegant dinner with candlelight for tomorrow and now it's ruined! Ruined!"

Irma Jonas had brought her painting school to Ajijic, and Lynn and Nicolas and I were its teachers. She had come the year before to make arrangements and understood the manner of artists in Mexico and in Portofino, where she had another summer school.

Nicolas cuddled up to me and put his head on my chest. "Damn that Lynn!"

17

"Oh, come on, Nicolas! She's probably seen more queens than you have. She's no naive." He would not be calmed that night, but late the following day he reappeared in his own house, where Irma sat with her twenty-six students, only two of whom were male. They stayed in Ajijic six weeks, loved it all, and were very generous with everyone. I myself received an offer from the aged wife of a Hollywood producer to live with her and two swimming pools in Bel Air.

When the students left, our own parties continued, full of young men, rich and beautifully built. I always felt inferior and knew no way to raise myself. Sometimes I lost myself in fantasies in which I too was handsome and attractive. Once I dared drop a sleeping pill into a drink for Lynn after a fight with Nicolas. He wept and sobbed hysterically. When he quieted down, I petted him, kissed him, and rubbed my hand over his groin. He had always allowed me these liberties, but they were incomplete and I wanted more; I wanted more in those moments of his suffering. He had come to me and was in my arms seeking comfort, and I wanted to comfort him by unbuttoning his shirt and rubbing my hands on his chest, by opening his trousers and reaching inside with my hands and mouth. But "Shit!" he said. "What the fuck did you put into that drink? It tastes of sleeping pills!" He frowned and fell asleep, woke up and said, "Are you trying to rape me or something?" He fell asleep again, and I remained awake throughout the night in shame.

By the time these liberties were extended to open attendance on his body, Lynn's drinking habits were already affecting his sexual abilities and he became impotent. He coughed incessantly and learned he had cancer of the throat but told no one. He smoked additional cigarettes each day and drank himself senseless at night. We never talked of this and I didn't even know of his illness. I was already back in New York when he shot and killed himself; I learned it through a letter from Nicolas, describing the gruesome necessity of cutting off Lynn's feet before his long body could fit into the coffin.

Nicolas left Ajijic years after I did and went to California, where he worked as an interior designer. He came to visit me once in my eleven-dollar-a-month apartment in New York. I opened my door to find him, dressed more elegantly than ever: Brooks Brothers suit, shirt with button-down collar, Sulka tie, bowler hat, a silver-handled cane. He laughed at the way I lived, and when we walked down the six flights of stairs, he pointed out the trash on steps, the puddles of urine and their smells, the disreputability of the building. I never heard from him directly again, but I knew he lived alone in Los Angeles, rich, isolated, and introspective. Zoe wrote to me in 1977 that he had died mysteriously soon after he lost his job; he had been discovered sitting in a chair three days after his death.

When I needed change or renewal for my painting, I made excursions from Ajijic into the forest of Tabasco and Quintana Roo, looking for orchids, Maya ruins, and ways of strengthening my inner being. In the forest, an immediate disturbance set itself up inside me. The forest prickled and baited me until, shortly before I left Mexico for good, I went down to Chiapas to a group of Indians I had read about, the Lacandón, who had been discovered living around the ruins of Bonampák in 1947 by Franz Blum. When I visited them three years later, the men still wore their long, uncombed hair down their backs and carried bows and bundles of arrows in their hands. They had remained almost completely isolated and had no contact with other Mexicans.

Being with the Lacandón even briefly brought back to the surface my compulsion to search for the wild man. I liked looking at the men, I liked sleeping in their huts, and their odd attitudes about order, health, and sanitation only served to implicate me further. I was with them for only a week, but their effect on me was profound; they reminded me of needs that had lain dormant for years. My body responded to that alien life as if it had lived it before, and the journey had served to trigger old responses. I was rushed back in time and felt as if I were sitting outside myself, another body taking part in the daily routine of the people, making the gestures of their lives, and I wanted to stay on. But the money I had lived on for so long ran out, and the few paintings I sold gave me no more than a few added weeks.

On my way back to the States, I stopped in Mexico City and stayed at the house of a friend, sleeping in a large bed with a young American of whom I was very fond. Many years later, in New York, the FBI called one day and said that someone I knew had applied for a job with the State Department and given my name as a reference. Would I be kind enough to come for an interview?

"Of course," I answered.

The meeting took place in the post office building on Eighth Avenue and Thirty-third Street, in a large room with a long table that almost filled it. The room was empty of people when I entered it and sat at one end. I was intimidated by the size of the room, and when a Mr. Fitzpatrick entered with another man, I was intimidated by their aggressive presence, their physical size and carriage, the manner with which they roughly, noisily pulled the chairs out from the table. Mr. Fitzpatrick introduced himself, thanked me for coming and doing my duty as a good citizen of the United States, and said nothing of the other man, who remained silent throughout the interview.

"Tell me, sir," he began, "is it true that you spent a night in Mexico City in June of 1950 at the home of Jane Alton?"

Seven years had passed since then, and I had to think back to what he was talking about, but I remembered and said, "Yes, I do remember the time."

"Do you also remember that another person, our applicant, spent the night there as well?"

"Yes," I said slowly, suddenly frightened of where this might be leading.

"Do you remember sleeping in the same bed with him?"

"Why are you asking me these questions?" I'm sure my nervousness could be heard in my voice.

"Don't you want to help your country?"

"I don't know what you mean. Didn't you say that my name had been given as a reference and that was why I was asked to come here? Isn't that what you said on the phone?"

"Are you trying to give us trouble, sir? We know about you. We know about your sexual practices. Just answer my questions, if you please. Now, what happened in bed that night? Did he make advances to you? Did you make advances to him? What kind of sex did you have together?"

In shock and rage and fear, I was tongue-tied and inarticulate. He demanded sexual details; he demanded that I lie to save our country from corruption and Communism. I never found out how he interpreted my denial that anything had happened between us, but he assured me that I would never again be permitted to work for the U.S. Government.

*   *   *

I had been intrigued by Gore Vidal's *Williwaw,* a book about a small naval vessel in the Aleutian Islands, at the time I was searching out job possibilities and had discovered that, on paper at least, I was suited for work only as a radar mechanic. There was an opening available at Elmendorf Air Force Base in Anchorage. Despite Mr. Fitzpatrick's dire warning, my application was approved by Civil Service in Washington and I was sent up, arriving there at a time when the temperature was minus thirty degrees and the heating system in the dormitory to which I was assigned was broken. I slept in all the clothes I owned and piled three blankets on top of me. During the night, the covers were thrown off and two men stripped me naked and tossed me out into a bank of snow. They rubbed me down with ice and laughed. When I went back inside, panting, shivering, one of the men handed me a water glass full of whiskey and said it would warm me up.

The head of the radar shop was a blond, handsome Air Force captain from Arkansas who read my papers with a certain unpleasant emphasis. "What kind of *name* is *that* you've got?" he asked. I explained my origins and my religion. "Well, you'll not get on here, you know. You might as well go right back to where you came from."

My complaint that afternoon to Civilian Personnel did not surprise them; they'd had similar ones before. They wanted me to make a formal statement before the board; instead, I signed up with the Military Sea Transportation Service as a messman in the galley of a tramp freighter, the *AKL-33.*

I had never been to sea and had never sailed farther than the Staten Island ferry could take me. I quickly adjusted to the roll of the ship and came to enjoy the storms we weathered; but it was a curious and absurd time, living on a ship in a climate that was as far as possible from the heat of the jungle that attracted me, living in an atmosphere more foreign than my time in the war and stranger than my first weeks in Mexico. The men with whom I worked and lived, the companions of every moment of my day and night, were rough, homeless, unattached, for the most part uneducated and inarticulate, all of them characters I'd met in O'Neill and Nordhoff and Hall. They got drunk in every port, were fired regularly, and were signed back on because there was no one to replace them. They were friendly to me, even when belligerent with each other. I liked them all, though

I was frightened by their violence when drunk in port. We sailed the Aleutian chain, went to Nome and Kotzebue, St. Lawrence Island and Point Barrow. I left Alaska when the *33* burned and sank just south of Adak Island, seven months after I joined her. I was sent down to Seattle to make salads and coffee aboard a troop ship, the *General Meigs,* that went to Frisco and sailed to Kōbe, Sasebo, Inch'ŏn, and Pusan, plying between Japan and Korea at the time of the Korean War. In my easy role as assistant cook, I had shore leave from the moment we docked to the moment we set sail. I learned about geisha houses, boy houses, pillow books, opium pipes, netsuke figures, Silla pots, prints by Shunsho, Hokusai, and Utamaro, Nō plays, and Kabuki, and I read the whole of *The Tale of Genji.* The crew was not much different from the one on the *33* and spent their free time gambling on the deck of our fo'c'sle.

With money I'd saved aboard ship, I returned to New York in 1952, settled into painting, and had my first one-man show at the Ganso Gallery. My father came to the opening, was surprised at the number of people there, and commented on how many gentiles were friendly with me. I applied for a Fulbright Fellowship and chose Peru as my destination because of an exhibition of photographs I'd seen at the Museum of Modern Art. The photos of Machu Picchu had impressed me with the remoteness of the site, the vertical shape of the landscape on which the ruins sat, the jungle covering the cliffs down to the Urubamba River, the worn textures of the buildings and their affinity with the land around them. Not wanting to fly over Central America and see nothing of the countries below, I took a bus down to Mexico City and went on slowly through Guatemala, El Salvador, Honduras, and Nicaragua and swam and waded across the western half of Costa Rica when Hurricane Hilda rushed by. I went by small boat to Balboa in Panama, took a smaller one to Guayaquil in southern Ecuador, and rode the back of a truck to Lima, arriving there with five dollars in my pocket. I had an introduction to a gallery director, Bob Gesinus-Visser, who invited me to tea in his bedroom at the Quinta Heeren; when I entered the room I found him sprawled on a great bed amid a lavish cluster of silk pillows, looking like the doctor in *Nightwood.* He arranged for me to stay in the villa of vacationing friends, an establishment that had a large swimming pool and a Great Dane who swam only with company and pushed me into the water every morning when I passed by on my way to the garage where I painted.

I moved across the country, to archeological sites in the desert, to Chavín de Huantár in the snow-covered Callejón de Huaylas, made a short trip on a whaling vessel out of Ica, and wandered along Lake Titicaca with a fakir who put long nails through his flesh and lay with his back on broken glass while I split boulders on his chest with a sledgehammer. I went into the yellow sands of Nazca and saw the long, straight lines that have been called the runways of extraterrestrial visitors. I examined the curving lines of trenches that formed gigantic birds and fish and other figures, decided that the trenches were dance patterns, and was laughed at for thinking so. It seemed so sensible to me—a trench that outlined the form of a sacred creature without ever crossing over itself, so that hundreds, even thousands of celebrants might follow the line without running into one another. The trench was exactly the width of a foot, rain never fell to destroy the image, and wind never shifted the sands to cover it. And why not dance the shape of your totem as well as dress in its skin, its feathers, or its leaves? Why not honor the conformation of your deity, the animal whose strength or flesh you hope to possess, the plant whose fertility you wish to increase, the ancestral spirit whose magical powers you are invoking?

I stayed for months in and above Cuzco, in the ruins of Machu
Picchu, Pisac, Sacsayhuamán, and Ollantaytambo, sketching everything everywhere, reveling in every day that brought new wonders to
my eyes. The buildings of Machu Picchu grew out of the rock of terraces on the edge of a cliff that dropped fifteen hundred feet straight
down and was all that I imagined it and more. Dr. Corvacho, of the
University of Cuzco, took me out to draw ancient sites he'd discovered himself and put me in touch with a Father who described the
way to a mission deep in the rain forest, giving me the direction,
"Keep the river on your right." A truck took me over the Andes,
crossing at seventeen thousand feet to the other side, where suddenly
the jungle grew almost from the peaks, sweeping three miles down the
eastern slopes to the floor of the forest, which stretched on past the
curve of the earth to Bolivia and the great expanses of Brazil. The
slope was so steep, the road so poor, that traffic was permitted only
one way, going down on certain days of the week, going up on alter-
nate days. The truck zigzagged its way down to Ocosingo, beyond
which was the wilderness and an overgrown trail that ended some
days away at the mission. There Father Moiseis, in a long white beard
spotted with crumbs and wearing a torn, stained cassock, welcomed

me with loud shouts, pressed food upon me, gave me his own mosquito net, and talked for days, stopping only for mass and sleep. Manolo, a lay missionary from Spain, came into the small dining room that first evening with his beard trimmed short, his buttonless shirt open to the waist, and his freshly washed jeans belted with vines. He spoke softly, was humble and charming, and we quickly became friends. Like the Machiguenga and the Wachipaire Indians who lived in and around the mission and were able to retain their own mores only away from the eyes of Father Moiseis, Manolo and I could talk only when out in the jungle. We were close, and I might have stayed on with him but for the desire to go farther into the unknown.

A man appeared one day—Wassen was his name—naked but for feathers stuck into the flesh around his mouth and a string around his waist that held his penis up against his abdomen. He told of the decimation of his people, murdered, all but the women and children taken captive. I listened, and a force welled up inside me, driving me toward those who had killed, giving me hope that the wild man existed among them. I went out into the forest and three days later found a gathering of men sitting against a wall of trees, awaiting my arrival as if they'd always known that I would come. I went among them as if entering into luxury, the physical pleasure of their touch as they examined me more gratifying than any pleasure known before.

They took me in, and I lived with five young men, who taught me ways of life that had not existed in me before, showing me the freedom of a body without clothes, the simplicity possible in an act of touch, in embrace, in rest and sleep with limbs entwined so easily we knew each other as I might have known a long-time lover. We lived in a huge, oval hut; our group shared a small open compartment next to other small groups of men in sections that lined the inside wall. The women and children clustered around fires that ran in a row through the center.

The men were my friends, lovers who filled me with their sympathies and sentiments and made my daily life a dream in which I acted out my fantasies. I learned to shoot a bow and arrow, to run barefoot through the forest, to subsist on the life around me.

My small group was always the same, huddled together in warmth and affection. I loved them and wanted to be their equal, learning whatever my body could be trained to do, moving into their lives as I had never allowed myself to move before. They accepted whatever I was, though I could have been no more than a curiosity at first. They allowed me to settle into their intimacies, and I submitted myself to them without thought of consequence. They did not reject what they saw of me with their eyes; they did not reject what they touched with their hands; and because they did not reject my ugliness, I felt no need for shame.

Later, they became the basis of my life; they became the way I wanted to go. "You are ugly," my father had said, and I have never

been able to rid myself of the feeling that I *am* ugly. I cannot look into a mirror and see myself. There is no face there, only a comb combing my hair, a razor shaving my beard. Moe, my fat brother, was considered the beauty; Bernie, as youngest, was the favored one and in reality was the only handsome one among us. In Mexico I had begun to lose the sense of living only in my interior, of being alone and isolated. Among the men of Peru, there was no question of ugliness or beauty; my face and my presence dazzled them for no reason but that I was there and was in no way related to anything they had known before.

Surrounded by strangers and strangeness, I was more open, more alive and responsive. My lack of knowledge of the language forced from me gestures and movements that were as clear and understandable as words. My body learned to accommodate itself, to give as well as to receive. The fact that the color of my skin was different, that I knew nothing of local customs, that a band of white flesh appeared where I had worn a bathing suit, and that I carried pens and pencils and made drawings on paper, all combined with my shyness and my homeliness to give me a new feeling for life. The curiousness of me did not compete with the warmth the men of Peru exuded or the wonder they exulted in. They took me past the surface of their lives and gave me confidence and a new reality. The freshness of their world was so stirring and vital, was so much the breath of life, that I wanted to live inside them, to live the whole of their lives, the whole of their past and present.

Darinimbiak, to whom I gave my deepest affection, took sick, and I thought to cure his dysentery by taking him to the mission and its store of drugs. Other sick ones went with us and did well, but Darinimbiak died and was buried in the jungle. I returned to our village with the others but remained depressed for weeks.

One day, unknown to me, we went on a raid. We went into the forest as on other days, but there were more of us and we stayed longer and went farther. They committed the violence I had originally wished for: They killed men and brought back women and children. They had accepted me completely and took me into the deepest part of themselves, but I saw that I was not yet ready to go there myself.*

All my life I had been alone, lonely, unknowing, dispassionate, and

* See the author's *Keep the River on Your Right* (Grove Press, 1969).

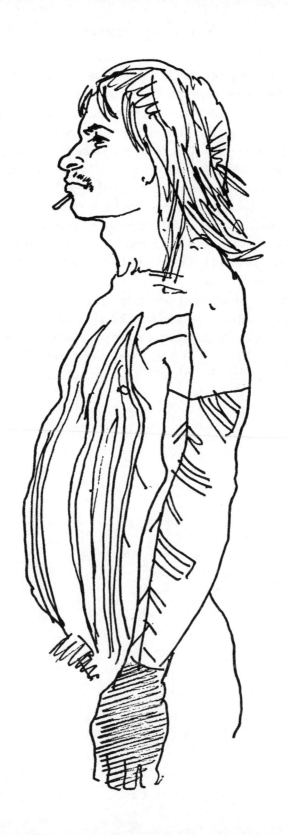

suddenly I was part of a people. I had wanted to burst full-grown into their knowledge and experience. I had wanted to *be* them, to relive all the past of my own life. They had given me completion and satisfaction, and when they filled me with it, when I was sated with what I thought I needed, I left them. After eight months of eating, sleeping, hunting with them, of submerging myself and trying to disappear into their lives, I left them without good-byes. As I had been compelled to seek them out, I was compelled to return to the world that had given me the obsession. Having learned to cope with my loneliness, I went back to search it out again. What they had given me had seemed enough, and for a moment I had fooled myself into thinking that I was one of them.

I left my friends in my dream of them, keeping them as they were, as they are, though all are dead now, killed by the coming of the road across the continent. More than twenty years have gone by and still I wonder why I left them. It is not clear that it was only the violence that disturbed me. Sometimes I think a loneliness came over me there, too.

Chapter Two

The childhood memory of the sign THIS WAY TO THE WILD MAN OF BORNEO had made Borneo a wildness beyond all others. It was where I would meet him, touch him, be touched by him, and thus become him. That he might kill and cannibalize me did not occur to me; or if it did, it occurred as a hope, a suggestion that always underlay the strength and virileness that I expected of him.

Yet for a time I avoided Borneo, as later I avoided New Guinea, holding each island in reserve, savoring the knowledge that the wild man was there. I tantalized myself with journeys elsewhere, allowing the wild man to permeate my every pore, letting him lodge inside my body while, in self-denial, I tried to shake him out. I wanted a peek at him, to look only for an instant, to shut my eyes and feel him there, to imagine the power of him and the control he had over me. I could not bear to look and find him gone and therefore myself empty; I could not bear to look into his eyes and find there nothing more than myself. If he was nothing more than my own myth of him, the world of my creation would vanish.

I therefore kept myself on edge. I kept the present far ahead of me, though his image was always there. I went to South America, to Africa, to Asia, picking up and following allusions to his presence but never satisfied.

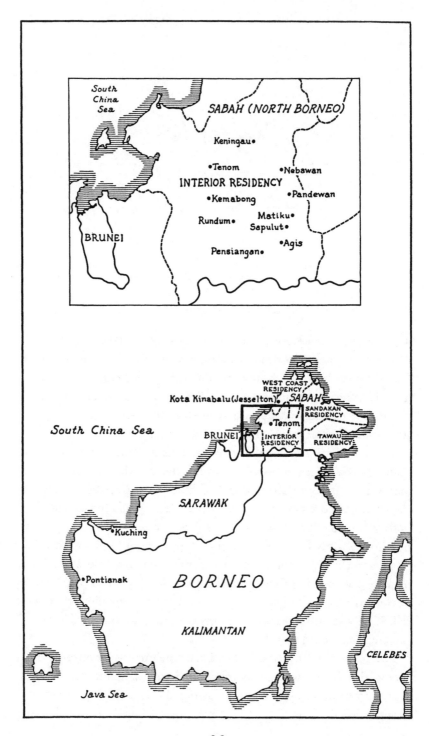

Moving from place to distant place was an integral part of my life, but it could be done only when there was enough money in hand. What I lived and traveled on I earned in New York by selling paintings through the Peridot Gallery, which took me on when the Ganso closed, and by working for Tiber Press, a greeting card company that allowed me the freedom to come and go as long as I was there for the Christmas season. I worked four or five months of the year, painted during the other seven or eight, worked again, and then took off to renew the landscapes of my interior and of my canvases. I had thought the journeys necessary as inspiration for my painting, but with time I came to understand that it was the journey itself that fired me and that the canvases were not the ends but the means of nearing the source of my pleasures; I was always running from my loneliness, rushing on to scrutinize the trails that led me deeper into myself, toward the wildness of the wild man. I hardly knew what pleasures I sought; I knew only that a breath of jungle air could thrill me beyond all else, and that the sight of the wild man incited in me a feverish response of longing.

The months in New York became an interruption of that other life, though they were a time of being nourished by friends, who always took me back into their world with love. They offered pleasures that appeared ephemeral because I had learned that my gratifications could be more profound elsewhere. Just as Roger Fry suggested that art is never enjoyed for its own sake but for its evocations, so I, trembling at the sight of a Sepik River mask, am aware that it is not its surface beauty that impassions me so much as my desire to enter into the consciousness of the mask itself. Looking at man in Borneo or Central Africa does not fill me with his beauty so much as evoke a vision of myself inside his body.

When at last, with those tentative sojourns in remote places, I had prepared myself to face the wild man's presence or absence in Borneo, I went there. I made my formal contacts at the office of the Permanent Secretary of North Borneo and set off by train from Jesselton, capital of North Borneo, for Tenom in the Interior Residency, the area least touched by the outside world. The Muruts, formerly headhunters, were said to be the most isolated people on the island.

The train had one car with wooden seats for passengers, one car for

freight. The few passengers wore sarongs. One man led a cock in by a string tied to its right leg. A young woman entered with a parrot on her shoulder. She sat apart from a group of three men but talked with them as if they were all of one family. They had tattoos on their arms and shoulders and on their chests.

The jungle materialized soon after we left Jesselton, after we passed the gray forests of rubber, and reached and moved along with the Padas River, a mass of boiling white water rushing over hidden boulders, by black rocks along the bank, and past the trees that grew from the water itself. When the narrow-gauge train went through a tight cleft in the hills, the plant life on both sides pushed its branches and leaves into the windows. The gorge went on, and the roaring of the river almost drowned out the other sounds: the boughs scraping against the metal of the cars, the cock across the aisle crowing at every station, the men behind me whooping it up with a bottle of brandy. I thought back to Mexico and Peru, walking again through their jungles, for outside the window were the reminders of the bamboo *paca* with its razor-sharp leaves and the long thorns that had made shreds of my clothing. Yet, my attention focused on the beauty: the streaks of sunlight landing on leaves and spotting up the darkness with circles of yellow moving in the slight wind; the parasites and epiphytes spurting from high branches; the occasional block of sky we could see, when the river was wide enough, above the forest on the far side; or the small blue butterfly coming to rest on my open, unread paperback Marquand; or the sight of four people getting off in the middle of what looked like wilderness, the girl carrying a record of Elvis Presley under her arm.

I could barely contain myself and allowed my thoughts to wander—but not into my deepest, darkest self and its hidden recesses, not too far within the maze where I hide and hesitate. It was too soon to reveal its secrets, too soon to open even to myself what I was looking for. Instead, I looked outside and strained my eyes and saw the back of myself running through a patch of forest and disappearing behind the leaves. Sometimes, decorated with feathers and bones, a bow and arrows in my hand, I was squatting on a branch, looking down at myself; not yet seeing a Murut there, only my own embellished, camouflaged self. Then I was on the train again, with the future not yet wanting to be known. I tried to force indifference onto myself, though the nerve endings of my fingertips tingled to touch what lay ahead.

Mr. A. M. Grier, Permanent Secretary of North Borneo, had wired to Tenom of my arrival. Gordon Douglas, the district officer of Tenom, was delighted to be of help, and Mrs. Douglas, a very pregnant and pretty woman, made tea, and took me across the parade grounds to the rest house, where I slept inside what looked like a cage—a screened-in room that had a bed, a table, chairs, a sink, and two bureaus. Mr. Douglas was not only congenial; he was also well-informed about the area. Both he and Mrs. Douglas relished the idea of a visitor and debated the directions in which I could go from there. He finally suggested what he thought would be the most provocative: the circular route from Keningau to Pensiangan, then to Rundum, to Kemabong and back to Tenom.

"Not only can you do that," he said in a way that gave me the impression that he wanted to go along, "but Mathurin Daim is the assistant district officer in Pensiangan and you can go around that whole area with him, to all the villages right on the border of Indonesian Borneo. Mathurin's a peach. You'll like him.

"As far as I know, no one's done this whole route. You can go from Tenom to Pensiangan in eight or nine days. Not too much of a problem. I've done it myself in the dry season. It will be messy now with rain coming down every day but you can manage, I think. And then the Japs had a road from Tenom to Rundum. Not much then and pretty bad now, I'm sure. All overgrown. But what interests me is what it's like from Pensiangan to Rundum. The Muruts do it, I know, because they tell me, but no white people have been there. I'd go myself, but I'm too busy now. Another time, maybe."

Mrs. Douglas insisted that I stay and celebrate Christmas with them before leaving. Every night until then, groups of young and elderly men went around Tenom from house to house singing "Silent Night" and "Adeste Fidelis" in both Malay and Chinese. Mr. Williams, manager of the Sapong Rubber Estate, invited me to Christmas Eve dinner, a sumptuous meal, and I spent Christmas Day at the Douglases', where there was sherry with the grapefruit, red wine with the turkey, and sweet champagne with the flaming pudding.

I walked to Keningau, a town larger than Tenom that boasted

Schmedann 66

shops selling tobacco, clothing, rice, and some hardware. The New Year's festival delayed me four days, but Ben Stephens, one of the few Eurasian district officers in British Borneo, took me to the races, to the blowpipe contests, and to all the dances. He introduced me to an Australian Evangelical missionary, Alfred Tharratt, whom he disliked simply because of his profession.

Mr. Tharratt worked with the Lundaya in Lawas, Sarawak, teaching them that alcohol was evil and that music and dance were sinful. The evangelical missionaries in British Borneo, mostly Australians, were trying to stop everyone from drinking *tapai,* the local wine made from rice, and they often succeeded. This not only made the Lundaya a dull people, at least temporarily, according to Mr. Stephens, but made them a hungry one as well, since the men decided that, if they weren't going to make *tapai,* there was no point in growing rice. This didn't bother Alf, as he insisted I call him, since he felt the experience would teach them discipline. Mr. Tharratt had come to Keningau to talk to the Muruts, who had not yet been missionized. He had set up a stall in the crowded marketplace to sell religious tracts in English, Malay, and Lundaya. Later, I learned that Gordon Douglas followed such missionaries, took along a case of Scotch, and asked for *tapai* in the villages the missionaries had passed through.

The trip from Keningau to Pensiangan took eight days. Dinki, my first guide, was a complainer. After saying my gear was too heavy, he put it into the long carrying basket on his back. I carried the ten pounds of beads plus the tobacco for presents and trade goods. I had bought the beads in Singapore, the tobacco in Tenom. It was late when we started off, nine o'clock, and we didn't get very far before we had to stop for Dinki's own belongings, and then we stopped again whenever we met anyone along the road. Dinki chattered and complained about the weight on his back, though it wasn't even half the official load. His friends laughed at his complaints, but it was not an auspicious first day. I felt depressed and irritated.

Nonetheless, that day was the easiest of the eight. We walked along a road that could be traveled by jeep during the dry season as far as Besanon, a village farther on, where we intended to spend the night. But early in the afternoon, a heavy rainstorm forced us to take shelter in Togup, a group of four shacks, all in disrepair, used only by travelers. Inside one of the huts, we removed our dripping clothes. Beneath his shorts, Dinki wore a loincloth wound high around his waist and under his legs, leaving his buttocks and hips bare. His body was hard and sinewy. He made a fire from wood in a corner of the hut and put water on to boil for rice. The shack was on a hill, just above a river that was not visible at first because of the rain and heavy forest growth. When the rain lightened, we went down to wash the mud from our legs. Dinki unwrapped his loincloth, cupped one hand over his penis, and splashed water over his body with the other. He looked up to stare at me, and I stared at him. Though I was annoyed by his slowness and his grumbling, I was invigorated by his naked body in the river and by the sight of him in his loincloth crouching to cook our rice.

When the rain stopped, Dinki fretted that his back ached and said he could go no farther, so we stayed in the hut. I slept well on the bamboo floor, wrapped in the thick blanket Mrs. Douglas had lent me.

We spent the next day climbing up and down a muddy track through the forest. Dinki often belched and expelled gases, but he had the grace to drop behind before he farted. We stopped at the kampong of Sook, not an interesting village, for I slept in a Western-style house on an uncomfortable wooden floor and was fed only rice in exchange for beads and tobacco. Dinki left me there, though I didn't know it until the next morning; he was already on his way back to Keningau before daybreak, and someone else showed up in his place.

Bumbulok was different and was proud to be with me. He made no complaints and joyously lifted his carrying basket as if he were returning from a successful hunt. During the seven-hour walk to Nebawan, we stopped four times, each time only long enough to smoke and remove the leeches from our legs and arms. Bumbulok talked on happily while we walked and never seemed to tire. It pleased me that I was not singled out by the leeches and that as many attached themselves to him as to me. Once they properly fastened themselves onto my skin, they were not easily removed. Like the vampire bats of South America, they inject a fluid into the bloodstream to prevent coagulation, causing the bite to continue bleeding long after the leech has been pulled off. They are repulsive and slimy, an inch or more in length. They can stand up like thorns, unnoticed on a leaf; they can

39

roll themselves into balls, stretch out or shrink, or arrange themselves to squeeze through the cloth of a pair of trousers. They sit on leaves waving their heads around, sending out beams of radar to locate whatever prey is around. Because so much of the forest growth reaches low across the trail, they most often attack the legs, but I also found them on my neck, shoulders, and abdomen. Bumbulok and I would sit to roll tobacco; I'd take off my sneakers and there would be six or seven of them nestled together, sucking at my blood. The heat of a cigarette usually forced them to loosen their hold, but sometimes I'd have to pull them off, squeezing tightly with my nails to prevent them from slipping through my fingers. I often wondered what they ate when there were no humans or animals around.

There was rain every afternoon, and often during the whole of the night. In the morning, water covered everything and the mud was deep and slippery. Sometimes the vegetation opened out into grass-land, with sharp-edged leaves that were tall and dense enough to hide a man. The jungle was always intensely there, not only to be looked at and stumbled through, but also in the sounds that provoked and stirred me, though I could identify only the high-pitched *whup-whup-up-up* of the gibbons. I saw hornbills and brilliantly colored birds and heard calls that varied from whistles to screeches to stunning songs, and even to the piercing sound of an insect in the late afternoon, which might have been the whine of a dentist's drill. The trail in good weather would not have been difficult, but the ankle-deep mud on the near-vertical climbs and drops was slippery and exhausting. The rain thundered onto the leaves during the brief, heaviest showers, and the leaves continued dripping water for hours afterward, the sound like the rain itself. The dank smell of rotting vegetation, all green, black, and orange leaves underfoot, pervaded everything. My ankles were scratched and scraped by grass and sharply pointed twigs, and there were cuts on my thighs and arms; but nothing was ever painful or irritating. I did not think of abrasions except to note their presence. They gave the journey an element of threatening danger, and ignoring it proved my hardiness and daring.

We crossed wild streams and rivers, sometimes on simple bamboo bridges, sometimes on slender, slippery logs, but most often by ford-ing violent rapids. Once, we passed over the Panawan River on a sus-pension bridge of wire and wood that bounced and swayed as we moved along it. Somewhere on the track between Pandewan and Matiku, there was a splash of sunlight where the forest opened out, and dogs came splattering through the mud. They stood in front of us and barked. A man appeared on horseback with a rifle in his hands. He wore only a sarong that was pulled under his groin, so that he seemed naked within the wooden saddle that curved up and hid his hips. A *parang*, his long bush knife, was slung across his shoulder, and feathers of red and black stuck out of the small bag on his back. Walking barefoot behind him was a woman in a black and red sarong, her breasts bare except for beads. She held a silk parasol high against the sun or rain. Men carrying heavy loads in baskets on their backs followed behind. The scene was out of *Rashomon*, except that the woman should have been on horseback instead of the man. Their sudden appearance within the forest and the graceful movements of them all were eloquent and intriguing. We nodded and smiled and greeted each other: *"Salamat pagi!"* Good morning! *"Salamat pagi!"*

Where the track was narrowest, the leeches seemed as numerous as the leaves, and my legs and arms and shirt were covered with spots of blood. I tried to minimize the impact of that world with its impending exultations, but the scratches, the blood, the abrasions, forced onto me pictures of Harry Carey and Robert Preston trudging through the savage forest in the enervating heat, rifles across the crooks of their elbows, clothes in shreds, sweat pouring down their faces and staining armpits. They were pushing on to gold or diamond mines, or off to rescue golden-haired princesses held captive by leopard men or by painted Zulus known to trap and mutilate all whites, tearing off their genitals and eating them to gain the white man's strength and magic. But I wanted it reversed; I wanted the wild man inside me, masticated, swallowed, absorbed.

We were following a river in Borneo, going deeper into darkness, going farther from the outside world, turning corners, penetrating recesses, so I thought. The river churned and roared with tremendous force, itself a wildness that stirred up passions I refused as yet to allow to surface. As we went farther on from Keningau, the villages became more out of the past—in the present, yes, but built in olden ways without the use of saws and nails, with floors and walls of bamboo tied with vines. Strange foods were served on leaves: pieces of wild boar still covered with all its bristles and fat, roasted mouse deer,

Schweinsann '60

roasted cassava, cucumbers mashed with sugar, a sticky glob of some unknown substance that stuck to my spoon, stuck to my teeth, and stuck to the roof of my mouth. There was rice thickened with sugar, and superbly delicious fruits: rambutan, a wild lichee covered with soft bristles and looking like sea urchins dyed red, foul-smelling, tasty durians with cream-colored pulp and pits that could be roasted, pineapple, and mangosteens. There was a pickled fish that shocked me by its similarity to my mother's schmaltz herring. The food was part of the uncontrollable wilderness, voluptuous in all its yieldings, and I was eating it all with lust, having expected its strangeness as part of the unknown to come.

Dinki, at five foot two inches, had been the tallest of my guides; Limbawang, a mere four foot ten inches, was the shortest. Dinki was the only one I didn't like, perhaps because he lived too close to the world of shops and government offices and schools, with all their influences, good and bad. He got up late, he never smiled, and he seemed to disapprove of me. The others were always cheerful, pleasant, and glad to be of help. But in a way, I wanted myself alone. Alone, I'd gone to the mission in Peru; alone I went on from there and met an untouched people. I wanted to repeat that time, knowing it wasn't possible, knowing there were no virginal groups in Borneo; I'd come too late for that. Yet, the jungle was exquisitely inside me, pressing through my veins and sinews, adding one small reaction to another, setting up vibrations throughout my body and building to a climax I could not expel.

I spent nights in houses, huts, and shacks. The villages were much alike, except for the first one where I had slept on a proper wooden floor. At Nebawan, I slept alone in a huge room without walls laid out on three levels, with enormous Chinese jars filled with *tapai,* the rice wine, tied to posts on one side, awaiting the next occasion for a feast. All the buildings were up on stilts, five feet or more above the mud, with ladders of logs cut with notches for steps. In Pandewan, an orange manx cat slept with me next to a bamboo wall patterned with spears and blowpipes. Hanging from the rafters were fish traps, a Christian cross, a rusty head-hunting knife, and feathers of various sizes and colors. In Sapulut, with its one hundred fifty people, slightly larger than the other villages, we slept with other travelers, two men and two women. The men carried spears; one of the women held a baby and a small gray monkey. The diseased skin of one of the men was flaking off as if from dryness, from ringworm, a fungus that can be treated and cured by pills taken regularly. I was repelled by the look and smell of the ringworm and wanted to move away, but I was also attracted and wanted to run my hands over the man's body, like John Pettit, who worked for years with lepers and caressed their sores and wounds as if with sexual pleasure.

The hut was surrounded by a mass of huge, yellow fern. Behind the fern, the foliage dropped down to the Panawan River. On the other side immense trees shot up bare of limbs until the trunks reached above the densest undergrowth. Thick vines with sharp edges curled, cork-screwed, looped, and attacked everything within reach. Great masses of thin vines hung straight down.

Mayan, my guide of the day, sat next to me on a rough board outside the hut, took out a bit of cloth, a shard of porcelain, and a scraped section of bamboo, and with them quickly made the fire to light his cigarette. I saw his face, but the features did not register on me. The other travelers were more a mood than a fact. When they offered spoiled meat from a bamboo container, I ate it and hardly knew what it tasted like, but I felt a closeness with all of them. The monkey sat on the shoulder of one of the men and picked lice out of his hair. He examined each louse before plopping it into his mouth. One of the women was cross-eyed.

My guides were good, but none remained with me more than a day or two, and because I wanted to be alone in the forest, I almost avoided looking at them, forcing their personalities to mingle into one. Only Dinki had worn Western clothes; the others wore only a *chawat,* the loincloth of bark or manufactured cloth. The features of the men remained hazy, so that I could not put faces to villages, only names. Limbawang took me to Pandewan, but I cannot imagine his appearance, nor that of Mayan, who took me to Matiku and on to Sapulut. I went to Agis with Angkashang and made the last lap to Pensiangan in a canoe with four paddlers, all of whom were nothing more than shapes. I spent most of the day walking behind the men, and in the evening I was still too new to everything to be aware of all that I looked at.

I enjoyed the walk to Agis with Angkashang. We'd have enough *tapai* the night before to get slightly drunk and dance together and

then to sleep on past dawn. There had been only a brief shower the previous afternoon and no rain that night, so the track was almost dry. Bright sun the next day cleared it completely. The heat would have been oppressive to others, pushing in from all sides, but it stimulated me. At times, I was able to look up from the trail into the jungle and examine it while walking. Angkashang and I, exhilarated by our effortless movements, raced along at top speed, and I was going as if toward my ultimate goal. We stopped only once for a cigarette.

The day was a blinding one of contrasting sunlight and shadow; meshes of vines that hung like gray fishnets in front of the deepest shade. Occasionally I could see the sky, cerulean blue with swirls of white cloud; below, streamers of foam, remnants of rapids upstream, floated on the surface of the river. We stopped in the late afternoon at a solitary hut, where two men slept in a corner. When awakened, they greeted us with surprise and good humor and went off, at Angkashang's direction, to the *orangtua,* the headman of Kampong Agis, to tell of my arrival and the need for a canoe and paddlers the next day. The rest of the journey was to be made by river.

That evening, I sat in peace on a rock, with my feet in the Talankai, a river that moved swiftly there and almost in silence; upstream, its cataracts and falls had made deafening sounds. The constant hum and buzz of insects became louder. The hills opposite were covered with luxuriant growth. The river turned sharply left immediately below where I sat, and there the muddy greens and browns changed back to the white water of the rapids. The peace I sat with moved into joy and urgings of release as I wandered dreamlike through the gamut of my feelings of kinship with the wild man. This was Borneo and I was close.

The *prao,* a long and narrow canoe, arrived with the *orangtua* and four paddlers early in the morning. We shook hands formally and started down the Talankai, sweeping along with the current through cascades, passing great black boulders barely beneath the water's surface. An hour later we reached the junction with the Tagul and began to move up its wilder waters. Cramps attacked the muscles of my legs from sitting cross-legged in the canoe, but then I discovered that I could lie down in comfort, and I stretched out and looked up at the passing overhang of trees and bamboo. The passage was hard and slow, more and more difficult as we went farther upriver. The paddles

Schneebaum '68

were useless against the strong current, so the *prao* was poled along the shallower, stiller water close to the river bank. The cataracts were often so high and rough that we waded through the violent surge to pull the canoe into calmer waters. I bailed for hours, not because of leaks but because small waves came into the canoe from all sides. We passed huts and kampongs and heard gongs announce our arrival and departure. Occasional *praos* went by with seven or eight people standing, waving and shouting at us. When we stopped for lunch at a muddy bank, a canoe came up and a man offered rice and fruit. The jungle sometimes shot straight up from the river, forming the walls of a canyon against which the sound of the paddles striking the side of the *prao* echoed. We went through tunnels made by branches and clutches of bamboo that fanned down to the water. There were monkeys jumping up and down in the trees and screeching their excitement at our going by. Birds flew up in pairs and sometimes in flocks.

Late in the evening, at the confluence of the Tagul and Siliu Rivers, we spotted the white buildings of Pensiangan, and my heart jumped while I flushed and wondered what lay ahead. Pensiangan was a town of two hundred people, not yet where I wanted to be, but a starting place. We tied up at the right bank and climbed the hill to the house of the assistant district officer, where I was welcomed like an old friend.

Mathurin Daim was an enthusiastic host and couldn't resist renewing his offers of fruit and meat and rice. He could not sit still but constantly got up from his rattan chair to hold out bowls of food, and he shouted toward the kitchen for other delicacies or for tea or coffee or orange squash. Mrs. Daim, who moved with the swiftness and silence of a deer, told me her name three times, but she spoke so softly in her shyness that I was never able to hear it. She did not eat with us and rarely served at table, preferring to remain in the kitchen preparing our food while a young Murut girl waited on us. The Daims were Kedazans, a subgroup of the Dusans, one of the largest groups of related peoples on the island, and came from the town of Papar on the west coast. Both were beautiful to look at, with short straight noses, full lips, clear skin, and sharply focused eyes. Mrs. Daim's face was round, while Mathurin's was almost square, with wide cheekbones that accentuated his Oriental eyes.

Schneebaum '60

Mathurin and I, in a curious way, became friends immediately. He told me later that he'd never had a white friend before, and that he was first attracted to me because I gave off no repellent odor. He was imaginative, full of energy, intensely interested in his work, fascinated with the Muruts, delighted with his wife, and absorbed in life in general and in the excitement of North Borneo's coming independence. He'd been sent to Australia under the Colombo Plan, a fellowship like the Fulbright, and he had liked being there temporarily, but for him the Australians, like all Caucasians and most foreigners, had an unpleasant smell that always put him off any relationships other than distant ones. When as a child he'd attended the Catholic primary school in Papar, his first days were excruciating because he got sick whenever approached by the priest who taught there; the smell of his garments, combined with his body odors, was repugnant, and Mathurin often stayed away from class because of it. The sensitive nostrils of the local people, he said, were even more horrified by the pungent aromas of the creams and oils used on the hair and bodies of the Indians, the Sikhs and Tamils. Cleanliness among foreigners, in fact, was completely at variance with local customs, and Mathurin was particularly repelled by the European habit of holding up a rag, blowing one's nose into it, and then putting the rag back into one's pocket. How much more sanitary to blow one's nose between one's fingers, Mathurin said. No less revolting was the idea of sitting in a tin container and washing with dirty water instead of bathing in the cool rivers. Nor did he think it hygienic to wipe away feces with a piece of paper; water was cleaner, simpler, and more sensible. He could not help but laugh at the British, who constantly insisted on proper sanitation and yet had customs that the people of Borneo found odious and unclean, and I could not help but laugh at his apt descriptions of our strange practices. Among the people of different races I'd met who were educated in Western traditions, he was a rarity; he was honest with me, allowing himself to open up and reveal long-repressed thoughts. Of course, it helped that he was so articulate in English.

"But why don't you object to my own body smells?" I asked him. "Or are you just being nice?"

"Oh, no, I'm not being nice. You don't have that smell about you. Even my wife talked about it, which is something we never discuss, the unpleasant characteristics of white people. I'm not sure why you are an exception, but it's probably because you've been around this part of the world so long, living and eating the same way we do. Unlike the British, who always take their own food wherever they go. And I don't like the long bumpy noses and big ears of Caucasians. They're so ugly."

As always, I regretted my own long nose and large ears and held my hand to my face in embarrassment, but Mathurin was not seeing me and was unaware at that moment that I was the ideal example of the physical type he was describing. "Then tell me who you *do* think is beautiful."

"Our women, of course. They are the most beautiful in the world." He thought for a minute, then said, "James Dean was very good-looking. I like Pat Boone, too. They both have short noses. And among the women, I like Elizabeth Taylor and Sophia Loren and Marilyn Monroe."

Mathurin welcomed the idea of my making a side trip upriver in his district to sketch the people before continuing on to Rundum and returning to Tenom. He mentioned the names of several villages—Siatu, Katuntul, Samantabawan, and others—but their sequence did not register, and I was prepared for a trip that might take days or weeks. He assured me he would help find a *prao* when I was ready to leave. The next morning he took me around Pensiangan; we stopped at the dispensary, then at each of the five Chinese shops, and ended up in the last one drinking cocoa with biscuits, eating mangosteens and durian. A teenaged Murut boy with long hair brought glasses of *tapai* on a tray. Asau, the owner of the shop, urged us to drink, and I fell into a semistupor after three glasses. The boy pressed more *tapai* onto Asau and then sat next to him on a bench. Asau surreptitiously, almost unconsciously, put a hand inside the leg of the boy's shorts, gave a squeeze, and took his hand out again. Mathurin's skin, the color of cool sienna, reddened when he saw this, and he moved uncomfortably around in his chair.

"Is it really true, all those things I've been told about Hyde Park?" he asked in a low voice.

Somewhat taken aback by the suddenness of the question, and not sure that he meant what I thought he meant, though he was staring at Asau's hand, I asked what he had in mind. He nodded at the Chinese and said, "That kind of thing." He had stiffened and was not his usual easy self.

"Yes, I think so, Mathurin. I've never been to England so I can't tell you about it firsthand, but I've heard the same stories and I'm sure they're true. There are places like that in New York and San Francisco, in Singapore and in Bangkok, and in almost every big city in the world. And in most small cities, too."

"But how can that be? Is it really true? It is difficult for me to believe. All my life, the Church, the English Church, has taught me that such things are sinful, and all my life I had been horrified at the idea of men having sexual contact with each other. My people never do such things. Children sometimes play that way together, but it is nothing more than a game. The men never do it. When I was in Australia, the men were always putting their hands on me in a way that frightened and disgusted me. I knew very well what they wanted, but how can they do such things? It is very wrong. The women, too, they were just as bad in the way they touched me. And when they came close to me, I was always nauseated by their smell. It was the only serious problem I had in Australia."

Mathurin was thoughtful that evening, silent during most of the meal. Mrs. Daim caught his feelings and didn't offer seconds. The conversation had disturbed him in some way that I could not bring out of him. I sat reading for a while, and then he brought out a book I had asked about, *The Birds of Borneo*. He pointed to the birds I'd be most likely to see. In his silence he was gentle and tender.

Mathurin's house was on a high knoll that sloped steeply on two sides down to the water. From the veranda, I could see the Siliu winding through the forest-covered mountains, and if I turned my head slightly to the right, the Tagul was meandering up to where the rivers met, two or three hundred yards away. The hill directly opposite was covered with wild cane, except for the space of a couple of huts, a small grove of coconut and banana trees, and great clumps of tall grasses. The light and the quality of the air were always changing. White clouds and black ones moved constantly across the sky, dropping their blue shadows onto the brilliant green, the shadows curling around the mountains and undulating over the rolling shapes on which they fell. In the early morning, the mist that had settled in the

Schwinnbaum '60

night rose from the rivers, unveiling the surroundings like a lifting curtain. Moonlight burst out for the first time, and the Siliu sparkled with reflection, glaring brightly under black hills silhouetted against the sky, from which the long clouds of gray mist rolled down to the water.

One morning, I took up my drawing pad, went down to the river, hailed a passing *prao,* and was taken to the other side. I sketched vines and trees and jungle growth, thrilled at where I was and with the drawings I was doing. The variety of the bird life fascinated me. Having searched through *The Birds of Borneo,* I was beginning to know the yellow-crowned bulbul, the bird I heard most often though I rarely saw it; and I easily learned to identify, by their bright colors in all that green, the fairy bluebird, the white-rumped shama, the magpie-robin, and the black-winged flycatcher shrike. I sketched at the water's edge where the trees were full of birds. When I was ready to return, another *prao* conveniently appeared and came in answer to my call. In my excitement, I missed a step and slipped, fell into the water, and groaned as I watched my drawings float downstream.

I left Pensiangan with Peter as interpreter. He was the son of Sigoh, the headman second to Mathurin in command of Pensiangan District. There were also four paddlers, and two young men of the malaria gang, who rarely were with us, spending most of their time in houses spraying against mosquitoes. Our first stop was Katuntul, four rapids upstream, where Gayang, the *orangtua,* and five men with gongs were waiting for us at the edge of the river. We had heard the gongs discussing our arrival long before we reached the village, so it was no surprise to be greeted by them. Gayang was dressed in his loincloth of bark. He welcomed us with handclasps and led us into the village's largest hut, which was built of bamboo and thatch. We sat on the floor near the entrance, while a hundred or more people sat or stood behind us in the huge, open room. Food was immediately placed around us in bowls of coconut shells. There were several kinds of fish in various shapes, sizes, colors, and textures, water buffalo meat, pig meat, venison, soup with chicken, mountainous portions of rice on rattan trays, and seven or eight different kinds of fruit. We ate with our hands, and when we were finished, coconut shells full of *tapai* were brought. Three men took up brass gongs and began beating them in dance rhythms. The women, who had been dressed in sa-

rongs, were changing into elaborate costumes—black skirts with intricately patterned beadwork in triangular designs and waistbands thick with beads and bone, and headdresses of beads and feathers. Their breasts were bare except for strands of shell and seed necklaces. Some of the men changed from the simple *chawat* to a more festive one of cloth, painted with zigzag designs, and put on jackets covered with cowrie shells, and headdresses of argos pheasant feathers or white eagle feathers. They began to dance, and I was drawn in, not realizing at first, because of the crowds, that the dancing was on a platform in a square hole below the surface of the floor, in the center of the long room. I stepped down onto this *langsaran* and bounced up and down with forty-three men and women, trying to keep my balance. The *langsaran* was like a trampoline, a bamboo platform about fifteen feet on each side set onto long flexible bamboo poles tied to stakes at the far end. Everyone was holding on to his neighbor and was singing and moving slowly to the right with each jump. I was instantly caught up in the exhilarating action, though it took a while to find the rhythm of the jump.

It was not long before I was led off the dance floor to the *tapai* jars, four of them standing along one wall, the smallest two feet high, the largest about four feet. They had a fine green glaze and were Ming export ware from northern Thailand, traded inland from the coast two or three hundred years earlier. They had quickly become part of the women's dowry and looked starkly refined in that jungle setting. I knelt down and sucked from a bamboo straw, sipping until a leaf tied below the surface appeared and I'd had my full portion. Water was poured in to raise the level above the leaf and the man behind me drank down until it was dry again. The wine remains in the jars covered with a cloth until an occasion for drinking arises, my visit being such an occasion. The cloth had been removed and I saw maggots swimming in the mold on top. Water was added and bamboo used to stir it. The mash began to bubble and work immediately. As a visitor, I was forced into drinking more than anyone else simply because all the men wanted their turn at drinking with me. It is a game everyone thoroughly enjoys, although the guest is usually the first to pass out, which I did.

The dancing looked simple at first, hardly any movements to the feet and just a waving about of the arms, or so I thought before I understood the hand movements and the meaning behind them. When I later demonstrated my technique to Mathurin, he laughed and explained that my gestures were all wrong, that I was chasing the women away with my fingers. I cannot have had a very good time, he said, thinking of the intimacy I had missed with the women. "The fingers must always curl into the palms while the hands face upward, signifying consent. If the palm is down, as you have it, it means rejection." I wondered how many women I had dismissed in this way.

Often there were four or six dancers, men alternating with women; at other times, only women danced, or only men, or a man would dance alone, moving with astonishing grace, or a man would dance with one other man or a woman. I wondered whether the men's movements had any meaning when they danced together, but I could not understand them. Most often, the dancers all faced the same direction, in single file. The movement was up and down on the balls of the feet, with everyone moving slowly forward. At a signal from the dancer in front, everyone turned around. A ring of onlookers formed as small a circle as possible around them, usually jumping up and down and singing the same song over and over:

Andui, andui kulindangan,
Yasoi, yasoi di domidison,
Sandu yuki lindung bolindung,

which roughly translated means: Love something, love everything, love nothing.

During the dancing there was a lot of shouting, patting on the back, and pushing of the shy ones into the circle. The gongs did not stop at all; at least one player continued when the others were eating or drinking. There was a sense of everyone's giving of his whole self and working for the delight of the guest and of the entire village. I was offered delectable bits of raw, roasted, or pickled meat, selected from a bowl and dropped into my open mouth. I was pulled into the dancing group by the men, sometimes by the women, or I was dragged to the jars of *tapai*. When I sucked at the liquor, the men watched and let out a long yell that lasted until I'd finished my portion to their shouts and applause. The noise was thunderous, and the gongs could probably be heard for miles around. There was no way to avoid the drinking, until I learned the trick of remaining on the dance

floor even when I was too tired to dance. The dancing required more effort than I originally supposed, because the bouncing of the *lang-saran* was exhausting, but no one was forced to the jars from the dance floor. There was also the wiser trick of going out to empty my bladder and not returning for half an hour.

Peter and the paddlers were treated with the same amiability accorded me, though the paddlers, used to entertaining and being entertained in the same way, remained in the background but enjoyed themselves thoroughly. None of them had trouble sleeping; they simply stretched out on the floor, put their heads down, closed their eyes, and fell asleep. In spite of the great quantity of liquor I'd consumed, I slept no more than one hour that first night. The noise and the dancing never stopped, and the floor was always shaking. At daybreak, with my head aching and beads of perspiration above my brows, I went down to the river and sat in its cool waters to refresh myself after the heat and energy of the house. When I returned the gongs were silent and Gayang was having everything cleared up but the *tapai*. Coffee and boiled eggs were brought, and Gayang sat with me and Peter while we ate. For the first time, I noticed the two skulls above my head, hanging from a crossbeam. They were covered with decayed cloth and vegetable matter and had obviously been there for years. I had a sudden vision of Gayang and his men raiding the nearby village of Dobolon or Samantabawan whenever heads were needed for ceremonies or for the consecration of a house being built. They brought their captives home tied up with vines and put them into cages of bamboo so tight around them they could not move, each victim in his own cage. Then Gayang and his men, and the women as well, screamed and beat their gongs. They surrounded each cage, one after the other, and taunted the men inside, jabbing them with spears and arrows and long knives, each thrust accompanied by a screech of invocation to a spirit of the dead. "O great hunter of heads and boar, give me prowess to kill!" the men would cry out; "Make the pigs and our bodies grow fertile!" the women would pray, while the steel of their weapons penetrated the victim's flesh, not deeply enough at first to kill, only to wound and terrify, but then prodding deeper until the prisoners died in agony and were decapitated.

While I sipped my coffee and watched the eager, smiling face of Gayang, there seemed nothing but joy in him and the pleasure he was offering me as his guest; yet, I knew that he had been homicidal at times and had taken part in rites that I thought of as violent and cruel. When I pointed to the heads above me, Gayang laughed and said they were Japanese killed during World War II. Peter showed disgust as he translated, and Gayang laughed at him.

When I finished my food, I took out my drawing paper and pens, but before I had a chance to sketch, I was pulled back to the *tapai* jars, and the sound of the gongs began as loudly as ever. Celebrations lasted three days or until the wine ran out. On my fourth and final day in Katuntul, my hand was shaking so badly I could do no work. This had as much to do with lack of sleep as with drinking *tapai*. The five gongs were carried outside the long house and everyone of the village lined up on the bank above the river to bid us farewell. The paddlers, who were as weak as I was, had trouble poling the *prao* through the three rapids upstream to Samantabawan, where again all had been prepared for our arrival, and again we were lavishly entertained. Three mornings later, we went to Siatu, and on the tenth day after leaving Pensiangan, we reached Babayasing, the largest village, where we had our biggest reception.

For me and the men of the *prao,* and certainly for all the villagers, the days were happy ones, though Peter and the boys of the malaria team usually looked as if they would have preferred to remain within the comfort of Pensiangan. I rarely thought of the wild man and I rarely thought about being in his world, though there was a continuous excitement that came from being there. The color and texture of everything had a sensual quality, as did the air itself. I breathed in warmth and memory and desire as if the inside of my chest could experience the qualities that my eyes were taking in. Soft blue hung low in the morning mist and greens sparkled on foliage flashing in filtered sunlight. The curve of the long, lustrous leaves, the vines dripping from high branches, the rare glimpses of animal life, and even the presence of leeches, all became the very essence and reality of myself, authenticating the universe I dreamed into. Without people, the sights and sounds would have been enough to fill me up, but there was more, much more, for the whole atmosphere of the kampongs during the drinking and dancing was unconstrained and deeply erotic. Not only to me but to everyone, though eroticism for the others was a feeling to be acted upon immediately, not thought about or repressed, and I often saw couples disappear into darkness and return with renewed vigor. Unlike me, they hadn't been raised with the restraint of a Judeo-Christian ethic; they were freer than I was, though I wanted to go their way. They had codes no less rigid than ours, but different, mixed up with ancestors, gardens, genealogies.

The men, even those no longer young, had hard, muscular bodies that impassioned me, and I yearned to envelop them with my own body. "Take me!" I wanted to shout. "Give me!" I wanted to yell. "Let me inside your lives and your ferocity!" The men had a forceful masculinity that was basic to their character, alive and instinctual. They were masculine without self-consciousness, while I was at the other extreme, not a man of ruggedness or muscle or virileness but some half creature, thin and weak, not frail but vaguely feminine, not at all a man of wildness. I was living not outside, like them, in displays of physical prowess and emotion, but inside, where only I was aware of my pain, and of my pleasures, too. In my youth I had been incapable of outdoor sports, incapable in my head, of course, because I never tried them, though once in the schoolyard I was forced to play stickball and swung the bat for a homer; so incredulous was I, I lost my bearings, and only after my teammates had yelled directions did I run and touch all bases and return home to overwhelming slaps on the back. Later in the game, I caught a fly ball out in center field, even more amazing because I had tried to hide myself out there, shrivel into nothing, but blinded by the sun, I closed my hands and the ball was there. This was my only experience of sports with other students. Musclemen and athletes were the pride of the school, just as at home my father wished his son to be a wrestler. Yet I was good on parallel and horizontal bars; alone I seemed to manage well.

The Murut men did not need to assert their masculinity but simply accepted it, and I longed to ask about their sexual lives. The women too were attractive, with round, cheerful faces, eyelids lowered in shyness, unrouged lips, ample breasts like globes, the dark nipples high and prominent upon them. They walked with a haughty grace and a charm that was almost irresistible to me.

There was in everyone, in all the men and women of all the kampongs, a delicacy and gentleness, a capacity for laughter and happiness, a kindness in their attitude toward me and toward each other, and an honesty in their naturalness that made me feel inadequate. I had only beads and tobacco to offer, and I had little knowledge of their customs. Everything I did was awkward, and they laughed at me, bringing out my own laughter. They were even amused at the slipperiness of my feet, for there was no traction in my bare soles, no balance in my body. They themselves gave everything there was to be given—their wine, their food, their love; they emptied their larders and their hearts with no thought but to give pleasure and to rejoice in it. They did not think into the future to what might happen because of their generosity; they would have no regrets for what might have been. Missionaries there that I met scorned the Muruts for their drunken orgies, calling them the most intemperate people of Borneo, but to me they seemed to be living their moment to its fullest.

Peter was different. He was seventeen and had an air of arrogance that disturbed me. His hair was cut short in the European manner of the time. He wore an undershirt, over it a white long-sleeved shirt, jockey shorts under khaki shorts, and a new pair of tennis shoes. He might well have been carrying a tennis racket under his arm. The paddlers and I wore sandals and shorts, and a shirt in the cool of morning.

Like all Muruts, Peter was short; he had finely arched brows, black eyes that he used effectively to command in spite of his youth, a wide mouth with full lips that were usually shaped more toward a pout than a smile, thin nostrils, and tiny ears that looked pressed against his head. He wore a ring of clustered rhinestones on the middle finger of his right hand, and on the wrist of the same hand he wore a thin band of spotted skin to ward off the attacks of poisonous snakes. He was strangely silent and aloof most of the time, keeping himself at a distance from everyone, including me, though he was usually at my side during the day. Unlike Mathurin, who came from the coast and was therefore considered to be an outsider, Peter was with his own people, but he seemed to have no interest in them. Throughout our four weeks together, his reclusiveness was often in my mind. He was the son of the headman of Pensiangan, where he had spent his earliest life. He had gone to Catholic schools in Tenom and in Keningau and had only recently returned to Pensiangan to take his place as eldest son at his father's side. Mathurin, with his innate sensitivity and intelligence, and perhaps because of his different teachers and influences, used his schooling to advance and expand his mind. He knew he was not always successful. Peter acted as if schooling in itself made him superior. He was not interested in the life around him and, at least on the surface, he seemed as inexperienced in jungle lore and people as I was. I questioned him about the bone and vegetable charms that men and women wore on strings around their necks or hung over doorways or from ceiling beams; I asked the names of birds and plants and trees, but he seemed empty of such knowledge. In the *prao,* when an unknown bird flew over, I would ask, "Peter! What's that?" and he would shake his head and shrug his shoulders. At my insistence, never through his own initiative, he would ask one of the paddlers, and the name would roll lovingly from the paddler's lips.

I could have learned a great deal from Peter. I had hoped at first that in his youth, he would willingly speak on any subject, but even sex, so openly talked about by everyone in the villages, and so available, too, was not a matter for discussion. He knew nothing about it, he said, and had never had any experience. He didn't care to know, either. Polygamous marriages, he kept insisting, were no longer possible under the new religious law, though the number of wives a headman had was immediately obvious when we were introduced to the women as we went from one kampong to another. Was he lying to impress me? Was he trying to make me think he had risen high above his own people and was so westernized that he knew nothing of their culture? Had he learned in mission schools that Europeans question everything, and did he think he could raise his stature if he too were ignorant of the same things? He looked down on his kinsmen for their lack of education and for their lack of what he thought of as civilized clothing and civilized ways. He did not drink the wine. His reactions to the way of life he had been born into made me wonder again about missions and governments who forced cultural changes without giving a hint that not everything Western is ideal and perfect or that something of traditional life might be good and useful. Mathurin understood a great deal; he will learn from the mistakes of others, and from his own, as well.

Sometimes in the late afternoon, a group would go down to the river to bathe. We would strip and flop into the water and laugh. Peter stood apart, still wearing his shorts, washing himself with a cake of soap. I never had any intimation of what his thoughts might be,

though several times I tried to question him. I was the only one to call him by his Christian name; the others called him Lasir.

At Kampong Dobolon, up the Sibangali River, an appealing young man named Anginsu appeared in the hut soon after my arrival. He had been out hunting and had returned with a rhinoceros hornbill splashing its colorful feathers across his shoulders. He held a blowgun in one hand and wore a torn *chawat* into which he'd tucked his dart case. A *parang,* his long hunting knife, was also tied to his waist, and there was a carrying basket on his back. His hair was short and wild, and his enormous eyes were surrounded by long lashes. His face was wide, square, hard, good-looking. His body, too, was hard and well shaped. In a rush of passion, I made a sketch of him. He laughed at the drawing and I gave it to him. I made another, and then we drank at the jars side by side. I was shivering with the desire his closeness produced in me and went out to empty my bladder. He turned up at my side and we relieved ourselves with our shoulders touching and looking down at one another with interest. When our streams stopped, I slapped him on the back in a need for contact and then, in a joking way, I touched him. Instantly, instinctively, he drew away, then threw an arm around my waist and laughed. He reached to my groin and we examined one another. He was surprised by my circumcision and noted that he was smaller. Later, I saw him describing out mutual interest to a group of young men, and still later to another group.

The eroticism of the kampongs was compounded for me by the fact that someone was always putting a hand on me, touching my arms, my legs, my chest, my back. Older men often sat next to me, gently stroking my arm and inner thigh in a sensual, not quite sexual way. They never went further than this pleasant, affectionate touch, and I did not know how far anyone might have gone if we had been alone and I had pursued it. I was convinced that this had no sexual meaning and was a gesture of warmth and curiosity, no different from the manner of their movements with each other. The two malaria boys slept curled up tightly together inside a double length of sarong, and young men made jokes of grabbing at the bulge of one another's *chawats,* but I saw no contact between men more intimate than this. I returned these signs of friendship in as normal a way as possible for me, though I could not remove the implications from my mind and body. When I was sitting on the floor and a man rested his hand on the bare flesh of my upper thigh, I could not help the quiver that ran across my skin.

That night, I was resting in a corner, flanked by spears and blow-pipes leaning against the bark walls that were painted with abstract designs in red and black. There were monkeys and dogs and children wandering through the remnants of food scattered everywhere over the bamboo. My head was reeling and bouncing against the floor that was going up and down with the jumping of the men and women. Suddenly, I saw clearly for the first time that the dancers were birds, that the men were flying around, strutting, attracting females. Their headdresses of feathers became living plumage and their waving arms became wings. They were soaring through the sky and floating on the wind. I got up and became a bird and entered the dance, rising on an updraft, hovering high above them all, gliding through the airstream, swooping down and gathering up in folded wings the sense of exhila-ration. I was hot and covered with the sweat that poured out from the alcohol inside me. The women disappeared from my vision, and the men, a group of them, no individual man, but the whole of the men there, every one of them, all with their bodies shining in the firelight or silhouetted against it, naked but for the brief *chawat,* their muscles quivering with dance, their eyes open and glittering, sent forth from within themselves a lust that shot into me like a spear, a sensation that flooded my body with passion and overwhelmed my weariness. I wanted to throw myself within the bodies of the men, to burst apart in all directions. They were the wild man and his hand pulled at me, a strong hand that pulled me to my feet and took me to the *tapai.* I sucked deeply and swallowed, and when I breathed again, I sat back and saw that he was Anginsu, an answer, I thought, to the urges within me. I fell back onto the floor and laughed.

It was late then, two or three in the morning. I got up and went to the door. It was raining lightly. I went down the notched log and walked to the edge of the clearing. From the hut came the sounds of song and dance. The rain brought out the fetid smell of earth and leaves and fallen limbs; it was the smell of musk to me. Anginsu mate-rialized, suddenly holding my hand, taking me through a grove of coffee trees in bloom. We stopped under a coconut tree, shielded from the house by foliage. There was mud and stone underfoot. Anginsu pulled his *chawat* to one side, pulled at the waist of my shorts, and leaned back against the tree. His body, naked, excited, was wet with rain. He touched my chest with fingers like feathers and I leaned onto him. We stood there, moving belly against belly, our arms clasped around each other's backs, breathing deeply, luxuriously, as the rain came down more heavily. We rubbed our bodies together and soon released the forces within us. In the rain, cooled and calmed, we went down to the river to wash. At the house, there was no sign that anyone had noticed our absence. We went to the *tapai* and drank. Anginsu was flushed. He went onto the *langsaran* and began a frenzied dance that was different from other dances, more angular, more violent, and I wondered if there was any reference to me in his movements.

I was drunk, or I had been drinking enough to make me drunk; I had just had a moment of deep pleasure; I was living in a suspended world that had no connection with my own past world and had nothing more than a peripheral relationship to the world of those around me. I was living instead the excitement of a dream, my dream of the wild man. For a moment, there was nothing there but him, immense and overwhelming, hovering horizontally above me, floating, coming down to rest upon my body and then sinking into it, calming me with his presence. My brain was tranquilized, accepting him, accepting myself, my place, the existence of the wild man inside me; he was there that instant but unclear; I could not grasp him, only recognize him. My vision was expanding, contracting, pulsating, unseeing. I was stretched upon the top of my sleeping mat with my arms straight back. I was breathing only from the top of my breath, and for another instant I was alone, falling through space, my head falling backward, dizzying me, falling deep into a giant telescope with my brother Moe at the eyepiece, his mind reaching into his future, into his own distance ahead, light years ahead into stars and galaxies. He was stretching away from me, falling the opposite way into depths of sky while I was falling into depths of jungle, he reaching into the future, I into the past. We reversed and were spinning around one another, binary stars revolving around a central cherished theme. He shot off into unknown universes, I was swept into the edge of a whirlpool, swirling around the wild man, accelerating with each turn, the wild man changing into Anginsu, Anginsu there in front of me, dancing, looking as I'd first seen him, blowgun in hand, hornbill over shoulder.

Schneebaum 1960

He was still and I was swirling, around, around. He was changing aspect, poisonous fluids suddenly dripping from darts behind his ears, a length of bone stuffed through his nose, streaks of red painted on his face, feathers cirling his calves and arms. The blowgun was no longer at his side but up against his mouth and he was turning slowly, following me with his eyes, aiming the blowgun at my stomach. His penis, now monstrous in size, was also aimed at me, but the weapon disappeared and he came up close, was on top of me, pushing and pushing. Anginsu, the real Anginsu was pulling me and pulling me, pulling me up to dance, and I was bouncing on the soles of my feet, happy. But the vision gone.

On my last night there, I gave the headman some tobacco, and beads enough for all the women. When he called the women to share the gift, a great uproar burst out of shouts, screams, and beating of gongs, and the *tapai* jars were refilled. In the morning, with everyone lacking sleep and slightly drunk, we slid down the muddy hill. The women were singing and dancing in the mud at the edge of the river, in the water itself, in the *prao,* over me, over the paddlers, refusing to allow us to leave. The paddlers gave a sudden push with their poles, upsetting the balance of the standing women. The *prao* turned over and dumped us all into the still water.

As we traveled along the Sibangali River, the exuberance of the men increased in a way that left me exhausted but only added to their own energy. It was as if the liveliness of the paddlers, even when sluggish from lack of sleep, intensified with our arrival at each new kampong. Men were caught up in the festive spirit and came along with us, adding new *prao*s to our growing fleet. We were a flotilla of eight canoes by the time we got to Bantangon on the border of Kalimantan. The canoes were poled along in single file, with shouts and songs to brighten the way.

One night, I tried to sleep outside, a shocking breach of etiquette. Until then, I had been able to manage only catnaps. In Bantangon, even these were impossible, for the men and women danced where I was trying to sleep. The violent movement of the floor never stopped. That night, I picked up my mat and my blanket and, to everyone's surprise, went out and spread the mat on the ground, covering myself with the blanket and falling asleep immediately. It was not long, however, before I was awakened by the sound of coarse breathing and heavy steps coming closer. Soon I felt the breathing on my head and a tugging at my blanket. I opened my eyes and looked up at an enormous water buffalo. I sat up and the animal backed away. I picked up my blanket and returned to the house, to be greeted with hoots of laughter and embraces from everyone.

From the time Anginsu first gossiped about the differences between us, a group of men accompanied me whenever I went to the river to bathe. They stared at me and made me nervous. I knew that their frankness, their openness, their curiosity, and their timidity, too, were their way of life and were what I hoped for in myself as well. As long as nothing in *me*, the object of their interest, threatened them, I in turn could be equally free with them without embarrassment, with nothing to hold me back but simple courtesy.

As they stared at me, so I began to stare at them. The candor and trust were part of the joy of being there, and I thought about it often. But thinking could also sadden me, as it did on occasions when it took me back to youth, to a series of photographs that haunt my memory, a progression in which each photo remains still for a moment, then jumps to the next one. It is not slow motion in any sense, but an advancement in a time sequence. In the first one, my mother is laughing; I am also there, aged ten or so, and we are going somewhere important. In the next photograph, we are standing at the bottom of the gangway of the S.S. *Pilsudski*, looking up at the deck for someone. Next, there's a picture of a man in a steward's white jacket coming down the gangway; I know he is a relative, and it is exciting to realize that we are smuggling him into the country. Another photo shows the three of us in a taxi crossing the Brooklyn Bridge; and the final one is of me on the floor with this man, fighting him, beating him on the shoulder or biting him on the leg. There's a pause in the time sequence, a blackout, and then the movie of my mind begins to roll.

I am at the kitchen table in the back of the store. I am drawing and am deeply involved in my work. Suddenly, the man has taken me by the arm and is scolding me, pointing to the store, where I sense my father has been calling me for some time. I shake off the hand and return to my drawing. Then I am on the floor with the man, fighting him, beating him on the shoulder, biting him on the leg. The movie reel jumps ahead and the man has taken me to the Loew's in Bay

Schnebaum '60

Ridge. The time is winter and we sit in the darkness of the theater with heavy coats over our laps. His knee is pressing against mine. He takes my left hand, moves it under his coat and into his open fly. The shock of touch attacks my hand, thrills me, and causes me to tremble violently. On the screen there is movement but no sound, for I hear only the booming of my heart and the throbbing in my temples. We go to other movie houses, and we ride in his car and stop in Owl's Head Park to perform simple rituals. During these times together, he never touches me, never looks at me. It is as if the relationship did not exist. There is no acknowledgment of anything but seeing a film or riding in a car. I yearn for something closer, to be able to touch his face, to be able to talk to him, and I ask nothing more complicated than why he chose me rather than one of my brothers; but somehow I know that a word would destroy it all.

He never looked at me, that man, but the men of Borneo openly stared and I stared back in pleasure. It was a liberation, being able to stand there while they stared, and staring back was even more so. Tiwason in Bantangon had been more curious than others about me, watching me, following me out to urinate, following me down to the river, sitting with me, dancing with me, insisting on our drinking together the whole day. In the evening, he spread his mat for us both to sleep on. With the firelight low, with the singing silent for the moment and the floor at rest, with the night sending in its insect sounds and the house giving off its vibrations of peace and stillness, we covered ourselves with my blanket. I curled myself against his back, put my hand onto his bare stomach and rubbed it. He made noises of pleasure that reverberated through my arm. In anticipation, I reached farther down. Gently, he patted my hand; gently, he brought it up to his chest and into his armpit. He held it there and fell asleep, and I slept on with a great sense of well-being, trust, and even hope.

Chapter Three

Often in the brilliant moonlight, moments of startling beauty would strike out at me from the shadows and shapes and colors, from the black fantasies traced and blocked against the deep blue of the sky or the shining white of the river. Standing under the trees, swaying in a half stupor, gazing into nowhere while I emptied the *tapai* from my bladder, my eyes would suddenly open wide and stare. A virginal vision of my surroundings would flare up and I'd jump back and try to impress it on my mind: the sharp outline of the huts, the slow movement of the palms, the swift passage of the clouds, and the calm of the dark, dormant mass of the forest, almost reversing the animal aliveness of the day, when my sight was clearer and my mind fresher. Sometimes when I was bathing, an awareness would come up within me of the men around me, of their brown bodies awash in the green water, with black rocks and tangles of jungle behind them; and overhead a flash flight of shrieking parrots would burst up from the trees and settle down like tossed clumps of red clay. Everything was dulled by my drinking the *tapai*; everything was sharpened and reinforced by my presence in a world that was so insistently a part of my life.

I sat in Pensiangan on the porch of Mathurin's house, staring out at a landscape that was more beautiful each time I looked at it. I made realistic drawings of the views, working a whole day on a single sketch, while rain and mist blurred the forest. One morning at six, I said good-bye to Mathurin and his wife and got into the *prao* with four men, two women, and two children. We traveled up the Salio River, passing neither *prao* nor hut during the twelve-hour journey. The rapids were long, frequent, violent. Six or seven times, I got out with Ilanu, one of the men, and with the women and the children, and we walked through jungle while the others, waist-deep in the river, pulled the *prao* over the rocks and through the furious water. The forest was solid with thorns and vines and overgrowth. Ilanu cut our path with his long *parang* and we climbed hills and waded over stones at the river's edge. Whenever we were close to deeper water, Ilanu threw his circular net upstream and drew in small fish, which he stuffed into bamboo containers.

There were tiny sunbirds flying in pairs and resting on branches, twittering out their discordant calls, and small-headed birds, tan and white, perching, bobbing their bottoms as if practicing the bumps of stripteasers; screeching eagles sailing high on the wind; flying foxes against the sky in the evening, moving from treetop to treetop; and the river itself rushing down at us while blue butterflies and black darning needles hovered above our heads. Once, when we'd stopped to scrape the leeches from our legs and arms, Ilanu saw the fresh prints of a mousedeer and went off with the other men; they came back half an hour later empty-handed, but with no sign of disappointment. At sunset, we arrived at Tumunkasi, where I was led into a house whose walls were decorated with the jawbones of wild boar, the long tusks still curving from the bone. Spears and blowpipes leaned below them. There was no dancing that night, and I drank only a few bowls of *tapai,* but when I put my head down onto the bamboo of the floor, it began to spin. I meandered lazily through my past and future. The wild man had seldom revealed himself to my consciousness but had become a subcutaneous presence that underlay my thoughts. Why hadn't he overtly appeared among those former headhunters, those men who stung me with their touch, the men with whom I sat and talked and drank and danced? They'd been around me, the men of Borneo, and I was there within the orbit of the wild man; yet, only in the dream was he alive and real. The men in Tumunkasi that night were settling onto mats and curling up in pairs. I was on my own mat, easing myself into the sleep that brought again the hallucination of my penis tatooed, a bone through my septum, a skull hanging by a strip of gut from my neck.

The fantasy never lasted; instead, it moved on like a swelling wave, heaving and undulating with ecstasies. I looked back and I looked forward; I look again and suddenly, without warning, the present is upon me, is with me now, and I am here writing this page. I am still full of *tapai*; I am still lying with my head on the bamboo floor; I am still reaching.

When wasn't I reaching? When wasn't I pursuing untouched corners of my brain and soul? When wasn't I seeking out resting places for my energies and passion, my melancholy and depression? I lost interest in my Judaic beliefs in early adolescence, after my mother's death, and spent my spare time reading Lin Yutang and Evans-Wentz, delving as deeply as possible for me then into the Upanishads, the *Bhagavad Gita* and the rest of the *Mahabharata*, the Tibetan Book of the Dead, the *Dhamapada*, the *Book of Tao*, feeling my solitary way into the philosophies of India and the East, paralleling, substituting, enriching my search for the wild man in this other way. These philosophies spoke of a way of living with which I felt a harmony, a way that was honest and unpretentious, a way unlike what I thought of as the wasteful life around me. I had not yet begun to paint in earnest, and my life still lacked that sense of fire kindled by working on a canvas. It was a time of Gandhi's truths, and he epitomized many of the needs of my own soul, though there was no apparent connection between his life and mine, hardly more than a yearning in me toward the darkness of his skin, the emaciation of his body. I knew only that he represented truth and truth was among the things I thought I searched for. I projected myself into his suffering and into his idealism. I steeped myself as well in works not quite related to him, in Ouspensky, Gurdjieff, and Mme. Blavatsky, studying the mysteries of everlasting life and the pleasures that come from within oneself if one knows the secret of their release.

That time was lived in blindness, for I never knew the direction in which I needed to go. Unarticulated urges alternated with peace and serenity, but nothing was realizable; nothing was consciously gained. It was an exorcism of the dybbuk that had entered me early in youth and demanded release only when there were forces to absorb its spirit, a place for it to inhabit. India might have been an exorcism, I thought; Gandhi might have sustained me as another part of the wild man, both a yin and yang, opposites that would come together and solidify me.

By that time in my life, through reading and the demands my body made for fulfillment, I had primed myself into an obsession with the marvels and beliefs of India, and when my plans to go to Borneo seemed to be going awry, it was to India that my mind immediately turned. I had written to Tom Harrison of the Sarawak Museum in Kuching and to the Chief Secretary in Jesselton, North Borneo, knowing that visas were difficult to come by. Tom Harrison had written back saying that I was not a qualified anthropologist and therefore would not be welcome in Sarawak, and when the months passed with no word from Jesselton, I gave up on North Borneo as well. I thought then to cross the whole of Asia from Istanbul to Singapore, spending most of the time in India.

Two days before my freighter sailed, a letter arrived from the Chief Secretary assuring me he would be happy to help if, in exchange, I was willing to give the government of North Borneo some of the drawings I would do. I agreed, but decided that Borneo would come after my journey across the continent.

Three months after landing in Istanbul and traveling on trucks, buses, and foot, I crossed the border from Lahore in Pakistan to Amritsar in the Punjab. I spent my first ten days sleeping with thirty or forty others in the courtyard of the Golden Temple of the Sikhs, on a cot lent me by an attendant named Balwant. That first night was so complete a fulfillment of my dreams of India that a sensuality seeped along the surface of my skin. On the cot to my right was an ancient bearded man whose face was like the face of the rabbi who taught us Hebrew at our kitchen table behind the store. His full, white beard was like the rabbi's, and the odd tic of tilting his head as he talked was also the same. I knew nothing of the rabbi or of his life, nothing more personal than that the wrinkled black suit and the black hat he always wore smelled of age and dried perspiration. He was our teacher; he came and went; there was no nonsense while he taught, no instant of revealing how he lived at home. In India, I saw the guru on

his cot, his long tangled hair untied at night, covering his bare shoulders like a purple robe in the light of the room. The rabbi had sat at the table stiffly bent over, nodding the rhythms of the Pentateuch; the guru lay there beside me with his arms loose, his legs slack, the whole of his body so relaxed that he rested in perfect ease, in the freedom and tenderness I imagined were everywhere around him.

It was the guru who took me into the Golden Temple in the morning. There was a long line of pilgrims along the narrow causeway across the great pool, waiting to enter the gilded two-story shrine. We passed the crowds and entered a room in which three men in white turbans sat cross-legged on thick carpets along one side, chanting, the oldest in the center reading from the huge volume of the Granth Sabib, using his fly whisk at the line like a reader before the Ark of the Covenant with his pointer in the Torah. To me, they were three Oriental Jews from the brush of Rembrandt! I dropped a rupee note into a basket and received a lei of jasmine blossoms and an orange; I held them in my hands and shook them as I used to shake the citron and palm leaves in the synagogue.

Surrounding the temple, far more varied and rich than the ghetto of the Lower East Side, was the area of the bazaars: narrow streets hung with long, colorful banners; fat men naked to the waist squatting like Buddhas behind their pots of steaming foods; bicycles, ox-carts, tongas, and buffalo and sacred cows sitting in the street and blocking the traffic. There were Sikhs everywhere. The men were oddly unattractive in beard nets or with string tied into facial hair to curl it; the women looked lavish with rings and diamonds in their nostrils, their ears cluttered with jewels, their arms and wrists and ankles covered with masses of bands and bracelets. Occasional saddhus carried begging bowls and staffs, and other holy men went by with faces streaked with yellow paint or gold. Flute players and drummers were followed by placards announcing the latest movie; hawkers sold mangoes and fruits still unknown to me. My first stop in India had all the color and excitement anyone could have imagined or wished for.

The next day I was out with my sketchboard, wanting to draw everything in sight, unable to draw anything for the exhilaration that made my hands shake. A holy man wearing a blue G-string, a *rumali*, was some yards away with his back to me. He was elegantly bent, with his arms and begging bowl stretched out to receive an offering. I began to draw and he turned, a startling man with deep black skin and a long black beard, a mass of hair on his chest, and hair circled in layers on his head, each layer dyed a different color. He saw me with my pen and paper and put a hand in front of his face. As if frightened, he ran down a flight of stairs and disappeared, only to reappear, poking his head out of a door to stare and smile a curious, wistful smile and disappear again. The shopkeepers around had been watching this with interest and amusement. Several motioned me to follow him. I went down the steps to an open passageway, where he seemed to have been waiting, leaning against a wall, almost posing there, not quite sure what to make of me. His head began to shiver slightly, and suddenly he was going up a flight of stairs toward an open door. Again I followed, into a small room with worn carpets, where three men sat drinking from saucerless cups. They turned to look at me, bowed their heads, smiled, and went back to their conversation. My saddhu from the street was off in a corner unwinding his hair, unwinding it almost without end. In the color of rust it touched the floor, a length of blue, and then a length of dirty, olive green. With his head bowed and his hair falling to one side and down to the floor, with his hands at the nape of his neck, his elbows out, he was a slender, ascetic version of a voluptuous bather by Degas; and I stood watching him in silence, moved by the slowness of time, by the murmurings and laughter in the room, and by the noises from the street. I was still for a moment, suddenly still, quiet inside myself. I did not hear the sounds in the room, though someone had come up softly behind me.

"Would you like a cup of coffee, sir?" It was an old man with a wrinkled chest. He led me to another room with plush pillows on the floor, and I sat on silks of orange and ochre. The coffee appeared, and I sipped alone while staring at the cracked walls covered with photographs of men seated cross-legged.

A rotund little man came in and introduced himself as Suri Anantananda. The man I had followed came to the door and stood there hesitantly, watching, listening, both of his hands in the black of his beard. Suri Anantananda motioned him away with a toss of his head and said, "He's a *harijan,* an untouchable, and is not allowed in this room. We must keep the castes separated." In meticulous English, he explained that I had entered a Hindu monastery and that visitors were not permitted. He was the chief disciple and heir apparent. The Master, who was ill, would die within the week.

"It is a small monastery. We are only twelve saints here," he said with pride. "We become saints at the age of eight, when we are chosen to live in the monastery, and from then on we are bachelors. We do not think about women or worldly goods. We are not permitted to cut our hair in a normal way, but we must either shave every particle from our bodies, from head to toe, or we must never cut any of it." Suri Anantananda had chosen to shave his hair. His head and body were smooth and polished. He wore a white dhoti wrapped around his thick waist, leaving his lower thighs and shins bare. His upper half bulged with breasts and folds of flesh around his waist, around his neck. Kohl outlined his eyes and there was a red caste mark on his forehead. He pointed to the photos of the men behind him. "These are our former Masters." All the men were shaved and hairless, plump and sexless.

Suri Anantananda got up, already taking leave of me. "When you return to your country, please tell your people how beautiful we are. Please tell them that we are saints and send them peace." He called a servant to let me out, turned, closed his eyes as if in prayer, and went down the corridor.

The lowly *harijan* was at the bottom of the stairs, with his head bent. He peeked up to look at me. I put my palms together, nodded and said, *"Na masté."* As I was about to enter the street, I turned to wave, but he was gone.

I had stumbled into a monastery into which I should not have gone, and my reception by the chief disciple was certainly more than I deserved, yet it left me curiously dissatisfied. It was not a meeting with a saint that I could have imagined; it had interested me more to be with the *harijan,* whatever he was. I was trying to make up my mind about the incident and was walking through the gate of the temple when an old man came up and shook a fist in my face. "Nehru is not good! A bad man! He's nothing! A monster! We must destroy him!" He was already within the temple compound before I recognized him as the revered guru, my own rabbi, who had slept next to me in the courtyard. We had talked the previous night about Sikhs and their religion, comparing it with the other main religions of India, Hinduism and Islam and Buddhism. He had been gentle and kindly, talking in a soft voice that sounded in the night air like the whisper of wings.

"Our founder was the great Guru Nanak," he had said. "He was like your Jesus Christ. He died, he went up to the Lord, and then he returned to earth to spread his teachings. He said to his followers, 'There is no Hindu, there is no Muslim.' And he said, 'There is only one thing that matters; unless Truth enters the soul, all service and study are useless.' "

The moon lit up the courtyard and shone in tiny lights in the guru's eyes. He was stretched out on his cot, leaning on his left side. There was nothing moving around us but the slowly creeping shadows of the walls and the entrance gate. Occasional voices drifted on the wind as pilgrims lined up to enter the temple and pay homage.

"The time of Guru Nanak was five hundred years ago, when the

Muslims and Hindus were almost at peace with one another in the Punjab. The Muslims came to India with violence, destroying temples and killing people and trying to force Islam upon us. But they could not change the religion with war. It was not until the Sufis, one of the Muslim sect, came that there was peace."

My mind went back to Persia and its greatest poets, Hafiz, Omar Khayyám, and Saadi, all of whom had been under Sufi influence.

"The Sufis were a gentle order of Muslims and did not believe in violence," he went on. His voice had none of the harshness or the singsong quality of the voice of my rabbi. I listened and learned.

"Guru Nanak found much to admire in their ways, for they believed in one God, and they did not believe in the caste system. But they disapproved of all who did not believe as they did. Guru Nanak discarded the Sufi rituals that had no meaning; he saw no reason for anyone to isolate himself and be an ascetic; and he said, 'There is one God, His name is Truth,' and this is what we teach."

The guru sat up in his cot and looked at me, no longer with such gentleness, and succumbing to the tic of tilting his head—precisely the gesture of the rabbi at the moment I made a mistake in reading the Book of Esther. "Eh? Eh?" the rabbi questioned. Clop! went his thumb and forefinger on the top of my head. Clop, again! The guru shook his fist, and I thought of the Sikh army and its militarism; I thought of God demanding the destruction of Jericho, of the battles to take the land of Canaan. "But we are in another time and we have other problems to be solved. Look at how Nehru fears us! Why should he treat us so differently from all the other states of India? Only because we are Sikhs and he fears our troops! All the other states have their own language equal to Hindi, but we are not permitted to use Punjabi officially. Why is this? Tell me, why is this? We are more Sikhs in the Punjab than any other people, and we should have our own language! Nehru is an egomaniac. It is like his not wanting to give up the Kashmir because he was born there. The laws of partition should have given it to Pakistan because the religion there is Islam, but he will not let his birthplace go to another land!"

The newness of everything overwhelmed whatever negative thoughts might have entered my mind. I was prepared to move in any direction and decided to visit the area where the Dalai Lama lived. I remembered hearing that this was a place called Dharamsala in the Punjab and that it might be possible to see him.

Dharamsala was a series of hamlets that hung on to steep slopes of the western Himalayas. The high mountains, sometimes hidden by cloud, were sharply peaked and ridged with snow. Jungle and pine forest grew below the snow line, and the air was fresh and cool. The British had used the region for weekends and vacations from the heat of the plains. Lord Elgin himself died and was buried there. I arrived during the monsoon, the season when the hills capture the clouds for heavy, almost constant rain, where waters rush down the mountainside to the valley and flood the villages below. The people of Dharamsala say with pride that they have one of the heaviest rainfalls in India, one hundred sixty-six inches a year, a substantial amount, but not comparable to the nine hundred five inches of rain that fell in 1861 in Cherrapunji in Assam, on the other side of India, a thousand miles to the east, where three hundred sixty-five inches of rain had deluged the land during the month of July alone. I liked the rain and the mysterious quality the clouds and mist gave to the surroundings, hiding, then unveiling, the forests. At times, the clouds rolled away and offered glimpses of the mountains and valleys that stretched on into the distance.

On my first morning, borrowed umbrella in one hand, sketchboard in the other in case of a break in the weather, I climbed to McLeodganj in Upper Dharamsala, where many Tibetans had settled. In the dry season, a bus goes there, taking the long way around through Forsythganj, a distance of six miles. Via the Nowgojee Road, the steep footpath, the distance to McLeodganj is only two miles. The whole of the area is known as Dharamsala.

I stopped for tea under a cypress tree and continued up the mountain to Suwarg Ashram, where the Dalai Lama lived. I registered at the police station, as all visitors must, and was given a pass. The buildings and gardens of the ashram were enclosed by a high wall; inside, I was directed to a small wooden house and was greeted by Sonam Topgay Kazi, interpreter to the Dalai Lama. His face was round but not soft and had sharply angled cheekbones; his smile looked permanent but was not fixed or empty. His face showed kindliness, sympathy, warmth, intelligence. We sat in overstuffed chairs sipping tea while he questioned me and asked why I had come. I was ashamed to answer, in truth, that twenty years earlier I had seen the official photograph of His Holiness at the time of his investiture as Dalai Lama when he was a boy. He was enveloped, almost hidden, within his robes and winged hat, sitting on a great purple pillow; and that photo, seen only once, had remained clearly in my mind, evoking memories of mysticism and the mysterious East, the occult, yogic ecstasy and astral bodies of Shangri-la and even Genghis Khan and Marco Polo. Instead of mentioning those memories, I said I hoped to ask His Holiness about the work CARE was doing with the Tibetan refugees in India, a worthy subject for an interview, I thought. Sonam listened and seemed satisfied that I was no threat. He made a phone call, and a thin man with a shaved head came in. He wore the same brown robes as Sonam and was introduced as the personal secretary of His Holiness. He set up an appointment for Saturday, three days away. When he had noted it on his calendar, I got up with him and started out the door, but Sonam asked me to stay on to talk of Western painting.

There were six Berthe Morisot reproductions tacked to a board over the mantelpiece. "I saw them in a magazine and liked them, so I cut them out and put them up. We do not often see the art of other countries here." Sonam had been born in Sikkim and had gone with his family to Tibet when he was five. "That was many years ago, and I have been with His Holiness ever since. When we first escaped to India, we came to Mussoorie, and now we are here. The ashram is very beautiful. There is no life for me outside it." We talked of my being a painter, and then about Renoir, Manet, Bonnard, as if I were comparable to them. "I have not yet advanced to an understanding of Picasso," he said. "But perhaps that too will come."

The next morning, I went back to see Sonam with some drawings I'd made in Afghanistan of the giant Buddhas carved into the great wall of Tolwara at Bamian. He looked so enviously at them that I gave him one.

The night before the appointed Saturday was a restless one. I got up earlier than usual that morning and had breakfasted by six. When I arrived at the ashram, a long line of Tibetan men and women were waiting outside. Several monks stood together, all wearing brown robes over mustard-colored sleeveless shirts. They all looked between the ages of seventeen and twenty-five. Other, older men were in darker robes, with winged or sheepskin hats on their heads and prayer beads around their necks or wrists. The hair of most was uncombed, while others had shaved their heads except for a long pigtail. The women braided their hair and wore dark woolen garments brightened with silver or bead necklaces. Almost everyone was wearing a photograph of the Dalai Lama on a button like a campaign button pinned to his jacket or coat. A man with his head bent as if deep in thought walked along twirling a prayer wheel, each revolution offering the litany *"Om mani padme hum."* The men and women waited calmly, while around them was a confusion I had not seen before. Uniformed men were rushing about, climbing in and out of trucks, and directing soldiers in what seemed chaotic fashion. At eleven thirty, according to plan, I telephoned Sonam from the police station.

"I am most sorry," he said, "but His Holiness is not well today, and it is not yet certain that he will be able to see anyone. But you will wait there, I think, and I will call you as soon as a decision is made."

At noon hunger pangs reminded me that there was nowhere for lunch but back down in McLeodganj. A number of flustered policemen suddenly entered the station house and demanded everyone's papers. The papers were carefully examined and all names written on a ledger sheet. Everyone but me was physically searched. At two o'clock we were herded to the ashram and told to wait outside the gate. After a while, we all sat down on stones at the side of the road. Indian officials were running about, their faces grim. By three, most of the visitors had given up and had drifted off. A cold wind came up with rain, and I shivered in my wet clothes. I went back to the police shed and sat with four men. Some time later, I telephoned.

"I'm most sorry," Sonam said in a sadder tone than he'd used earlier, "but you will not be able to see His Holiness today."

"May I see him in the morning, then?"

"Oh, no! In the morning he will be at his meditations."

"Can you tell me when I will be permitted to see him?"

"I'm sorry, but I don't know, sir. You will have to be patient."

Cold, wet, hungry, frustrated, and exasperated by the delay, I shouted into the phone, "Is this the way you usually treat visitors to the ashram? Don't you think it was rude to have kept me waiting so many hours without having had the courtesy of offering some explanation?"

"Oh, please, sir, wait! Wait there, sir! Wait right there!"

Relieved by having given in to my anger, I sat down again. Sonam arrived five minutes later, drenched with rain; so upset was he by my outburst that he had forgotten his umbrella. His face was contorted as if he were in pain. He led me into a side room of the police station.

"Those were cruel words you spoke to me, my good friend." Tears rolled down his cheeks. This was probably the first time anyone had spoken so harshly to him. My apologies were honest and deeply felt, for I was thoroughly ashamed. How could I talk that way to a member of the Dalai Lama's court? Sonam, simple, singular man that he was, accepted my apology, and in a strange instant, we not only returned to our former familiarity but went on to an intimacy that was rare and soft and compassionate, expressed in nothing more than a look between us and the touch of a finger on my wrist. He too must have been irritated by the day's events and could not have eaten lunch; he had been busy in the office of His Holiness.

"Please wait only a few more minutes. There must be word soon, and then you will come and have supper with me." Sonam returned to the ashram.

Content because he had quieted me with his look and with the sound of his words, I put off the cramps in my stomach by smoking one cigarette after another until I emptied the pack. I decided to go down to the Rest House and had begun to write a note to Sonam when his call came through and I went to his rooms.

"You must be very angry with me."

"The truth is that I'm too hungry to be angry."

He motioned to a servant who was preparing food. "You understand what happened today, don't you?"

"No, I don't. I only know that the police were rushing around."

"The thing is that there were suspects."

"Suspects?"

"There were secret agents from China trying to get in to see His Holiness. The police found four of them climbing the wall. They had guns and knives with them, so we canceled today's appointments and there was a search."

Tinned meat and vegetables came to the table, and we ate quickly. I wondered whether the canned food was served in deference to my being a foreigner. Sonam cautioned me to say nothing of the suspects, but on my way down to the Rest House, I saw a crowd following a truck. Standing in back were four manacled men.

When I phoned the next afternoon, Sonam told me to come up as quickly as possible. I went directly to his house, and he led me along a path lined with cedars to a small building in front of which several men were kneeling and bowing their heads. Next to them were men in robes tinkling small bells. They faced a porch where three lamas murmured and gestured blessings. The shining faces of the priests looked freshly polished and their smooth heads glossy and burnished, as if light came from within their skulls. When the group of bowing men backed off, Sonam took me closer. The three men on the porch looked so much alike that had it not been for the buttons with photographs, I might not have been able to distinguish the Dalai Lama. He, like the other two lamas, wore horn-rimmed glasses; he had none of the pomp and exoticism that had been the picture in my mind. But when I recognized him, I also recognized his spirit, for he had a glow around his head as if he had a halo, or I a "third eye" with which to see his aura.

Sonam and I climbed three steps but remained at a level below His Holiness. Through Sonam we talked, but for no more than four or five minutes. There was a quiet composure about him as he stood there, and I felt a tranquillity emanating from him and even piercing me. I could not think clearly, and no words of importance passed between us. I think he somehow understood that I had come to be in his presence rather than to interview him. I cannot remember whether or not I presented him with the traditional silk scarf, but I remember his saying that he hoped the U.N. would force the Chinese out of Tibet so he could return to Lhasa. The Red Cross was not being as helpful, either medically or with food, he said, as CARE had been years earlier.

Even in that short time with him, I was so awed that I could barely hear his voice through the ringing in my ears, and I could only mumble indistinctly. I took him away inside me when I left, and he remained there for several weeks. I often felt him flare up like a nova or a variable star, blinding me to what was around me, filling me with increased yearning for nonexistence, sanctity, and the Universal Self, states of mind I did not understand. But in fading, he allowed the surrounding life to impress itself upon me.

A horde of guides attacked me when I got off the train in Raja Ki Mandi to visit Agra and the Taj Mahal. I had to fight my way through the mobs, each member pulling at my small bag. They all knew the perfect hotel and would happily show me the way on foot or by trishaw or tonga. The manner of their descent on me put me in bad humor for the rest of the day, and the Taj, though stunningly elegant and simple in structure, seemed too richly decorated on the surface of the tomb and in the intricate lacework of the marble screens inside.

Outside the gate, lepers poked fingerless palms in my face and frightened me. An offered coin always provoked an onrush of beggars roughly pushing one another to close in on me with demands for similar grace. The torments, the frustration, and the sadness of the people were seen everywhere, but even with these depressing, almost continuous pressures, stimulation and excitement were there.

I continued by train to Gwalior, which was rich with good moments. It was a pleasant, welcoming town, though it had little to offer the tourist: a fortress sprawling along the top of a mesa, a number of Jain temples inside its walls, a grand palace on the edge of a cliff, and below, Jain statues carved into rock.

Three Indians and their guide were inside the fortress. The guide was speaking so loudly in English I could hear they were about to go down into the dungeons. Since I had forgotten my flashlight, I followed them. They did not seem to mind my being there and occasionally smiled at me. The guide's comments kept me in good humor for some time.

"These rooms," he said, shining his light around the gloomy tunnels and chambers, "were used to hide the women when a fierce battle was raging. And these hooks," he said, pointing to the tops of pillars at some iron rings that were certainly used to chain the arms of prisoners, "were where the swings were hung so the ladies could enjoy themselves while waiting." He put his flashlight into a recess in the wall. "Oil lamps were placed here to give the women ample illumination," he said, though it would have taken a dozen klieg lights to brighten that particularly dismal room. A deep, large pit, in which I could easily imagine crocodiles and other wild animals waiting for victims to be thrown down to them, "was used for bathing." I had a vision of all the women of the court sporting and enjoying themselves, swimming in the pool, swinging on the swings, and having a grand old time, while above them, their fathers and brothers and husbands were killing and being killed. The guide didn't bother to explain the purpose of a door in one wall that could be opened to let water in to flood the room.

That afternoon, Lord Krishna's birthday, a procession of painted elephants encircling a palanquin that held a golden statue crossed the road while I was on my way back to the hotel. No sooner had I entered my tower room when there was a knock on the door, and standing there was a man of whom I had asked directions earlier in the day. He invited me to dinner at his home that night. He had intelligent eyes, a sharp nose, thick sensuous lips, and a pleasant smile. He wore a white turban carelessly twisted around his head and a white dhoti covering his waist and thighs. I accepted the invitation, and he returned at seven.

Mr. Chandwasker lived several blocks away, in a tiny two-room flat two stories above the ground, with his mentally ill wife and seven children, all of whom slept in one room. When we arrived, Asha, the eldest child, a sweet and pretty girl of eighteen with jasmine blossoms in her hair, had just finished washing the wooden floor and was throwing the dirty water out the window. She brought two low blocks of wood for us to sit on, took up a handful of fine, white sand from a bowl, and, while her father and I talked of India, let the sand filter through her thumb and forefinger, moving quickly, making a sketch of leaves in front of us, as if putting down place mats. It gave me a strong feeling of welcome. Rice and vegetables, steaming hot, appeared, and Asha and her brothers and sisters sat around and watched and listened as we ate. Asha translated for those who understood no English. Mrs. Chandwasker was not seen or mentioned.

Mr. Chandwasker talked of his life as a part-time guru. He had a clerical job with the railway and usually worked a year at a time, saving as much money as possible; then he would set off to preach the *Gita* with nothing more than a robe on his back, a bowl in one hand,

and a staff in the other. When he returned to Gwalior, the job was waiting for him. It sounded like my own life. After dinner he sang one of his own poems, first in Hindi, then in English:

> Hark ye! Listen to the rumblings
> on the Mount of Sanchi.
> When questioned what is inside these stupas,
> the mountain answers:
> Oh, man of two thousand years, weep!
> For mankind has wounded me,
> and every stone of mine,
> every rock of mine,
> is a stupa—a place of pilgrimage.
> Oh, look at the shattered doors of my great stupa.
> Can't you hear the whining cry of the rock?
> The man-becoming-demon tried to destroy humanity.
> The world comes here every day
> to pay homage to the path of Ahimsa, of nonviolence,
> and finds the great tradition of Indian culture
> earned in the Gates
> in the form of stones from Jataka.
> But they have forgotten the Man
> who toiled for centuries
> to build up Man from a particle of stone,
> creating nonviolent humanity.
> Hark, ye man of two thousand years!
> Listen to the rumblings!

In Hindi, the song was electrifying.

Soon we were talking about my own family and life. When it was discovered that I had brothers but no sister, Asha brought a bowl of ash and dabbed my forehead with a fingertip. She tied silver tinsel around my left wrist, and Mr. Chandwasker mumbled a prayer in Hindi. Thus, Asha became my adopted sister, and I was a member of the family.

Days like these were satisfying but rare. Mr. Chandwasker was easy to be with for a few hours on each of the days I was there, but our relationship gave me only pleasure and not the insights and knowledge I hoped to gain. He was a guru, but he did not expand my thinking, though I opened my mind to whatever he might offer. He may have offered more than I realized then, but I was expecting too much too soon. Indian religions are more demanding than Western

ones; Judaism and Christianity are faiths of acceptance, requiring little effort or curiosity, only the acknowledgment of certain beliefs established by divine revelation. Indian religions require concentration
and inner search and are inseparable from Indian philosophies. The
Old and New Testaments tell of a definite chain of events; the Upanishads brood upon the meaning of existence, the meaning of God, the
meaning of Self. Nothing but death is certain in life, and death brings
no fear because it means rebirth.

There is a picture of Benares in my mind, of enormous blue cranes
tiptoeing through the rice fields as if afraid to get their feet wet, and
other birds almost tame enough to touch, flying into rooms and settling to nibble at crumbs as if humans didn't exist, of packs of monkeys in the temples, huge booming drums in processions of gilded
elephants, children on stilts twice their own height, magicians throwing snakes around and telling jokes, gurus at the ghats lecturing to
crowds. I sit and try to sketch this deluge of humanity, but the atmosphere prevents me. I sense I am invading a privacy, as if I am prob-
ing secrets better left unknown. I walk and turn and stumble over a
corpse wrapped so tightly in white cloth that its features are clearly
outlined. Dozens of bodies lie there, sprinkled with red powder and
tied to makeshift stretchers. A square of concrete projects into the
water, and on it men tend funeral pyres, smoking, chatting, laughing,
as if the dead were pieces of lumber. A saddhu walks by with a great
mass of flesh growing out of his temple, hanging down the side of his
face, almost reaching his shoulder. A woman sits and massages the
lower two of her four breasts, which protrude from either side of her
navel. Close to her sits a cow with a fifth leg arching from its back. A
man dressed in beads and loincloth, his body painted blue, a white
design on his forehead, his hair down to his buttocks, moves with infinite pain along the road, picking up a small stone, lying flat on the
earth and stretching out as far as he can reach. He leaves the stone at
the end of his fingertips, gets up and places his feet in the spot where
the stone lies. He picks up the stone again, lies down, stretches out
and replaces the stone on the ground at the end of his fingertips. For
how many miles has he been moving this way?

Are these people holy? Are they holy because of their infirmities?
Those naked men who sit in front of their begging bowls reciting
prayers to themselves for years, are they holy? I look at people who

walk on all fours like animals and I look at people slightly more erect, like apes, and India becomes a place not so much of the primitive as of the primeval, close to the beginnings of man, when Nature hardly knew in which direction its newest creature would grow. I was seeing a country of violence and suffering, of poverty and riches, of murders, slaughters, cruelty, of abandoned lepers and lepers who declined medical treatment in order to retain their beggar status, of castes of criminals and savage devotional rites; a country of the Ganges, in which shriveled, half-burned corpses float downstream and the diseased bathe for cures and take home phials of holy water for others to drink. It was the country of Gandhi's nonviolence and peace, the country that I had thought of as Nirvana itself.

It was in Benares that I stopped to reevaluate my thinking. My encounters with individuals like Mr. Chandwasker had been pleasant but never sufficiently satisfying. I realized that my own deficiency and ignorance were the cause, and I see now with the distance of years that I had been pushing myself without stopping to think, wanting everything at once, skimming the surface and looking nowhere in depth, wanting that fine philosophy—feeding the poor, caring for the sick, a gentle approach to contact with all people—to be obvious and available everywhere.

A long time passed before I began to understand that Gandhi himself was inconsistent, for he admitted later in life that his path to nonviolence might be too difficult for others. I had always thought that to be nonviolent, one had only *not* to be violent. But my own pretentiousness and ignorance betrayed me when I had my own moment of violence one night on First Avenue and Second Street in Manhattan when I had come home to find my apartment a shambles, the tenth robbery in eleven years. Several of my paintings had been slashed, and I felt the knife suddenly slashing into me as well. The paintings were for an exhibition soon to open. Days later, I was at the window, looking down at spring greening up the marble cemetery. From the corner of my eye, I saw a man on the fire escape entering the apartment next door. It was my studio, connected to the room in which I sat by two unlocked toilet doors. I thought he would try the doors and come in to where I waited. Quietly, I picked up a hammer. When an arm came through, I slammed it with the tool.

I see the hammer now and I feel the arm's pain. I held the man until the police came. They rolled up his sleeves and pointed to the needle marks in his veins, as if his being a drug addict excused my striking him. The days passed and I became more and more angry with myself, so ashamed that I could not go to court to identify him. A month later, I moved.

Gandhi said, "One cannot climb the Himalayas in a straight line." When I was in Benares I thought about entering an ashram to learn of true serenity and love. Within those walls, I would be kind, gentle, generous, loving, and I would have the peace to live out halcyon days. No forces would disturb the tranquility, and I would harmonize effortlessly with all that was holy and beautiful. I would have saintly examples in front of me, and I might even be under the influence of such a spirit as that of the Dalai Lama. I could study the books I had read at home and come to a new understanding and thus be able to act and react differently. But I did not enter an ashram. I had isolated myself all my life, building barriers to shield me; at that time, in India, I demanded serenity within myself, not in any ashram. Living in a monastery would have made it easy to shut out the world and see nothing of the India I had been looking at, slowly becoming aware that what I was seeing had nothing to do with sanctity or holiness, or with anything in the books that had been real to me.

Imagine an Indian reading the Old and New Testaments, saturating himself in Christian religions, and then arriving in the West to seek out the wonders he had found therein! Where would he find them? In what way is this different from what my reading had led me to expect? My concept of India had been that all Indians were in direct communion with God. Look at the mystics and seers, the gurus and masters and yogis who come to the West and prove the truth of their teaching by the way they live their lives, by the very look of them as well, the beatific, blissful faces, the long white hair and patriarchal beards that give them dignity and distinction. But they are Easterners who have transferred themselves to the West. I wonder now: Did they search in pain for spirituality from the beginning of their present lives, or were they reincarnated as gurus and masters because they had, in earlier lives, struggled through to their present grace?

"All that we are is the result of what we have thought" are the opening words of the *Dhamapada*. Tell me, if the mystics understand this so clearly, where is the result of that understanding? Where is the evidence of their wisdom? Tell me where to find the beauty of their books! Is it in an isolated saddhu? Is it in the whole of humanity? Is it in a beggar on the Ganges? Tell me, wild man, are you near me now? Do I seek wisdom in you as well as lust? If I lust for you, is it also lust I seek in Him?

Chapter Four

I paint, I work, I save my money, I look into new ways. The harshness and self-control of Zen attracted me and I decided to study it as revealed by Suzuki in *The Training of a Zen Buddhist Monk*. The Master of Zendo in New York, according to reports, had the capacity of retaining his dignity and his inner peace no matter what the outer circumstances; he could ride the subways at rush hour and walk the noisiest, most crowded streets with the same equanimity he displayed within his temple. I telephoned the Zen master Shimano for an appointment. Two days later, I was in a room bare but for a tatami mat on which were two black silk pillows separated by a low black table. The far wall was a sheet of glass that looked out into a meditation garden of swirled sand and black stones. I sat on one of the pillows and thought of the stillness the garden created. I imagined myself in black kimono walking within that spare and graceful space. Ten minutes passed before the master came in and shook hands. He raised his elbows as if in benediction, and the wide sleeves of his black robe moved up like wings of a butterfly. His head was shaved and his eyes were black crystals. The line of his mouth barely parted as he whispered his greeting. We sat down in silence. I felt humble and lowered my eyes. I sensed a movement as he turned to look into the garden. I too turned and we continued in silence. The garden asked for restfulness, demanded a look into my soul for eternal understanding; but my mind was too active for repose at that moment. I wanted to discuss my future, to talk of the beatings meted out to dozing acolytes, the pain and anguish necessary for discipline, the need to train the mind toward perfect concentration; I wanted to talk of the various monasteries that might accept me, and of the beauty of their gardens. I did not want to sit still and wonder whether this silence was a test of my ability to remain so. I spoke of the stones and sand beyond the window, and of my desire to enter a Zen monastery, forgetting that a monastery would keep me in isolation. I was seeking advice on where to go in Japan and what training was necessary before I left New York. I realized the absurdity of my questions before the words were out of my mouth. He looked at me and stared inside me.

"But why do you want to go to Japan to study?" he asked. "Why can't you do it here? What is it you want?"

I had already spoken without thinking, but I could not stop. I blundered on about the importance of being on the right spot to become involved in the disciplines forced onto Japanese initiates. My needs could not be satisfied through Western religions, and I was attracted to the serenity and meditative life of Zen.

"I don't think you will be a Zen monk," he said. "You must learn to discipline yourself here. You must learn to live here. There is no place for dilettantes in Japan."

The interview was short and depressed me for weeks. I failed because I was shallow and infantile. I opened Suzuki's book again and learned that the way to Zen is not only through discipline but through overcoming stumbling blocks as well. Had the master thrown such obstacles in my path? Had he suggested in an indirect way that only by persistence, only by returning again and again, each time receiving that same rebuff, could I begin to see the proper road? I sent him a small painting with a note of thanks.

I realized I was not ready to return to him; I was not ready to content myself with the complete seclusion necessary for trained control. Instead, I escorted bulls across the Atlantic, sketched the great bath of the Queen of Sheba at Axum and the churches at Lalibela; I painted the black desert of the penis-hunting Danakil of Ethiopia; I crossed the Sahara through Libya and Chad, sailed the Congo down to Brazzaville, and shipped to Gabon to visit Albert Schweitzer, by then a senile old man.

My readings in Eastern philosophy again evoked sensations of serenity and love, and my feeling for India returned to its original state of credulity. I sought out information on India's remotest regions and read of aborigines in Orissa and primitive man in the Andaman Islands. The islands are in the Bay of Bengal, curving southward from Rangoon to the Nicobars, which continue the chain down to the northern tip of Sumatra. The Bay of Bengal Pilot of *The Mariner's Handbook* of 1966 gives this information on the people of the Andamans:

> There are two main species—the forest dwellers, who comprise the Jarawas and the Sentenelse, and of whom little is known as the tribes are hostile and avoid all contact with civilization; and the coast dwellers, who comprise the Onge and Andamanese. The Jarawas will kill on sight.

Those last words were the ones that interested me, for I instantly saw myself on their beach rushing toward their speeding arrows, rushing toward their arms, extended as they pulled their bowstrings back. I was invulnerable, not suicidal; no arrow, no spear, no bullet, no love could enter me and do me harm.

I made inquiries about the Andamans at the Indian consulate and the tourist office in New York, only to find that no one knew anything about them, though a man at the consulate was certain that a permit was necessary.

My plans were necessarily vague until definite approval or rejection was forthcoming. But nonetheless I returned to India. I heard tales of why permission would never be given: Political enemies of Indira Gandhi were interned there and were being badly treated; the Indian army was in training on Little Andaman Island with the newest weapons; the Russians were secretly building an atomic base; the natives *were* hostile to all visitors and *did* kill on sight; the natives were beggars in such a poor state of health, even compared with the rest of India, that the government would not permit anyone from the outside to see them. I listened to the stories with a certain air of contempt, suspecting that there was no truth in them, but also realizing that there might be hints of the facts if one knew where to probe. In

Bombay, I was told that the permit could be granted only in Madras, in Madras that it was granted in Calcutta, and in Calcutta that only the Department of Internal Affairs in New Delhi had the authority to issue it. By then my mind was elsewhere, among the Toradja of Celebes (Sulawesi) and with the Asmat of West New Guinea, people who lived in remote places and remained with their traditional life. In the meantime, I moved around India.

The thirteen years between my two journeys had altered my awareness, and I was looking for things that shyness, laziness, youth, and even puerility had hidden from me on that first occasion. If I truly revealed myself in every way, philosophically, religiously, sexually, artistically, lovingly, not only would I expand my sympathies and absorb more from the outside, but the outside—the people, the landscape, whatever I looked at and responded to—would in turn view *me* more sympathetically.

My first visit had been limited to the northern half of India, where Muslim influence was strong. I was told that if I wanted to see life as it was meant to be lived in India, the way it had been lived for thousands of years and continued to be lived, I must go south to Madras and Madurai, to Cochin and Trivandrum, to the temples of pilgrimage, Tiruchirapalli, Sri Ranganathaswamy, Sravanabelagola, Tirukkalikundrum, where the mysteries and beauties I had hoped for would come forth. Those names, when I saw them on the map and rolled their syllables over the tip of my tongue, incited fresh outbursts of passion that canceled whatever I may have learned from my earlier visit. I created fantasies that often took hold of me inexplicably as part of my loneliness, a loneliness I connected with a religion that could only be thought out in seclusion; it was my solitariness, my moment, a time, a lifetime unshared that embodied the asceticism and self-restraint that was my concept of Gandhi.

I moved in temples with crowds of devotees, heads shaved and smooth, foreheads streaked with ash for Lord Shiva; I watched the priests at *puja*, the religious rites, the lids of their intense eyes blackened with kohl, their garments simple G-strings, their black bodies shining with sweat and oil; I sat with beggars so misshapen they sometimes looked like spiders, their heads attached to shoulders without a visible neck, their black limbs extended and folded in four directions. The mass of India was there with its extreme devotion to ritual. Did they flock to temple, I wondered, for atonement and to thank the Lord for present blessings, as the Jews do, or were they more like Christians, praying for help, always asking aid in times of crisis?

In temple compounds, ornately carved buildings with halls of a hundred columns stood wherever one looked; walls and surfaces were covered with leaves and patterns of abstract designs, with human figures and animals telling tales from the *Mahabharata* and the *Ramayana,* legends of saints and devils, heroes and villains; everything incised, chiseled, molded; everything painted, frescoed, embellished, as if the artists believed that the more surfaces their designs occupied, the more complex the pattern, the greater the beauty achieved. The ornamentation offered no relief, no resting place for the eye, as if the constantly moving crowds had flowed up onto the walls and had suddenly been frozen there.

A single breath of purity appeared on the Bay of Bengal in Mahabalipuram, an ancient group of temples, hardly used for worship any longer, a wall of rock covered with fine reliefs, and huge stones carved into single animals: an elephant, a cow, a lion, each one alone, with nothing more than space around it, allowing it to breathe. The chasteness of the sculptures brought to mind my first pilgrimage to Italy, when the thousands of photographs I had studied in books turned real on the walls of churches and palaces, in piazzas and on buildings wherever I turned. It was a revelation when those tiny black-and-white reproductions, which had given no sense of size or place, took on their true lives in their own homes. Pompously, I evolved a theory stating that a basic opposition existed between Western and Indian art: In the Western world each piece of art would be most beautiful if left in its original site, in the place for which it had been made—the frescoes in Pompeii, the Elgin Marbles in Athens, the Giottos in Assisi; the reverse was true in India, where a work would take on reality only if removed from its surroundings— decoration so vast and excessive prevented the viewer from isolating a single piece in his mind; to appreciate a Bodhisattva seated in lotus position one would have to separate it physically from the clutter of intertwining leaves and figures around it. This grand hypothesis I related to my new conviction that Indian philosophies and religions became more valid outside India, where they could be examined and practiced away from the swarms of hungry people whose condition of life seemed to negate the beliefs and teachings, though they were the life through which those philosophies were formulated.

One day I was walking through Sri Meenakshi Temple in the city of Madurai, largest and most important place of pilgrimage in the south. The profusion of ornamentation pressed in from all sides, but I happily wandered with the crowds, charmed by the colors and smells and varied costumes. I came to the huge tank, the bathing pool, with wide steps leading down to blue water, and I sat there, hoping to merge with the scene, inhaling, and trying to sense the direction in which to lead my mind. Laughter and the murmuring of prayers came to me; bells tinkled and rang; the muted sounds of the mass of pilgrims moaned on the air as they passed through the courtyard and halls.

Religious intensity and fervor expressed itself in every part of the temple. In front of me, men were at ablutions whose physical aspects were as complicated and ornate as the carvings around them. A young man, with his dhoti wrapped high around his waist, stood in water to his knees, gesturing in formal prayer movements that were more complicated than those of the other men. He crossed his arms, pulled his ears, bounced up and down, then bent to splash water to his face. He crossed his arms again, held his nose with one hand, an ear with the other, bounced again and splashed water. He noticed me watching and smiling. He looked up again and again, as if to make sure I was still there. Each time he looked, he turned and made a different gesture, hoping thereby, I think, to continue to attract my attention. His *puja* lasted another ten minutes, longer than that of anyone else in the pool. He wiped his chest and arms with his shirt, smiled at me, and came over and sat down.

"Hello!" he said with great enthusiasm. "What is your name? Isn't this a beautiful place?" His name was Somanada and he was twenty. He lifted the thread indicating his high caste that was looped over his chest from his right shoulder to the opposite side of his narrow torso. "Which country are you from? I am a Brahmin and I come here three times a day to pray."

"Don't you go to school or have a job?"

"Oh, no! I have no job at all. I have finished school and want to be a teacher because my father is a teacher, but we are Brahmins and it is very difficult to find a job. It is no longer as it used to be in India. Everything is changed, and now it is the *harijans*, the untouchables, who get first chance at all the jobs and apartments. It leaves nothing for us. We are like the ancient Hebrews, who were always discriminated against. No one wants us any longer. I have to live on baksheesh."

"Baksheesh?"

"Yes, there is no other way for me to make money, and my father does not earn enough to feed the whole family. I have nine brothers and sisters and I am the oldest. We do not know when I will be able to find a job."

Somanada's eyes were black and bright; they sloped toward his ears and were touched with sadness, as if he were burdened with past incarnations. I looked into that blackness and saw remoteness and humility, secrecy and shyness. He was part of the atmosphere of the temple, and I was pleased to be with him. I got up and said I was going back to my hotel and wondered whether he would accompany me. "Oh, yes!" he said with a marvelous sparkle in his voice, in his eyes, in his walk. We went through the crowded streets, and he talked again of his lack of funds and how he needed to find baksheesh that very day, that he had made nothing so far.

At the hotel, I discreetly asked if he would like to come upstairs. As I had hoped, he said, "Oh, yes!" It was a small room in a cheap hotel, but there were two chairs as well as the bed. I locked the door and sat on the bed. Somanada immediately sat down next to me. He put his hand on my thigh. "That ritual," he said in answer to my question, "is performed at noon *puja* and is the longest of the rituals. I take longer because I am a Brahmin priest and have more prayers to say than another else." I put my hand on top of his. His face was long and thin, just as the rest of him was long and thin. His eyes were set back beneath his brow, separated by the sharp edge of his long, pointed nose. His mouth was a line that had been curved into a smile since we first met. He sat up straight and was slightly nervous. He clasped my hand and I made a more intimate movement. The bed bounced as if the whole room had exploded. "Oh, no!" he exclaimed as he jumped up. "Oh, no!" He went to the door and came back and sat down. "Oh, no! I don't do anything like that, sir. I am not like that at all!" He got up and went to the door again and turned and looked at me.

"No!" he said in a whisper. "Please!" He opened the door and stood there as if he could not make up his mind whether or not to leave. He stepped in, then turned, stepped out, and finally left.

After lunch and a sleepless attempt at a nap, worrying about having insulted and frightened Somanada over something that had little importance to me, I went out to Thirumalai Naick Palace. I sat in the shade of a coffee stall, thinking that I would never learn anything about this country. Somanada was suddenly triggering something in my past, and my face was beet red before I recognized the thought. My childhood was rushing into me; I gasped at the memory that was coming forth and tried to reject it. I had delivered bread or beer and was on Ovington Avenue on a dark, spring night, not cold. A voice was calling, "Hey, sonny! Come here!" I turned and saw a man sitting on a stoop, his pants open, something sticking up, a hand beckoning me, asking me to come closer. My heart was pounding, my face burning. I knew; I knew. Was I eight? Nine, perhaps? "Come on up!" he invited. I stared at the flesh shining in the light of the lamp above the door. I went up closer, attracted, horrified, wanting to look, wanting to touch. The man reached up and took my head in his hands and started to push me down. "Come on, sonny!" I resisted but my lips were close, about to touch the stiffened flesh. "You know what I want! You know what to do!" I felt dizzy and pulled away. I ran to Third Avenue and stopped at the curb and vomited. At the kitchen table I could not do my homework. My mother put her hand to my face and said I must be coming down with the grippe. I don't remember my dreams that night, but I wondered now about Somanada's fears and dreams, about whether I had pushed him close to that same terror.

When it got dark, I returned to Sri Meenakshi for the nighttime rituals. The temple was only a few minutes' walk from the hotel, and the streets were full of people. The shops and stalls were brightly lit by oil and pressure lamps. As I approached the West Gate of the temple, I felt a hand on my forearm and turned to see Somanada smiling at me. He took me by the elbow and led me into the compound. He began talking of the sculpture and described the various ceremonies as if we had parted under the friendliest of circumstances. He was affectionate and kept an arm on my shoulder. We went through the courtyards and buildings that were open at that late hour and then sat on the steps of the tank at which we had met. He had come for nine thirty *puja* and had prayed that I would appear. He was watching for me. His day had been empty and depressing, since he had nothing to do and he had no friends. He was afraid that I would be angry and would not want to talk to him again. The temple was his second home, but he knew no one he could talk to there. He had been thinking of what had taken place in my room and was angry with himself for having shown his irritation. I apologized for having made a move that had annoyed him so much, and he said that it was a bad thing that I wanted to do. "Do you not know about electricity?" he asked. "If you do, then you know that in electricity, opposite poles attract, just like men and women attract each other. They are opposite in all things. In electricity, like poles repel, so that men cannot have anything sexual with one another. They are the same."

"But why do you think that humans are like electricity?"

"Oh, yes, sir, they are the same. It is very simple. Our brains send out waves of electrical currents that run through our blood streams in veins like wires."

I apologized again and explained that the word "baksheesh"* had set my mind in the wrong direction. I had thought that he was willing to come into my bed in exchange for whatever I would give him.

"But I am a priest! And men do not take money for such things!" He was quite vehement about it. "It is only women who think in that way!" He gave himself a shiver of repulsion, as if women might be capable of anything and I as a Westerner should have known it.

Just then a horn blared outside the sanctum sanctorum. For a moment, I thought it was the sound of a ram's horn. We got up and went into the building from which the blare had come. Several flabby men were carrying instruments: the horn just heard, small cymbals, bells, and a one-stringed instrument held vertically. The men were naked above the waist, their chests shining with oil, their faces and shoulders

---

* In mid-February 1978, I was on a bus going down from Saratoga to New York City. I was reading David Jordan's *Nile Green* and was startled to come across a reference to a passage in Baedeker's *Egypt and the Sudan*, 1914, on "Intercourse with Orientals." The passage, in part, reads, "The average Oriental regards the European traveller as a Croesus, therefore as fair game, and feels justified in pressing upon him with a perpetual demand for bakshish. Travellers are often tempted to give for the sake of affording temporary pleasure at a trifling cost, forgetting that the seeds of insatiable cupidity are thereby sown, to the infinite annoyance of their successors and the demoralisation of the recipients themselves."

streaked with ash. Hundreds of carved columns and sculptures depicted humans, animals, gods, demons. From the blackness of shadow, faces and carvings stood out, reflecting the dim light of an occasional weak bulb, oil lamps, and candles. Everything moved together, the human beings, the elephants, the dragons, and I was transported to Sinai and the fires around the golden calf. In fear, I heard the thunderbolts and the shouts from enraged Moses coming down to break the tablets at the sight of the graven images. But in Sri Meenakshi, in spite of the harsh sounds, there was peace. Men came calmly from a shrine, a tabernacle, carrying tridents, their tines covered with oiled rags lit like torches, and other men appeared holding up a palanquin decorated with chased silver, like the ark of the covenant carried through the desert.

Priests emerged from the inner shrine with oil lamps held in front of them. Someone chanted and plucked the stringed instrument. Worshippers prostrated themselves on the ground, walked around the palanquin several times, turned around, sat down, stood up, were blessed. The palanquin was borne to the next shrine amid a clamor of instruments. Genuflections and obeisances continued. With torches lighting up eyes and casting shadows among the demons, the effect was weird, magical, biblical, half real, half Cecil B. De Mille. I said goodnight to Somanada at one of the temple gates and did not expect to see him again.

The following morning he was outside my hotel. I was on my way to Tirupparankundram, five miles to the east. He asked to go along, and I invited him for rice cakes with sauce before we got on the number 5 bus.

Tirupparankundram is a tiny village with an attractive temple at the foot of a vast outcrop of rock a hundred feet high. A procession was coming out of the temple when we arrived, and we followed along. It was the hour of bathing, and the procession was on its way to the tank, on the other side of the mass of rock. Somanada apologized that I, a non-Hindu, was not permitted into the pool because the water was sacred. I sat on stones a few feet from the water's edge and watched him take off his white shirt and white trousers. Underneath, he wore only a tiny black pouch. In Sri Meenakshi, he had worn a dhoti that covered most of his body below the waist. Now, he was practically nude. His skin was black, almost purple; he was slender

and elegant; his frame was narrow, and he moved with graceful gestures. He watched my eyes admiring his shape and turned to show
himself from all sides. His right hip jutted out, his hands moved up;
unaware, he was suddenly in the classical pose of Indian sculpture.
He washed with soap and caressed his flesh. No one else was near, no
one watched another bather. Somanada floated in the shallow water;
he stood close to the water's edge and soaped inside his pouch, not
looking into my eyes but off to one side; he tossed the soap to my feet
and fell back into the water and rinsed himself.

Later, we went into the temple for prayers, and then out to a small
shop for a cold, sweet drink. I asked if Hindus were circumcised, a
word I had to explain. "Oh, no! We Hindus do not cut the penis!
Only Muslims do that!" It shocked him that I thought Hindus might
have such a disgusting practice. "But I must tell you, sir, that I never
think about sex because there is nothing I can do about it. I have
trained my mind so that my sexual energy can be used as power to
foresee the future, to see what is happening to my family, and to help
them in time of need. I must keep storing up that energy. Perhaps
when I am thirty my father will bring a wife to me, and then, only
then, will I begin to have the sex feelings you talk about. I do not believe in going to the cinema or in reading books, because these sex
feelings will surely come up and there is nothing for a man to do. My
penis has never been hard. I have disciplined my mind and my body
completely. I am a vegetarian, but I do not eat everything that is vegetable. I do not eat onions or chili peppers or other foods that make
the penis hard. It is not difficult for me."

On the bus back to my hotel, Somanada held my hand. "Do you
suppose," he asked, "that if I went with you to your country and lived
there for a while, my skin would turn red like yours?"

The new town of Bhubaneswar, capital of the state of Orissa, is a
city devoted to government buildings, markets, and housing wholly
without interest to me. Bhubaneswar of old, on the other hand, is a
town of temples so appealing that I had to rethink my theory that Indian architecture is so overdecorated one cannot see the art itself.
Oriyan temples were different and had no connection with the architecture I had seen elsewhere in India. In the south and in the north,
temple complexes were immense in area, sometimes containing ten or

twenty buildings, all thronged with worshippers and clusters of priests and shrines, all heavy with incense. Thousands of pilgrims packed into these compounds. Oriyan temples were small and intimate enough for the worshipper to feel at home at once, without the overwhelming wonder of size. He could touch the spirituality that floated on the air and inhale its fragrance with every breath. He worshipped there alone or with a small family, for space permitted no more than three or four people inside the dark shrines. There was an integrity about the grounds, in the way everything grew and blended into oneness—the small buildings, the trees, the grass itself—all fitting neatly into a unity that asked for solitude. An awesome, sacred quality assured the celebrant of the presence of purity and devotion, of the existence of beliefs that he would ease into, beliefs in divinity and omnipotence. Even I moved there inside a halo of unearthliness, unlike the oppression of moving with massive crowds that caught one up in the emotions that held the mob together. There was instead the feeling of uniqueness and the presence of forces that spoke individually to everyone who worshipped there. It was a place in which I might have stayed on.

The old city is on the edge of a great tank, green with algae. In the center of the city, surrounded by street stalls of foods, is the Lingaraja Temple, largest of the temples in the region and closed to non-Hindus. A few minutes' walk away, on the edge of fields of vegetables and rice, is a group of three small temples, Mukteswar, Kadareswar, and Purasurameswar. The three are carefully arranged around an open courtyard. Their towers, shaped like phalluses, stand against the sky with elegance and power in the soft light. Immense, ancient banyan trees drip roots within which meditating yogis sit folded up and still. Mukteswar is the smallest of the group; its thirty-five-foot lingam tower is covered with floral decorations. Standing next to the tower is an arch with the forms of two reclining women carved into its lintel.

In a small bathing pool, three men were washing clothes; another was washing himself. Bird sounds slipped through the air, and leaves fell onto the water, dropping patterns of green and blue. Shade from the trees covered most of the temple, while sunlight glowed on the ground behind it. I felt then that I was looking at Art, that the whole of the temple was a work of art, and it moved me with a strength that made me shiver. It was my youth and the philosophies of India that were staring at me; I was there inside it, and it covered me like a tent. The whole of my frustrating past fell away, and I was living the beauty of my concept of this country. The face of everyone nearby was soft and round, fused with the air, melting into it, as in a blurrred photograph. My eyes were misting over and I gave in to my emotion and savored it. I sat on a low wall, staring without seeing, receiving waves of exaltation that bewitched my sense of proportion. The synagogue again caught itself into my trance, and I was with my brothers in a pew, stretching out the fringes of our prayer shawls to touch the velvet covering of Torahs being carried down the aisles, while singing chilled my spine. It was the temple in Brooklyn, it was Sri Meenakshi, it was Mukteswar, nothing seen, nothing visual at all, nothing but a feeling deep within.

A man's laughter broke into my thoughts, Somanada flashed through, and I was back thinking straight about the temple as Art. The decoration of the tower in front of me suddenly took on meaning. There was no individual carving that could be removed and isolated; horizontal bands of ornamentation varied but remained of a piece and formed an overall design that settled itself into the stone with restraint. The tower was a unit in itself, beautiful and serene.

The laughter came again and I thought I saw Somanada, but it was a man standing next to the arch, looking at me and smiling. He motioned for me to come over and leaned back against one of the pillars. He began to talk as soon as I started to move toward him, talking without humor, without preamble, telling me a history of the temple as if he were a guide. I was not interested in his lesson; I wanted the earlier silence, the atmosphere into which I had settled myself. I could not listen and broke into his talk as politely as I could. I preferred, I said, to gather my own knowledge and feelings, and to walk around by myself, looking at everything with my own eyes and thoughts. Later, perhaps, I could listen to what he had to say.

"Please do not think that I am a guide," he said in a voice so pleasant and understanding that it surprised me. It was as if he *did* know what I meant. "Or that I am looking for money from you. But you see, I am the priest here, and this is my temple. It is my family's temple." I apologized for thinking he was mercenary and asked him to go on with what he had been saying. "I laughed at the way you were so obviously affected by the temple, and I only began to talk to you be-

cause I have been watching you from the moment you entered. I liked
the way you walked, the way you looked at things, the way you
touched the walls and carvings. You did not look like a tourist, so I
decided to talk to you." When he first saw me coming through the
gate, he thought I was an Indian from another part of the country.
Now, knowing that I was not Hindu, he would be happy, if I liked, to
take me to the famous Lingaraja Temple, where no one would question
anyone he brought in.

Like most men in old Bhubaneswar and around this group of temples,
the priest wore only a dhoti. He was very good-looking and had
a muscular chest and strong arms. His skin color was lighter than that
of Somanada, and he too had the Brahminical thread looped over his
shoulder. He asked if I was married.

"No," I answered, and returned the question.

"No," he also said. "My father wishes me to marry soon, but I am
sure that I will never take a wife."

"Why is that?" I asked.

"You tell me first why *you* never married."

"Because I do not like women in bed," I said simply.

"Well," he said after a pause, "that is also my reason for not wanting
to marry." He asked again if he could take me to Lingaraja Temple,
and I declined, saying that I preferred to spend more time alone
there, and later would go back to the hotel.

"May I go with you?" he asked with surprising directness.

I answered, "With great pleasure." His name was Sarath and he
was twenty-six years old.

Sarath talked easily about his life. He had a great friend of eighteen,
his dearest friend, a priest at the Lord Jaganath Temple in Puri,
thirty-five miles away, four hours to the southeast by bus. "We have
been lovers now for five years, and we are able to visit each other for a
few days every other week. Usually, I go to Puri because it is more
difficult for him to get away, while my family can always be here to
take care of the temple." He and his friend were deeply in love and
hoped some day to be priests in the same temple so they could continue
their friendship for the rest of their lives. Sarath had never
touched a woman and had never wanted to. Women and girls had
offered themselves to him in the temple, but he had always found
being close to women distasteful, except for the women of his family.

His first sexual experience happened at the age of thirteen, when a younger male cousin came to visit his home and seduced him on his first night there. The cousin was nine and had already had two years' experience. They still saw one another, though the cousin was living in Cuttack and had a wife and two children.

Sarath was telling me all this as we lay on the bed in my room. He talked and I talked, but it was mostly Sarath talking, telling secrets he said he had never verbalized before, revealing all his inner life. It seemed to me that within those few hours we had become close, so close that I thought I was in love, knowing well enough that it could be no more than a momentary affair; but for whatever time it existed, it was real. For the first time in my life, I invited someone to accompany me on a journey; for the first time I allowed myself to think of traveling with another person. Within a few days, I was going to the Temple of Konarak, where I hoped to sketch. It would be nice to have a companion, if Sarath cared to come along. We would stay at the cheaper hotel, I told him, and he was delighted with the idea. In my head, it was an idyllic dream. Sarath was no teenager, and he looked and acted mature, seemingly satisfied with his lot. For generations his family had been priests of the three small temples, and so it would continue for generations, though Sarath would not contribute to the line if he remained unmarried. There was no reason to think he was shallow or that my own feelings were frivolous.

For some time, the ceiling fan was the only sound in the room. I had thrown the mosquito net to one side, so that it acted like a curtain in front of the windows. We dozed and dreamed. Sarath suddenly sat up and suggested going out for a beer, a suggestion that surprised me. In my fantasy, it would have been more suitable for him to be smoking ganja, the local marijuana. A Catholic priest might offer me beer or gin and a rabbi would have taken out the schnapps, but this was India and Sarath was Hindu. I was embarrassed by the suggestion. The law forbidding alcohol in India had been relaxed in some states, including Orissa, but I felt in some prudish way that a Hindu priest should have been above drinking it. I agreed to go out, but at the moment we were too indolent to move.

"I must tell you, my friend," Sarath said, "that I have a dream. May I tell it to you? It is a good dream, and I have been dreaming it for many years. It is to own a taxi. Think of it! A taxi! With such a car, I could make a lot of money, taking people back and forth from Bhubaneswar to Cuttack." My heart thumped, for I thought I knew what was coming.

"Of course," he went on, "I don't have enough money. I do have four thousand rupees in the bank but I need another nine thousand, which is more than double what I have, and I have been saving for years. Someone here in the marketplace has an Ambassador for sale right now. It is exactly what I want, but it will take me years to save the money, and by then the car will be gone. I always see myself, you know, driving with the car full of people. They all get out in Cuttack and another crowd gets in and off we go to Bhubaneswar. It is beautiful, my dream."

"Oh, yes, it is beautiful," I agreed nervously, afraid that he would press further. "Money is always a problem. I'd like to help, but it isn't possible right now. Whatever I have I'm using for this trip, and I have a long way to go. But I promise you that when I return to New York, I will send whatever I can."

"You know, I have a foreign friend. He sends me money from time to time. He is from Germany and is very rich. He was here two years ago with many cameras, and he took many photos of me. He was very kind and he stayed here for a week. I went with him everywhere. He is sixty-eight years old and could be my grandfather, but he is very kind. I have his photo. He writes to me every month and sometimes there is money in the envelope."

A slight wind came through the windows and moved the mosquito net so that it billowed against my hip. The shutters rattled. Sarath's hand went to my shoulder and rubbed it slowly. "Wouldn't it be beautiful if we both had gold chains to wear around our necks? Then, whenever we put them on or took them off we could remember each other and our love. We could think about our days together here in Bhubaneswar."

"Yes," I agreed, "it is a wonderful idea, but too expensive for me, Sarath."

"Expensive? Oh, no, it is not expensive. We can get the chains right here in the market. Even now I have a friend who can sell them to us tonight. It is not really very much money, three hundred rupees for one gold chain, thirty-seven dollars of your money, and you know that is not too much. And if you cannot buy two chains, maybe you could buy one for me, and then I would remember you for the rest of my life."

It had disturbed me to hear Sarath talk about buying a taxi. Driving a cab was not what my mind conjured up as part of the life of a Hindu priest. The needed nine thousand rupees had been in Sarath's dream, and I could not seriously connect it with myself. But a gold chain was something else, for he was suddenly asking for a present, asking for it at that moment, asking to be reimbursed for what had happened between us. I flushed and frowned and stuttered, not quite sure what it meant or whether or not I was reading it properly. I had made so many mistakes in the past. He was a priest, and that had nothing to do with taxis and gold chains. But was I misunderstanding? And, misunderstanding or not, which one of us was the whore? Hadn't I been taking something substantial from him?

"Let's go for the beer," I said, crawling over him to get off the bed.

We sat in a garden across from the hotel amid hibiscus in bloom. Sarath had three bottles of beer, talking all the time about the taxi and the importance of the gold chain. It depressed me to listen to him, and it depressed me to watch the alcohol taking effect. It also depressed me to realize that I must have been one among many, a common circumstance in his life.

I agreed to buy a dhoti, a good one, and we took a bicycle rickshaw to the market. It was past nine o'clock and only one shop remained open. It was where Sarath's friend worked. They showed me many things and Sarath got his dhoti. I refused to look at the fifteen-dollar shirts and the shoes they were pressing into my arms.

Later, I told Sarath how upset I had been by his constant talk of presents. He was startled, though I thought I had made my reactions clear by my manner. "But you would be giving me a present anyway, wouldn't you? What is wrong with asking for it when we were so close? That is a good time, isn't it? I was loving you and my love was accepting whatever you offered. Is there any difference between asking and giving? They are the same, are they not? So what does the time matter?"

Sarath would not believe that he had provoked me or that my uneasiness was strong enough to force cancellation of our arrangements for Konarak. "Is it possible that you think my only interest in you is financial? Do you think I went into your bed only to make money? Is that what you think?"

Sarath looked so tragic that I was tempted to reverse myself. He seemed wounded and I felt I had stabbed him. Was I making a mistake? Was it simply naïveté that allowed him to ask for gifts? All those fine philosophical thoughts I was always talking about, where were they then? Not inside me, obviously. I knew that manners, gallantries, obligations were different in India, and I could use no outside standards to judge him; yet, I was doing just that. Who did I think I was to criticize him, or anyone, for that matter?

Sarath seemed to be thinking in a similar way, for the expression on his face was one of profound shock. That our relationship had ended did not seem comprehensible to him, or to me either. I turned and went back to the hotel, as sad and sorry as if I had broken a long-lasting friendship. I could not sleep for thinking up excuses for his behavior and excuses for my own. It had been a romantic encounter—his being a priest, our meeting in the temple, the dream of being together in Konarak, even the contrast with Somanada. But I had destroyed it myself, for it was I who had invented it all.

Sarath would not be in the temple the next day. He had earlier said that one of his brothers would be there to attend the rituals in his place. I went back and walked around, cold nervous, my hands shaking. I think I went there hoping to see Sarath again, hoping to regain that lost love. I saw no one there, and it wasn't until I went out into the courtyard that I began to calm down.

A group of pilgrims were camping beside the entrance gate of Kadareswar Temple. I sat on a wooden bench beneath a mango tree, sipping from a glass of tea, watching the women build their fires, cook their food, and live in their normal way even though they were far from home. There was no confusion within the group, only laughter, and I sat there thinking that if I stayed there long enough, I would begin to understand the whole of India, that those pilgrims would enact the whole of their lives in front of me. Men, women, and children congregated there as if the temple were their soul, while the phallic towers enclosed them within the meaning they accepted as life itself. I saw a harmony between the flesh and the stone, between the meek and the unyielding, the sorrow and the beauty, and I saw that their lives would go nowhere beyond the ritual of their religion, that for them, this intimacy was all of life, and hunger and pain were a small price to pay for the sustenance of reincarnation. Which left me nowhere but on the outside.

Where then was my thinking? What had I been doing in India? My two visits had given me no clue to any understanding, either of myself or of the life I was looking at. I had taken as gospel some books about a humanity and universality that could exist, for me, only in my own self, and reading could do nothing more than bring forth those qualities in me. It was up to me to live them out. I could not believe that I had already conditioned myself to such a degree that it was no longer possible to break through to new sympathy and understanding. Yet I had destroyed the contact with Sarath! The pleasure I had had of him remained real and true, and I was already forgetting the unpleasing aspects. It pained me greatly to know that I had disillusioned him. Was I living only on my surface?

The original inhabitants of India were a black people who had been there before the coming of the Aryans, long before the beginnings of Hinduism. The invaders forced the indigenous population to make their homes in isolated regions for safety. Some, like the Senthals, were still living in the forests of Orissa.

I had corresponded from New York with a Professor Rath, a music teacher at a dance school in Cuttack, the former capital of Orissa, half an hour from Bhubaneswar by Sarath's imagined taxi, or by one of the many that plied back and forth each day. My arrival in Cuttack coincided with Professor Rath's journey to Baripada, near which the Senthals live. We reached the outskirts of the town in time to watch a flock of egrets in a mango grove poking their long beaks into grass and flying up in pairs. We went on to see the chief inspector of schools, B. K. Das, a heavy man with horn-rimmed glasses and thick lips, who arranged for me to stay at the Circuit House, a large comfortable bungalow reserved for government officials. He assured me that he knew the kind of village in which I wanted to stay, where people lived who had felt little or no Hindu, Muslim, or Christian influence. We went to the market and I saw my first Senthals, a black and handsome people. The dhotis and saris they wore made them almost indistinguishable from other dark Indians, though a closer look showed rounder faces and a more open sense of humor.

In the morning, I learned that a tour had been planned for me, and one of the teachers picked me up in a jeep. We went to the local primary school, where I was suddenly asked to give a talk on the differences between the American and Indian school systems, a subject about which I knew nothing. I floundered through fifteen minutes of nonsequiturs and half an hour of questions. With experience, I fared better at the local technical school, and still better at the secondary school. Chief Inspector Das came to see me during lunch and said that within the hour I would be driven north to Rairungpur for a dance that a group of Senthals was preparing in my honor. My bag was packed within five minutes, and I thought myself lucky to be going off alone, away from restricting officialdom. However, the chief inspector and his teachers were in the jeep.

Thirty miles north of Baripada, in the dimness of almost night, we reached a series of forest-covered hills. The road began to wind through them, and we pulled up at an *osuna* tree with a small shrine nested in its roots. There were smells and indistinct shapes that quickly gave me a feeling of protection and a sense that I was in some innocent, venerated place. We got out of the jeep, and the driver handed a coconut to a young bearded priest who was ringing a small brass bell. The priest broke open the coconut and poured its milk over the worn clay figures around him. It was too dark in the weak light of two small oil lamps to see what all the figures were, but images of goddesses, horses, and elephants seemed to be among them. Prayers were said while the priest continued to ring his bell. He took the meat out of the coconut and put a piece into the mouth of each of us and then dabbed vermilion on our foreheads. Having thus been assured of a safe journey through the mountains, we proceeded on our way, with the blackness of the forest on both sides of the road. I felt I was coming into new territory, a new sense of India, and I tried to dismiss my companions from my mind. The vermilion spot on my forehead was engraved there.

By ten o'clock we had reached Rairungpur, had had tea and cookies in the courtyard of the secondary school, and were back in the jeep on the rough road to Sansimila. We were moving through what appeared to be complete darkness and desolation when ahead of us a pressure lamp burst into light. It flared up inside me as well. We left the jeep at a bamboo archway decorated with flowers and mango leaves and were rushed by a crowd of men and boys. I was garlanded with jasmine blossoms, five or six leis looped over my head, thrown onto me in enthusiastic displays of hospitality. Smiling, laughing faces showed teeth tinged red with betel. Hands came at me to touch my shirt, my arms, and smooth the paleness of my skin. The excitement was infectious, and I allowed myself to be surrounded, shoved, carried along on the wave of eager men. A lamp held high to my face permitted everyone a good view of me. Drummers and cymbal players followed, and the crowd began to sing. From the first house came ten or fifteen men carrying decorated bows and arrows, dancing passionately to the rhythm of the drums and capturing the movement of the crowd. I wanted to dance too, to shout and wave my arms and give in to my own exhilaration, but the cool composure of the chief inspector and his teachers held me in check.

In front of the open door of every house was a brass bowl of mango leaves of welcome, and next to each bowl stood a woman who took up a conch shell as we passed and blew it and continued blowing. A great din sounded out against the drums and cymbals, getting louder as we went along, each new conch adding its voice to the others. We went through the village to an open area where five chairs were lined up in front of a space roped off for dancing. All the other villagers were already sitting, squatting, standing there. The men offered betel and fruit and cigarettes. Light came from gas lamps.

The dancers were all men, heavily painted, skin-color cobalt blue, dressed in silks and satins, bejeweled turbans, richly adorned saris, and scarves of floating gauze. Lord Krishna and his attendants played flutes on the bank of the Jumna, and Rama rescued his beloved Sita from the dreaded Ravana. The chief inspector had led me to believe that we would be seeing tribal *cchau,* but these were Hindu dances, legends from the *Mahabharata* and the *Ramayana,* beautiful but disappointing after the jubilant meeting and parade through the village.

Silence settled onto the empty space of the dance area, and a line of women filed on stage to form a half circle facing inward. Four men with kettledrums tied from their necks and shoulders beat a slow rhythm. The women took a few steps forward, a few steps back, at the same time advancing around in a circle. The drummers stood inside the circle in a row, shoulder to shoulder, moving back and forth and around according to the direction of the women. It was done with ease and great style, more eloquent through their unaffected gestures than the earlier, formalized, flamboyantly artificial pantomime. The movements of the women changed to bending and scooping something from the earth, and then into obeisance in front of me and the chief inspector. It was a *dubang,* a dance performed at harvest time.

Another silence followed. The crowd of onlookers was pleased with the effect of the performance and pressed more food and betel onto me. Shouting came from the distance, and in a moment a band of warriors thronged the stage, waving their bows and arrows, screeching out and jumping up and down, exuding exuberance and zest from their bodies. The villagers let out ululating shrieks. The dancers' howls echoed, and in my head I was one of them, yelping, dancing their elation, entering into anonymity, accepting, being all, my arms on shoulders of bearded men in black furred hats, fires tossed in Hassidic tradition, a groom, a bride, carried on chairs, encircled, exultant and rejoicing. I flew open into temple rites, Peruvian diversions, Bornean exaltations, Balinese delights, and we were all together, dancers, musicians, all the villagers of all the past, joining in songs of celebration, the chief inspector and his teachers lost in careless memory, and I singing in response to instincts thrilling with their wildness. Was I letting out a primal scream? I moved and danced, I followed them; I follow India, I am eternal.

Chapter Five

None of us learns from the past of his own life. How is it possible then to learn from the past of others, or from the people and past of other civilizations? Is it simpler to search out our own futures? Sometimes, unconsciously, I know something; I have a feeling that I'm ahead of myself, that I'm on the verge of a knowledge, of insights, of a kind of wisdom that will take me into another sphere of selfness, whereby I will sit inside myself and direct my senses into whatever I wish at any given moment, and that will encompass all the world, all love. I like being on that verge, that edge of not knowing, with the knowledge coming into being, not sure that I really want to go over into absolute perception. I reverse Kierkegaard's thought and I think that life, my life at any rate, is understood forward and lived backward.

I take my step forward and I see a future that eases my tensions and gives me moments of tender thoughts and distractions: a future in which I wander through the paddy fields of Bali with bare-breasted women splashing under waterfalls and rushing streams, with barong dances and music of the gamelan. I expected to avoid the island because I imagined its charms to have degenerated under Western influence, but Bali was on my way to Celebes or New Guinea, and I made up my mind to stop.

On the island, I was instantly charged by the visual treasures that were everywhere: pools of water lilies and lotus, women on the dikes of terraces stamping the paddy in baskets, moving as gracefully as if dancing, men trotting in lines with bundles of harvested rice on their shoulders, water of the sawahs, not yet green with shoots of rice, reflecting sky and mountains, clusters of palms and coconuts in corners and edging fields, great sweeps of ripe paddy leaning against the light wind.

I stopped in the village of Ubud and discovered it was the center of painting and sculpture, where tourists arrived in giant limousines for a glimpse inside the museum and a look into artists' ateliers and the shops selling their canvases and carvings. I was reluctant to be seduced by the island, but the warmth of the people delayed me, and I could not resist the chance to learn from the love and energy with which leaves, flowers, and foods were turned into aesthetic forms. I took a small house and settled down.

One day, early on, having heard that something of interest was happening in the late afternoon, I went down to Kutuh on the outskirts of Ubud, walking along a muddy lane lined with moss-covered stone walls behind which stalks of bamboo shot up beneath banyan trees, banana, breadfruit, mango, and papaya. The lane opened into a courtyard in front of a temple, on the side of which was a covered pavilion. Within the pavilion, groups of men were gambling, playing with small decks of cards and using painted boards for fan-tan. They were barefoot and wore only sarongs. Directly in front of the entrance to the temple, five men were setting long bamboo poles into the ground, tying on banners, covering a section of hard earth with straw mats, and building an entire theater within a few minutes; the proscenium arch appeared suddenly, a mass of foliage partly covered with a curtain of cloth.

No sooner had it been finished than the audience was seated. The straw mats were the stage; in front of it, the men of the gamelan, the orchestra, were sitting down with their gongs and xylophones of bronze, with drums and cymbals. The audience was all around them: children sitting on the edge of the mats, women behind them, the men in the rear. By the time the performance began, the crowds were everywhere, on temple steps, on terraces, on top of walls, in trees, on altars.

Inside the temple grounds, the actors and actresses were being

to Gordon & Joe, with lots of love
Bali   Tobias 74

made up in a small pavilion. The facial painting was done slowly, carefully, the whole process of preparation taking several hours. The long, loose hair of the women was threaded with white frangipani, and the line of the forehead was altered with soot to a sharp central peak. Their elegant bodies were wrapped in floridly decorated sarongs and glittering sashes. Elaborate headdresses were waiting on one side for the make-up to be finished. The men were painting beards on their chins, dabbing white on their cheeks and noses for comic effects, being wrapped in sarongs and chestbands, and adjusting their krisses, the long curved daggers. It was behind the scenes at the circus, watching the clowns convert themselves into short-lived jesters. It was myself pampered the only time in my childhood, standing on a chair, surrounded by relatives who were dressing me, taking the same care as these actors. The cousins were sleeking my hair back and scrubbing my face, paring and cleaning my fingernails, my toenails, too. With great exclamations they clothed my naked body in new white undergarments. A white satin shirt was carefully buttoned by Ada, whose dress sparkled with sequins, while Tante Yette, best friend of my mother, always certain to bring giant layer cakes in Rinso cartons for bar mitzvahs, adjusted the shorts and pinned the full waist. Ada brushed white liquid onto the spots of dirt on my white shoes. I felt a prince. They were adulating me, and Tante Yette laughed her great laugh and warned me not to run down the aisle but to walk slowly and sprinkle small handfuls of rose petals in front of the bride. It was Joe Gams's wedding I was being dressed for.

A signal that I neither saw nor heard was given backstage, but the actors were aware of it, and everyone was suddenly rushing through the gateway to take his place behind his instrument or to squeeze into whatever space he could find.

A man came out from behind the curtain and regulated each of the four pressure lamps that hung above the stage. The curtains parted once again, and three white-robed priests came out and knelt in front of the gamelan with flowers and bells and bowls of water for blessing the orchestra, the night, the crowd, the actors. No one in the audience got impatient with the delays; for myself, the play had been under way since I first arrived.

There came a silence, through which a dog walked slowly and unconcernedly across the area of stage. The overture began with a clash of drums, cymbals, and gongs and continued for fifteen minutes. The gamelan was brilliantly controlled, with never a misplaced note or rhythm. There was no music for the players to read; Balinese music has never been written down.

Finally, a voice was heard from the other side of the curtain, which shook violently with the violence of the hidden actor's story. He burst onto the stage, masked and costumed as one of the characters of Balinese history. He was the single actor in a *topeng padjegan,* performing all the roles of the play. He would disappear behind the curtain and quickly return as someone else, a king, a warrior, a minister, his mask and costume changed accordingly. The gamelan played furiously, and the actor danced, strutted, angled himself in accordance with the character he was portraying. The long monologue and comic episodes entranced the audience, even though, or because, they knew it all by heart. The play lasted over an hour and was followed by other dances that went on through most of the night.

When there were no festivities in Ubud or in the neighborhood, I went out walking. I sketched in temples, balanced myself along the edge of dikes, watched the men and women harvesting or plowing in the paddy fields and the bullocks in the sawahs sitting in deep mud, and once tried my hand at pounding rice with a group of nineteen women, who were very much amused.

On the edge of a terrace, I met two boys of eight strolling with short bamboo poles over their shoulders as if they were going fishing. Each carried a string of dragonflies threaded like tiny carp. They swung the lines at me and smiled, radiant with the pleasure of their catch. We stood there talking, they laughing at my attempts to speak Balinese, correcting my pronunciation with patience and humor, and storing up a funny tale to tell. A dragonfly came from out of nowhere, suddenly buzzing loudly, then flapping and whizzing at the end of one of the strings. The boy picked it up, pulled off its wings, and threaded it along with the others. The line at the end of the bamboo pole was baited with a lumpy substance, nothing more than the head of a dragonfly dipped into a sap that attracted the other fly. Later, I confirmed that fried dragonflies are delicious.

At Pusering Djagar, famous for its linga, I saw the only female symbol I noticed in any temple in Bali, a vulva next to a penis, standing isolated on the platform of a bamboo altar. Both were realistically carved in stone, the penis about eighteen inches high, the labia slightly shorter and squatter. Projecting from the ring of the penis were four knobs that looked vaguely familiar; several seconds passed before I realized that the knobs were *palangs,* like those I had seen in Borneo ten years earlier. They had not seemed real at first, but I had not known then that some men in Southeast Asia bored holes through their penises and inserted bamboo tubes; nor did my later reading mention the existence of this practice in Bali.

But I had seen them on three Kelabit men in northern Sarawak, up the Baram River. The men had been bathing in water above their waists, and I wanted to sketch them. Their earlobes extended down to their shoulders, and there was tatooing on their chests and arms. As they came out of the river to greet me, each one modestly cupped a hand over his penis, but when one of them took up his *chawat* to wind through his legs and around his hips, I could see something strange attached to the end of his penis. He laughed shyly when I asked to look more closely, and I was startled by the small, thin section of bamboo that went through the head of the penis and extended out on both sides. He slowly twisted the bamboo and pulled it out with such care that I assumed he rarely removed it. Later, in the village, he and the other men showed me small clusters of bristles that could be fastened to the ends of the *palang* when preparing for sexual intercourse.

I had seen photographs of Chinese and Japanese instruments of erotic pleasure; the Hittite Museum in Ankara had decorated gold tubes of "unknown use" that closely resembled the Chinese decorated jade tubes used for sustaining erection and increasing penis size; but nowhere in my reading had there been a hint of the *palang* until I read Tom Harrisson's *World Within* (Dufour Editions, 1959):

> The basic operation simply consists of driving a hole through the distel end of the penis; sometimes for the determined, two (or more) holes at right angles. In this hole a small tube of bone, bamboo or other material can be kept, so that the hole does not grow over and close. It is of no inconvenience once the initial pain has been overcome.

> When the device is put into use, the owner adds whatever he prefers to elaborate and accentuate its intention. A lively range of objects can be so employed—from pigs' bristles and bamboo shavings to pieces of metal, seeds, beads and broken glass. The effect, of course, is to enlarge the diameter of the male organ inside the female.

In Malaya I had seen a small collection of bone and gold *palangs*. There, the material varied according to the status of the wearer and was most common among royal families, whose women apparently tired of their men sodomizing each other and devised the *palang* to discourage entry into the anal passage. I did not learn whether the men continued their practice of anal intercourse with the *palang* in place.

Bali was magical and innocent. Scenes in front of me were sometimes of such beauty that I was not always sure they had really happened: A naked boy of four riding a bullock in a paddy field amid breadfruit and coconut trees could send such comfort into me that I would sit motionless until he went on his way. The bent backs of men and women, their feet hidden in water and mud, their arms stretched out planting shoots of rice, evoked the warmth and peace of Millet. In the softness of an evening, an aged man engraving magical figures on strips of dried palm leaf summoned up Masters etching plates, but, in slow perfection, filled the leaves not from a sketch, only from the image in his mind. Colors changed in air like silk, giving off other hues as angles altered and ruffles varied intensity and tone. A flock of ducks waddled by in single file, led by a boy carrying a long pole tipped with white cloth and feathers. He set the pole into the mud at the edge of a rice field and went about his other duties. The ducks scattered and searched for food. At dusk, the ducks had already gathered around the pole when the boy returned to take them home.

I felt at peace with the landscape and myself within it. I never entered deeply into the lives of the people, though I tried with Oka, who worked at the hotel. Days could never be planned, because events were often spontaneous, and I rarely knew of anything until it was happening. The gongs of a gamelan would always bring me out to investigate, and I always found affecting incidents.

Once, a girl of seven was being taught to dance the *legong* in the courtyard of a neighbor's house. She was dressed in silks and a gold helmet, with white frangipani in her hair. The full orchestra was there, though no one was paid to play. The teacher, daughter of Prince Tjokorta Gedé, whose family had ruled Ubud for centuries, wore a red sarong and a black blouse. Her hair was tied in a great bun at the nape of her neck and was also full of frangipani. She was standing behind the child, manipulating her by the wrists, as if the child were without bones, molding her body to the desired shape. Her hands were everywhere on the girl, moving her head, moving her hands, raising the elbows, adjusting the feet, all at the same time. There was no talking, no showing of movements by demonstration, just shaping her into the dance itself in time to the music, repeating the whole of it over and over until the girl was ready to move on her own. At a feast before I left, I watched this young girl in the role of Princess Rangkesari, who rejects the advances of King Lasem, danced by a child who looked her double, the two moving together with perfect control.

Most afternoons I went through a mile of rice fields to the holy forest, where monkeys gathered when someone stopped to feed them nuts or other edibles. A path led to a gigantic banyan tree with a wide gap in its center through which stone steps led down to a small wooden bridge over a narrow ravine. When I stood on the bridge, I was encircled by the roots that came down from the high branches. The path went through lush growth to a divided bathing ghat and finally to the stream itself. More often than not, when I was there, young men and girls arrived to bathe and eat rice, bringing offerings to the temple. They stopped and giggled, looked at my drawings, and invited me to bathe or share their rice. We bathed together, but we were separate, each with his own shield of privacy around him. The women were only a few feet away, but they did not exist for us until they were back on the bank properly wrapped in their sarongs. We were never so rude as to look at one another's bodies and, in spite of the invisibility ordained by custom, each of the men cupped a hand over his groin.

Once, at a festival, Dr. Werner Meyer said, "Come! Come, let us look at the man's feet!" The feet were those of an entranced priest, possessed by the god Gandarwa to drive evil demons from the village. He had been dancing over the burning coals of coconut shells with a small wooden horse between his legs. When he stepped onto the line of embers, I heard a sizzling sound and thought I saw a puff of smoke. He walked and hopped over the coals, back and forth, shrugging his shoulders. At times, he stood on the coals for several seconds without moving, screaming out invectives against the devils while a priest beat a drum, surrounded by other priests and the hushed, enthralled crowd. The medium rolled on the ground, jerked in an almost epileptic fit, and finally was calmed by priests kneeling on his chest and thighs, smacking him across the face, throwing water over his body, standing him up, and shaking him.

"You see," said the doctor, "not a burn mark on his feet." The soles were calloused and crisscrossed with ancient cuts, but nothing of his walk over the coals showed but bits of twig and dirt.

Dr. Meyer, who is head of the government hospital on the island of Celebes and has a private practice there that keeps him busy when not at the clinic, comes to Bali every year. He is a connoisseur of religious rites and rituals and never fails to attend a ceremony, no matter how many times he has seen it. He is considered godlike and is approached with head lowered, palms together and posture in an attitude of prayer and supplication, for he always arrives with his bag full of medicines and treats the sick without charge. He likes to talk and is easy to listen to.

"The people of Makassar," he said the next day when we were having tea, "they are funny. And very superstitious. Oh, very superstitious. Many years ago the Chinese, whom they dislike, as you know, brought a strange disease to the island of Celebes. Because of their superstition, men still come to me frightened to death because everyone on the island is afraid of this terrible disease. You see, they think it attacks the penis. They have it in their minds that the disease makes the penis shrivel up and disappear, that it gets smaller and smaller until all of it is gone. It is terrible, I tell you. I have seen it often enough. I see the patients in the hospital holding on to their penises, screaming out that it is getting smaller and they are losing it. But it is right there in front of them, right in their hands. They hold on to it and pull on it and tie a string around it, and still it gets smaller and smaller. There are no visible symptoms, of course, and I have no way of knowing that anything is wrong unless they tell me.

"Sometimes a patient arrives alone in such a hysterical state that he cannot tell me the problem, and I do not always think of it. The disease is rare, but men have even been known to die of it. One of the biggest problems is that the men and the families are so ashamed that they won't admit what is wrong. When they arrive at the hospital, they have friends with them who watch while they sleep. The friends hold on to the penis to keep it from disappearing. It is all very secret. And whether the disease is real or imagined does not matter, since something happens to them; they think it shrinks up into nothing and they no longer see anything in their groin. Sometimes with drugs I can cure them. They believe in the white man's magic. It is frightening and terrible, the way they feel, but they believe it. Of course, it only attacks older men, men over fifty, never anyone young. Oh yes, they are a wonderful people. You must come visit them."

"Oh, my life is very good," he said another time. "I work hard, all day at the hospital, all night with my private patients. But it is good. In Germany it was bad. I was in the army, but I would not kill the Jews only because they were Jews. They put me in a prison. After the war, I came to Makassar and my practice was good. My wife came, but she did not like it. She wanted cinemas and night clubs. After a year, she went back to Germany. A Toradja woman, very beautiful she was, came to live with me. She was with me many years. I see her sometimes in Toradja. She is there now with her nice hotel. You must come visit me, and you must stay there when you go. The Toradja are fantastic."

That night, we talked again of Germany, the war, and the holocaust. Dr. Meyer told of his comparatively easy life in prison, and I told of my easy life as radar mechanic in the States. Moe had strung telephone lines in the Battle of the Bulge, and Bernie had sweltered on Bahrein and in India. Most of the European members of my family had been killed during the war, but my cousin Lucia, the daughter of my father's sister, came to us at the end of 1946. My father had found her through HIAS, a Jewish refugee organization. Dr. Meyer egged me on to tell the story, and although I told it to him in the third person, I remember it better in Lucia's own words:

"It was not bad for us in the concentration camp," she used to say. "Mama was cook and we helped in the kitchen." The story did not come out all at once, but the pieces fit together easily.

"I was ten when papa was killed. I don't remember how. But my sister, Hella, and I were all right. And mama, too." She nodded her head and intoned the words like the ancient wife of an ancient rabbi, instead of the young, attractive woman she was.

"We were all right because they needed cooks in the camp and they didn't want to change them all the time, so we were not lined up and counted off. We carried the water, Hella and I, and sometimes we peeled the vegetables. We saw friends disappear in the camp and we saw them die. We saved the peelings and gave them away. The workers in the kitchen ate all right.

"But everything changed when the Germans knew they would lose the war. They began killing us more and more. One day, mama was chosen. They counted out, 'One, two, three, four, *you!* One, two, three, four, *you!*' One day Mama was *you!* and she stood in the line going to the showers. We knew it was not showers. Mama was in a line by the wall. Hella and I climbed the wall. We tried to reach down to mama but we could only catch her hair. It was very long. Hella pulled her by the hair. Mama couldn't make any noise from the pain, but Hella pulled her up onto the wall by her hair. Nobody in the line said anything. They were going to die but they didn't say anything. The Germans did not see. We saved her that time.

"Then we heard the Russians were coming. We were all afraid of them. The Russians would kill us and tell everyone the Germans did it. We heard the stories. But the Germans shouted one morning and they made us stand out in the rain, all of us, everyone in the camp, all together. Then the guns exploded. The guns and the machine guns and everyone was falling down. We were screaming. The Germans were shooting and killing us all before the Russians arrived. I was hit in the head and I don't remember anything. I don't remember how long I was there before the gypsies came. They came to rob the bodies. They were taking the clothes and the shoes. Everything. They saw that I was not dead and they took me too. The bullet hit me in the side of the head and it came out my mouth, knocking out my teeth. You can still see the hole here in my temple. The gypsies took me and I lived with them. They fed me and taught me to tell fortunes."

My father did not like Lucia and complained about her all the time. He expected her to do the cooking and the cleaning up. He had talked about her for weeks before she arrived, saying how good it would be to have a cook in the house for a change. This was before I went to Mexico, when I was working in his store.

"But I am not a servant!" she yelled at him after a couple of weeks. "I had enough of that in the camp!"

"But what did I bring you all the way from Poland for?" my father shouted back. "Ungrateful! How can you leave all those dirty dishes in the sink? Look at the dirt on the floor! And what about the sheets on my bed!"

Lucia wanted to get a job. "Job? Who would hire a dummy like you? Stay and do the cooking!"

Lucia did find a job, married a doctor, had three children and two fur coats. Once, while still living with us, she said to me, "Let me see your hand," and examined it carefully. "Oh, yes, it says it right here. You are going to travel!"

Dr. Meyer was always aware of everything of interest that was happening for miles around Ubud. His spirit was a good one and the Balinese liked to have him at their ceremonies.

In the dead of a night, he woke me up and told me to get dressed. A jeep was waiting and we drove south, past the village of Peliatan. We stopped to ask directions and were soon walking through the sawahs. The moon was so full we did not need our flashlights. We came to a temple that was in almost complete blackness, half hidden under great trees. As we entered we saw a clump of people huddled together in a corner, with two small oil lamps giving light. The faint glow gave the scene an aura of occult mysteries.

Dr. Meyer and I sat at a distance on the steps of a pavilion and watched. Two priests, *pemangkus,* sat in front of two girls of about ten.

All were on a single straw mat, the girls sitting on their heels, the priests cross-legged. The *pemangkus* were saying prayers for the girls, who were bent over braziers erupting heavy smoke and incense. Behind the girls sat a group of men and women. After some time, one of the girls began to sway back and forth. Soon, the other girl began to move in the same way. They lifted their arms and held their hands up loosely. They swayed from side to side and then back and forth.

When the priests were satisfied with the condition of the girls, they stood them up. Special chairs with struts attached were brought out and the girls were led into them. The chairs were lifted onto the shoulders of two men. The girls sat up straight and began the movements of a dance. Their eyes were closed, yet they seemed to know what was happening around them. The group moved out of the temple and into the sawahs, and we followed along as if entranced ourselves. Someone beat a drum, and the women began to chant. The procession moved slowly. Sometimes it went one way, sometimes another, wandering through the rice fields, frightening away the *leyaks*, the witches who come in the night with pestilence and plague. The girls sat in the chairs, their eyes closed, dancing in unison. They stood on the shoulders of the men and swayed at impossible angles.

"Now we will go to the temple in Peliatan, and the girls will dance all through the night." Dr. Meyer and I had not exchanged a word from the time we first arrived in the temple until that moment. He knew every movement the girls would make. "They have been living in the Temple of the Dead for months, spending all their time training to go into the trance on this very night. They have never danced before. They have never danced and look at them now with their eyes closed, dancing together so perfectly. But it is not the girls who are dancing; it is the heavenly spirits inside them who are making every move." Dr. Meyer believed in the trance, the *sanghyang dedari*, as he called it, and so did I.

The gamelan was already playing in the square of Peliatan when we arrived. Our procession continued down alleyways, around several corners, back and forth, making certain no *leyaks* were left. At the pavilion, the girls were lifted onto the platform and went immediately into the dance, still with their eyes closed, still with their movements in unison. It was three in the morning and the whole village had gathered for the ceremony. Groups of the youngest boys and girls

were off in corners sleeping on mats, while older children tried to stay awake. Just before dawn, the girls blessed the crowd, tossed water and flowers over us. They came out of the trance easily and with no sense of exhaustion, though they had been dancing for five hours. They were led back to the Temple of the Dead, where they would remain for some days before returning home to their parents. The crowd dispersed, satisfied that no evil spirits would destroy the village during the coming months.

Girls were always flirting with me, and the men and boys enjoyed walking and joking with me and offering their food. They liked to talk whether or not they understood English, whether or not I knew any Balinese or Indonesian. They tolerated everything, almost every strangeness of the foreigner. Of course, the *leyaks,* who appeared in the night as flames, knew there was something strange about the foreigners and never showed themselves when they were around. The Balinese like people and are quick to draw them into their lives and to invite the stranger to their homes and to festivals. They are shy and

To Sue and Gordon, with love and affection, Bali, Tchin 97

timid, gracious and trusting. Or so it seemed until the day of the meetings in Ubud during the election campaign.

The men had come in from all the villages around, the men I saw every day in the fields in their sarongs, always generous and gentle to me, but on this day different, all wearing shirts and trousers or shorts, which gave them a completely different aspect. There was another look in their eyes, in the expression of their faces, in the way they carried themselves. It was as if they were an entirely different race, not the people among whom I'd been living all these weeks.

They had come in by the truckload from all around, shouting slogans and lifting their arms in a fist salute. Loudspeakers blasted out political speeches while men on motorcycles and motorbikes made an incredible racket. With their dark glasses, their leather jackets, and their helmets and caps with chin straps, they looked sinister, like the most violent of Hell's Angels. That image of the people frightened me, because the duality that I was suddenly made aware of reminded me of my own violence toward that man who entered my apartment, and the violence in my hatred of my father when I used to put a kitchen knife under my pillow and think to kill him if he approached.

Yet the Balinese had rare discretion and understanding. The only times I noticed their tolerance of outsiders diminish were when they expressed estrangement from some of the young visitors. Most of the foreign youngsters who came to the island lodged along the beaches or slept in the sand in the tourist areas. Large groups never came to Ubud. A few young people would ride in from Kuta Beach or Sanur on their motorbikes and stay a day or two; others would arrive by bus from Denpasar and stay for weeks at Tjokorta Mas's cheap hotel. They slept there en masse and ate in the *warung,* the food stall in the marketplace. Those who were more independent rented small houses outside the town.

As well as being congenial, the Balinese are clean and neat, taking great pride in their fastidiousness. A shopping trip to the market, a stroll in the evening, attendance at a festival, all require a certain sprucing up—a bath, a fresh sarong, a clean shirt, grooming of the hair. This passion for tidiness is reflected in the beauty of everything they touch—in the manicured elegance of the rice fields, in the simple arrangement of flowers in a bowl, in the decorated offerings meticulously put together with extraordinary patience. So the Balinese looked at the red-faced foreign youngsters wandering their streets in ragged garb and shook their heads. Oka said he was always tempted to attack them with needle and thread or push them into pools to wash their hair and clothes. Most of them did bathe regularly; nevertheless, they always looked dishevelled.

A group of from six to twelve lived in a house not far from where I stayed. They ranged in age from seventeen to twenty-two, their numbers and sex varying from time to time as the clique exchanged partners with Sanur Beach. Many were attractive. Now and then, I talked to one or two, but my age was a barrier between us. When they needed specific information, they were polite and attentive, but at other times, more often than not, they drifted away in mid-sentence.

Two or three times a week, I was irritated by the noises and music that came from their house, usually the sounds of two transistor radios playing at the same time, or tapes of Dylan and the Stones that went on for hours in the middle of the night. Sometimes there were long silences from the house, the silence of drugged sleep.

One day I was sketching at the stream in the holy forest when two girls and a young man, teenagers and British, came and looked over my shoulder, stripped off their clothes, and went into the water. They soaped one another and laughed a lot. I wondered what the gods were thinking of this open intimacy. "Hey, kids!" I said. "You'd better not let the Balinese see you washing each other. They won't like it."

Their smiles turned into anger. "Fuck you, mister!" said the young man. "Who asked you!" he went on, and proceeded to soap the groin of one of the girls.

Another day when I went to the holy forest, I found wooden slats nailed across the opening of the banyan tree and a sign in English saying "Closed." I went to the Agung, the leader of the community. "They have desecrated the temple," he said. "They take off their clothes and they bathe naked. The boys and girls wash each other, and they make love in the temple. How can they do these terrible things in our holy places? Now we must wait until they leave Ubud so we can purify the temple. We cannot use it until they go back to school in their countries."

A week later, I was standing at the edge of the market buying peppers, eggplant, and peanuts, when the bus from Denpasar stopped to unload. A young man stepped out wearing a wide-brimmed Mexican hat, a colorful batik shirt, and fireman-red boots. I couldn't help staring. He lifted his knapsack onto one shoulder and came over to me. I was wearing a sarong, the most comfortable male garment I know.

The young man was tall and good-looking, with blue eyes and a wide mouth with full lips. He was smoothly shaved. "Well?" he asked. "What next?" His smile was friendly and warm, his accent Oxford or Cambridge.

"I suppose you're looking for a place to stay."

"Yes, please."

"Well, most of the kids are staying with Tjokorta Mas, so I'll take you there, if you like."

"Yes, that's the place I was told to look for."

"Have you been staying at the beach in Sanur?" I asked as we walked through the streets.

"Yes, how did you know?" He had a nice voice, deep and resonant, when I could hear it over the clumping sound of his boots.

"All the kids stay there when they first arrive in Bali." I introduced him to Tjokorta Mas and went on my way.

with lots of love
to gordon and Eve
Bali Tobias 74

I was sitting on the north end of the museum in Ubud, sketching the tops of the rice and the immense trees in the distance, an accurate, realistic pen-and-ink drawing that was taking some hours. Someone sat down next to me, forcing me to stop. I looked over and almost didn't recognize my friend of the previous day. He was bare-headed and was wearing huraches. He didn't say good morning; he simply sat down and sat there while I worked. His presence strangely did not bother me; he gave off no sense of impatience or boredom, or anything but a restful quality. I didn't become nervous, as I usually do when someone is nearby when I work. He didn't lean over to look at the drawing, and when I finished, I showed it to him. "Beautiful!" he said. "My name is Michael Healey." We shook hands and sat there for a while. He had taken a year off from Oxford to travel, he said, and had recently come to Asia from Mexico. He was majoring in music.

"What period?" I asked.

"Early music."

"Early? You mean like Guillaume de Machaut, or what?"

He was startled. In all his months of travel, he'd not met anyone who had heard of Machaut.

Michael was twenty-two—exuberant, brilliant, friendly, companionable—and had been lonely for months. He burst into talk and often reflected my own thoughts. His skin was a pale pink, in spite of the hot suns in which he'd walked, and his arms must have been exceptionally long, for they were always in his way, and he was always folding them or clasping his hands behind his back or behind his head. He would lie in the stillness of a field near me while I drew, and his talk often went off in mystical directions.

"I like the sky. I like the way we are part of it. I drift up into the clouds of nebulae and sometimes become that star that burst and spread the particles of life. It makes me exist in everyone and everything. I am part of the clouds up there, part of the universe, part of you, too."

The affectation of his talk never bothered me; it only touched the outer limits of my senses while I sketched.

"Do you never feel it? Do you never feel the continuity of the infinite? Sometimes I am the emptiness in the universe expanding, and from my nothingness I give forth atoms of life. If thereby I create life, why then can I not create love?"

He spoke these words as if some were capitalized—Emptiness, Nothingness, Life—and sometimes I thought he was quoting Thomas Mann or Hermann Hesse or even L. C. Beckett. But there was a quietness in him that attracted me, and I let him come with me on my walks.

Once, on the edge of a far kampong, miles from Ubud, we stopped to eat the rice we had brought wrapped in banana leaves. We sat near an irrigation ditch whose gurgling water flowed past us. My back was against a mango tree, while Michael lay on soft earth. I looked at him, and his eyes shone with unshed tears.

Into the silence and peace came a groaning from the distance, a sound of pain, at first, a moan of anguish. We looked around and saw no one. The sound began again, getting louder as we approached the trees. It had a weird cadence, an almost nonhuman wave of throbbing on the air.

There was no one that we could see within the grove. At the far end was an altar of bamboo. On it stood a wooden *tjili,* goddess of fertility. Nearby was a huge banyan tree. We sat in its roots and listened. A howling came up like the sound of a ghost carrying rattling chains in a haunted house. A lower voice accompanied it, causing cold shivers to run down my back. I got up and walked around but still saw no one. When the wind calmed, the voices softened, deepened, disappeared. For a while there was silence everywhere, a mysterious calm settling around us so serene I felt as if I were floating, drifting up into Michael's nebulae and becoming one with all the universe.

A voice groaned, the voice of my old friend Mary Miller, in an ambulance, groaning from her coma. No, I had promised her, no, you will not die anywhere but at home, but I was reneging, taking her to the hospital. From the trees came her groan again, jolting me. Then, from within myself came her agonized voice, loud and clear, the last words she ever spoke, "Where are you taking me?"

I stared at Michael and he, too, was transfixed by the moan, as if in frightened memories and dreams.

Slowly the wind came up again, and with it the voices returned. I looked up into the banyan and high up, hidden in branches and leaves, were two great tubes of bamboo of different lengths. Pipes played by the wind, frightening off the phantoms of evil!

Chapter Six

A man recently entered my life and told me things I never thought to hear. "I think of you many times a day," he wrote. Does he know, I wonder, that no one has written that to me before? And, because he tells me so, I know he has never said it to another. He had earlier said that I search for universal love, not the paired-off passion of two people but a love extending to all. Not so, sir, not so. Yet, if such a paired-off love, any love, your love, could come my way, would I recognize it? Would I accept it as my own? If it flooded me with tenderness and poignant pleasures, would I push it off and let it lie amid the waste of past griefs? Do I steel myself still to allow no individual love to enter? He writes and says these things of love and means them truly; but can he be prodded from his present to share in part a future?

Michael was young, intense, beguiling, but he was not in any sense like my new friend; there was nothing between Michael and me but time and place. The succulent life we could lead in Bali intoxicated like a heady wine and moved the days too quickly. He left Ubud in sadness, not in grief for leaving love, but in sweet melancholy for losing communion with a friend and countryside. He was on his way to Timor, Darwin, Sydney, back to London. Oh, yes, he wrote a letter—two, in fact—but to him I was Bali, temple feasts, and walks in paddy fields, and when they faded from his mind, I faded with them.

In Ubud, alone, I sought distraction and eagerly accepted Oka's invitation to attend his uncle's cremation ceremony in the remote village of Kedisan. Oka was an attendant at the Puri Hotel, where I had stayed when I first arrived in Ubud. He took me on his motorbike to temples, left me there to sketch, picked me up in the late afternoon. He had a need to talk, not easy on a bike, but he sought answers to questions about the foreign girls and men who had tried to take him to their rooms. None ever succeeded, he said. "I have my wife. I love my wife. It is enough right now. Maybe in a year I will be with other women, but never other men."

Oka was not good-looking. He was twenty-five and, like many Orientals, looked younger to Western eyes. His face, covered with a light down not quite dark or stiff enough to pluck, was narrow, not at all the round, full face of most Balinese. His skin was smooth and soft, unlike the tough, leathery skin of men his age who worked the paddy fields. He had charm and grace and moved his arms as if in dance, his hands turning at the wrist with special delicacy. To me his effeminate mannerisms implied a sexual attraction for other men, but I found I was mistaken. He told me this while riding along dirt roads, I, my arms clutched around his waist, listening with my cheek against his cheek, my ear focused on his voice.

"No, that does not happen here. I have been with the Agung in his palace many years. It was his home before he took in guests. Many guests come all the time. This is the Agung's palace and his hotel, and guests come from all over the world. Like you, like George from Paris. Some guests ask for boys, but none are here. They do not ask the Agung; they ask me, and they tell me of the boys in Java and in Celebes. Many are there, they say. They want to take me, too. But I send them to the Bali Beach Hotel. I send them to Denpasar. They will find them there, those who take money and hang around the big hotels. But none are here in Ubud."

Oka was silent for a while. Then, as if he'd thought things over, he said. "Sampeh? You have seen Sampeh in the *warung?* He is a *bentji.* Did you know that? He is a boy, not a girl, though he dresses like a girl and has his food stall like a girl. He cannot marry, but he lives like a girl and sometimes he is a girl with the men. He is nice. I like him. He is alone here in Ubud. There are *bentji* in other villages, but not here."

I told him of the American Indian berdache, who marry and live and work like women all their lives, and this surprised him greatly. Among some people of the world, I said, *bentji* become important priests. Some are sorcerers and some have operations that change their physical lives. He looked at me with shock and several days later told me that he'd had a long talk with Sampeh, and Sampeh had said that he was happy about his life and didn't want to change, even though men and girls sometimes laughed at him.

Oka drove me to Kedisan on his bike. Its cool streets of packed earth and rock were wide and clear. The brick walls were covered with dried mud, hidden under green moss. Stone steps led up to entrance gates behind which coconut trees, jackfruit, mango, banana, and banyan heavily shaded the houses of mud and thatch. Oka and I followed a group of men and women in gold-threaded sarongs through a gate into a courtyard. He introduced me to several relatives and left me on my own. Crowds were moving around, everyone cheerful and welcoming.

The courtyard contained several buildings with small porches in front. To the right of the entrance was an open pavilion with wooden steps that led up to the curtained platform on which rested the body of Oka's uncle. A smiling gray-haired man invited me up. I climbed the steps and lifted the curtain to see the body wrapped tightly in several layers of white cloth. A strong smell of decay hung in the air around the corpse.

Other structures close by also held platforms with altars. One was dedicated to the sun, another to Pradjapati, the god of cremation. In the center of the courtyard stood a tower with a bamboo floor twelve feet or more above the ground. A Brahmin priest in a white robe, with white flowers tucked around his ears, sat there chanting and blessing the offerings of food handed up to him, sprinkling them with holy water and ringing his bell. The offerings were of meat and fruit decorated with frangipani. Young men in sumptuous sarongs and flamboyant batik shirts carried trays of tea and coffee for the guests. Girls wrapped in brightly colored sarongs that covered their breasts held out palm leaf packages of sweet, pink and purple glutinous rice. The men and women in separate groups were sitting on porches, inside rooms, on the ground in shaded areas, gossiping and laughing and enjoying themselves immensely.

At noon, loud knocks on the village drum, the *kulkul,* signaled everyone to gather outside the gate of the house, and the whole village turned up to form a procession. The women, now dressed in red sarongs and blue blouses, led the way in single file, carrying on their heads bamboo gods dressed with frangipani and hibiscus. A gamelan joined them, and all went down the street to the main temple, where the men squatted on the ground or sat on steps while the women made their way down the terracing to a sacred pool, at the edge of which was a small shrine. The women disappeared inside the shrine and had their gods blessed. They came up half an hour later, and everyone returned to the courtyard.

"Do you like Bali?"

"Where are you from?"

"Tell us what it is like in America."

Lunch of deliciously spiced chicken and mounds of rice was brought on leaves, and I ate on a veranda with young men who asked questions about my life and the Western world. By the time most of the guests had eaten, other activities were taking place. The priest was chanting in his tower; almost immediately under him, women were chanting in a different rhythm, neither noticing the other. The wooden coffin was being prepared: Men were painting magical writings inside while at the same time other men continued carving with chisels and knives. I was not allowed to look inside the coffin then. Directly in front of where the body lay, across a space of courtyard, was a *wayang kulit,* an easily portable theater of leather puppets in front of a white screen. The manipulator, the *dayang,* was shouting out the voices of the many historical and mythical characters and beating metal against metal at the proper moments to indicate violence. (I had seen a *wayang kulit* several times in Ubud, but at night, when a white sheet was hung in front of the puppets and their shadows were cast onto it.) People were standing around, watching, eating rice and meat. Others entered the courtyard and arranged offerings around the tower—flowers, suckling pigs and roast duck, and great heaps of rice.

Oka came over and sat down, resting from the constant greeting of new arrivals. He was in an expansive mood, open and intimate, and began to talk about his wife.

"I miss her here. She did not need to come and I told her not to. She is very good, my Madé. She is very beautiful and she has given me a fine son, one and one half years old. She gave me another son, but he is dead. Maybe Madé did not wear her amulets one day, or she forgot the temple offerings. Who can tell? She would not have gone out at night. Of that I am sure. She would be too frightened of the *leyaks*. They eat the blood of pregnant women and the babies inside them too, so she would never go out at night."

Oka nodded his head, assuring himself that this must be true. "We met in school, you know, Madé and I. We liked each other and we were friends for a long time when we left school. Madé's father said to me, 'Why don't you take Madé to her room and talk to her?' and we went. We were both without experience but Madé knew how to stand and wash herself out when we finished. We were not wanting children then. We met many times, and our families talked and argued about the money, and my father agreed quickly when I said I would kidnap Madé. Then they went to the high priest and chose the day for the wedding. We will have many children and they will perform the rituals when I die."

As I listened to Oka talk about himself, my own world seemed far away and empty. The life in Bali that he described and that I saw that day and every day was full and richly textured. It had an air of well-being and wholeness, shaped by centuries of deep involvement in a communal, religious world. The people lived through all the manifestations of pain and pleasure, birth and rebirth, living every instant of time through experiencing the whole of their existence.

The priest stopped chanting, climbed down the altar, and disappeared behind the curtain with several men. They lifted the body from its bed and squeezed it into a coffin too narrow for it. The lid would not fit and was tied there with cotton belts. Women appeared from nowhere, a long line of them under a white cloth twenty feet long. They were crowding together, shouting, and pushing one another. The front end of the cloth was a padded section, like a bed. The cloth was whisked under the curtain by the men and came out almost immediately. It was taken up again by the women, who shouted and tossed it around furiously, trying to fool the hovering evil spirits into

attacking this false casket. Behind them, the men came down the ladder with the true container, screeching, barking terrifying noises, scaring what spirits might remain, scaring me as well, bouncing the coffin up and down in a wild, convulsive way, carrying it to its scaffold tower, which was covered with paper flowers around a golden mask of the wild monster Bhoma.

I was absorbed into the energy of the crowd, feeling the thrill of their attack on demons, devils, and witches, being kindled by their beliefs, led on by their excitability and devotion to gods and spells and incantations. The horrifying screams and howls intensified as the coffin was thrown upon the stairway to the tower. The men pushed the structure so it swayed and creaked, the coffin going to the top. A man jumped in frenzy there, tilting the tower while fifty men raised it to their shoulders and rushed onward, down terraces, up hillsides, screaming, squawling. The body was an encasement for the soul and was on its way to extinction, on its way to where the soul could be released, freed for reincarnation. This horde of shouting men, fearful of any evil that might enter the body before the soul was liberated, whirled along, running, falling into sawahs, going one way, then another, zigzagging and circling, onward to the village cemetery.

There, amid mounds of earth where other bodies awaited cremation, stood the painted sculpture of a bull upon another smaller tower. In a calmed mood, the men removed the body from its coffin, wrapped it in a palm leaf mat, and stuffed it into the hollow on the back of the bull. Masses of dried leaves and wood were packed under the bull and lit with a torch. The big tower was broken into sections and used to feed the fire. The flames flared up around the body, and the villagers began to move toward home.

I stood and watched an arm slip out of a hole in the side of the bull and the blaze leap up to blacken it. Oka, no longer participating in formalities, came over joyously and asked how I'd enjoyed the feast. He was full of the rapture of the day.

Then, more soberly, peevishly, he asked, "But why didn't they come? I told them about it last night."

"Who are you talking about?"

"Those kids who live in the house near yours."

"Oh" was all I could think to say at the moment.

The sarcophagus suddenly collapsed, sending up clouds of ash and smoke. The tower, the body were gone. Only embers remained.

But Oka was right to ask, and I too wondered why they hadn't come. I knew that most of them were too involved with themselves to care about the life around them, but there were others who would have liked the ceremony. The next day, I learned that a young couple had arrived in Ubud from Timor with a kilo of hashish and were very generous with it. The effects on everyone lasted for several days.

I felt a kind of loss for them, as if they had missed out on some important event, like the Peace Corps girls in Mayoyao, who had missed the skeleton ceremony in the Philippines some time before. We had gone to northern Luzon by jeep from Manila, they to inventory the hospital for CARE, I to look around and sketch in the land of the Ifugao, whose rice terracing was five thousand years old. We had no sooner arrived and settled in when a man wearing a loincloth and carrying a spear came with a letter inviting us to a ceremony the following afternoon. When our guide appeared the next day, the girls begged off, saying they were planning to play bridge. I took up my sketchboard and climbed down the terracing to a house high on stilts, where I was welcomed by crowds of men and women. A long line of them were moving between the stilts, under the floor of the house, where an open coffin was propped, displaying the partly unwrapped skeleton of a woman. Bits of flesh still clung to the bones and part of an eye stared out. Everyone in the line bent to kiss the forehead.

The body had been brought home from the cave in which it had rested for the past year. Its return was heralded with a feast of dancing, singing, and the ritual killing of pigs that went on throughout the night. I sketched the body, drank the strong rice wine, danced for hours, and ate my fill of pork and rice. In the morning the bones were rewrapped in ceremonial cloth and stored in the eaves of the house, along with the bones of other members of the family. On my way up to the hospital, I kept thinking of what the girls had missed and how disappointed they would be, but when I showed them the drawings and described what had happened, they were bored and horrified that primitive rites could take place so close to where they were staying. They didn't move out of the hospital compound until the day they left.

These incidents, like one involving an American girl on the border of Thailand months earlier, troubled me, partly because I saw some-

thing of myself in so many of the young I met. I sympathized with them and knew that I must have looked and acted the way they did when I first left New York for Mexico and in some ways still resembled them. Helen hadn't involved herself in anything but her own pleasures, but isn't that what I was doing, too? We both were walking from Malaysia into Thailand. Her hair was tied neatly in a bun and she had clear skin free of makeup and slender hands without rings. She wore jeans cut off at the calf and a blouse of Thai silk tied tightly around her breasts so that her waist was bare. I carried a small bag slung over a shoulder, Helen a knapsack on her back. We stopped at the small Customs shack, where two officers gave my bag a superficial search and waved me on. They went through Helen's pack more carefully, taking everything out and examining it minutely. Her purse and the pockets of her jeans were also searched. I waited to see if I could help her. "Shit!" she mumbled. "Fuckheads! Goddam gooks!"

Almost an hour later we were at the deserted railway station where the train began its journey north to Bangkok. We sat on a bench and waited. I asked about her travels.

"Oh, mine is the usual story, I guess. I dropped out of Brooklyn College for a year two years ago and here I am. An English major, no less. Imagine. Like, what was I going to do with English, anyway? I didn't want to teach or anything. I mean, Jane Austen's neat, but what was I supposed to do with her?"

The train arrived and three people got off. We were the only passengers to get on. The car was empty, and I arranged a section of seats for maximum comfort for the long night ahead. I took out the packages of rice I'd bought in Kota Bharu and offered one to Helen.

"Oh, boy!"

Even cold, the rice was good. Helen was putting a handful into her mouth when she suddenly burst out laughing, spraying the rice. "How about that! Those gooks! They were so sure I was carrying dope! They looked so disappointed when they didn't find anything!" She tossed the emptied leaves out the window, clapped her hands, put her bare feet up on the seat in front of her and drummed her hands on her knees. "Ha!" she laughed again.

"Here! Let me show you!" She took two pins out of her hair and unrolled the bun, then shook the long black hair loose, releasing a

small package. She picked up a plastic bag. "Ha!" she said as she put it into her purse. "I've been around Bangkok now for two years and have to go out of the country every few months to renew my visa. But that's easy, you know. I mean, I go down to Malaysia, like now, then to Singapore, and buy whatever I find there. Sometimes I go up to Vientiane. It's easy. I'm living on what I make selling dope to the GIs. They'll buy anything. I have this friend at home who sends me stuff in the mail. No one opens an air mail package here and I've never had any trouble. Like whatever price my girl friend says, I multiply it by five and there's no problem finding buyers. I mean the GIs never complain and it beats working in an office back home."

Helen had depressed me, and the kids of Ubud depressed me. Oka had no strong feeling about the way they lived. To him, they had the magic and mystery of other worlds, though they moved sluggishly about the town, seeing nothing, none of the art, none of the beauty and self-sufficiency of the people. They were exotic to him in the same way that the Balinese, with their astonishing ability to create beauty everywhere, were exotic to me. Why couldn't those young men and women see it? Why were they closing their eyes and minds? Why couldn't they too watch the quick, agile fingers of the women weaving fresh leaves around rice and feel a comfort in the constancy of their art? Men made the durable works—the temples, the sculpture, the reliefs, the paintings and the carvings for sale—but it was the women who made the art of daily life, the art with which they lived at home. It was a transitory, impermanent art; an art of the moment, so ephemeral that it disintegrated and disappeared within hours or days. Piety and belief in the world of spirits permeated every aspect of life and were reflected even in the tiny offerings of flowers and fruit that were placed like jewels in front of my door every morning to keep me safe from evil. Offerings were on all doorsteps and windowsills, in front of small and large shrines, on solitary altars in rice fields, in temples, even on the low walls of a house. It was a fragile art unknown to us.

"But if you like it here so much, why are you rushing back to your country? Why don't you just stay?"

"Yes, Oka, that's a good question, which I could easily avoid by saying that I don't have the money. But there are other things that I haven't really thought out. I complain because I feel sorry for what

Schnee baum '61

we've lost on my side of the world. I come to a place like this and I renew myself; I fill myself up with your trees and sky, with your people and your way of life, with your rivers and rice; and I take them back to New York to use inside myself."

They give me more life; they give me more death; they give me my own rebirth.

Chapter Seven

One day, I took the subway to a hall in Brooklyn for the wedding of my first cousin twice removed. He was the mute son of a Hassidic rabbi and was marrying the mute daughter of a rabbi, also Hassidic. The reception room of the men was crowded and noisy; the older men, dressed in furred hats and long black coats, were seated at a long table, positioned there like disciples at the Last Supper. Their gray beards and lined faces were out of sixteenth-century paintings or Persian miniatures, and out of India: the guru at the Golden Temple of Amritsar, and other saddhus and masters.

The ceremony was performed in another room, the men on one side, the women on the other, the ritual canopy in front. The wail of a solo trumpet chilled me and forced tears to my eyes as soon as it began, and I was transfixed by the procession coming down the aisle, led by three men stiffly tilted to the left and holding out candles. They kept themselves together like Siamese triplets, shoulders pressed tightly to shoulders, hips to hips, arms linked, the groom in the center in his white kittle, the shroud in which he will be buried one day, the others in black. His father was on his right, staring solemnly ahead, his mother's brother on his left, tears on his cheeks. The flames of the candles barely wavered as the men moved slowly to the slow tempo of the trumpet's plaint. The bride, hidden under layers of lace, followed on her father's arm. The chanted ceremony was brief and ended with the groom stamping on the wine glass from which the couple had sipped, shattering it to symbolize their break with the past, the breaking of the hymen.

The tables for the feast that followed had been set up in still another room, where a high curtain separated the seating of the women from that of the men. A long table on a dais was surrounded by the immediate families of the bride and groom, and with the most illustrious of the rabbis. The bride, her head already shaved and covered with a wig, was with her husband consummating the marriage while the guests waited for the stained sheet to appear, and when it did, the band burst into joyous music. The couple was swept up by friends and carried high on chairs, the bride circling the groom seven times. Men juggled flaming torches while balancing chairs on their heads, and everyone danced, the men and women separately, the oldest men dancing with the most abandon. It was an exhilarating time that might have been a wedding in Borneo or Bali.

All through the feast my mind conjured up scenes from ceremonies in Hindu temples and Buddhist shrines, comparing them with the equally exotic ceremony I was watching at that moment in Brooklyn. I was delighted to be part of it, delighted that, having rejected it, I could return and become involved and experience its vitality as I had done in my childhood. That I had moved so far away did not mean that I was no longer moved by it or that my excitement was less profound. In some odd reversal, as I watched the Hassidim dance and pray in exultation, I felt the same joy that I had felt as I watched and listened to the chanting monks in Burma, sitting in rows on the floors of temples, their heads shaved and polished, faces smooth and round, orange robes draped to leave one shoulder bare. Earlier, I had not been able to interchange those Buddhist monks with Hassidic rabbis in my mind (as I had interchanged aged Sikhs and Hindus with rabbis); my ideas of monk and rabbi were too disparate. I had never visualized myself as a rabbi, but I had sometimes seen myself in formal simplicity as a monk in temples of Burma, Thailand, or Japan, or in desolate places, living austerely on the mountaintops of Tibet or Bhutan. The monks were spare and lean, serene and calm, or so they seemed to me. They held in their emotions, as I had taught myself to hold in mine, showing their raptures only in their eyes or in the breathing of their bodies. Nothing of the wild rejoicing of the Hassidim was ever seen, nor the lively braggadocio of my wild man, either.

The Hassidim danced, but I was not seeing them. I was seeing instead a monk in my hotel in Mandalay in central Burma, leaning against a wall near my door, looking out through the French windows. It was the festival of Tazaungtaing, and the shrines were filled with Buddhas five to ten feet high, with men and women ambling through and kneeling to pray with palms together, thumbs touching their foreheads, the women wearing sprays of white blossom in their hair and carrying flowers to place on altars. A boy wearing a jeweled headdress sat on a dais with two golden umbrellas crossed behind him while men played drums and gongs to one side. Friends and relatives sat on mats, feasting on heaps of rice and vegetables. Processions paraded through the streets with percussion instruments, followed by children holding paper flowers and men carrying silk parasols in white and pink and yellow, with tinsel dangling from the edges. Monks and novice monks appeared wherever the eye turned, most with families who had come from distant villages to honor their sons and brothers. Those without relatives walked in couples, hand in hand. Gifts for the monks were hung on poles and flimsy altars along the street: robes, handkerchiefs, food bowls, utensils, soap, blankets. Monks in long lines held out their begging bowls, and women smoking long cheroots opened doors to hand out scoops of rice and whatever else they could afford.

The monk in my hallway was looking down at the crowds so intently that I was able to watch him for a few seconds before he noticed me. His bald head was shining in the slanted sunlight, and the color of his skin against the bright orange of his robe was tinged with bronze. His prayer beads were looped around a wrist. He turned and looked at me with a smile full of warmth and humor. He spoke no English but shook his head and reached out to touch my arm and said something I did not understand. I went into my room, and he stood at the doorway until I motioned him to enter. He sat on the bed and talked and looked down at his beads. His name was Aung San, he said, pointing to himself. He went on talking, though the words themselves meant nothing to me. But his soft voice and a sweetness in his eyes caused me to put my hand to his face. He leaned forward and laid his lips upon my cheek. His eyes were round and small, his ears large, his scalp glossy. There was a slight smell of sweat about him. Without embarrassment or even a thought of anything but sensual fancy, it seemed, he unwrapped his robe and revealed in the bright light of the room a smooth, hairless body with hard abdominal muscles and well-defined pectorals pointed up with black nipples. He was disarming, natural, childlike, and playful, and he laughed with gentle abandon. He accepted my ministrations and returned them with sounds as sonorous as a plucked bass string, emitting deep-toned quavers to ease the force of his energy. His eyes were closed and a faint smile lifted the edges of his lips. Soon he got up, put on his robe, said what might have been the Burmese equivalent of "Many thanks," and left.

A feeling of being with Buddha and God, an all-pervading satisfaction, quickly spread through me, as if being with Aung San had sanctified a relationship that had been on the verge of dissolution. It was a feeling that had never come over me before, and I remember thinking, This is what religion is about; why had it never come to me in childhood? Not the sexual act itself, but the feeling afterward, the sense of oneness, wholeness, acceptance, peace. I was more satisfied with Aung San in retrospect than in the act itself, for afterward I saw that act as sacred and profane, another yang and yin, the male combining with the female to make a whole. It was, I suppose, a feeling no different from that of worshippers using virgins or prostitutes in temples, the act of abstention or the act of sex releasing emotions like religious responses.

I had no supper that night, as if the fasting could help contain the spiritual tone of the event.

In the morning I went to Arakan Temple, which had huge leogryphs flanking the entrance and an ornate Buddha in the central shrine. I took the long walk to the Irrawadday, but the river had none of the excitement of its own delta downstream or of the rivers of India and Bangladesh, though I was wanting everything to be right and fulfilling and was looking at it all with indulgence. Two steamers with gray paint peeling from their hulls were tied up at a wooden pier, and four nondescript country boats were anchored in deeper water. Oxen and elephants dragged teak logs up the beach.

Upstairs at the hotel, Aung San was back against the wall next to my door, this time with a friend who was also in monk's robes. There was barely a word of greeting or introduction before they came into the room, and they were already disrobing as I was locking the door. It was all so quick and slightly shocking that I wasn't sure what was happening. They hung their robes on hooks on the wall and were instantly in one another's arms, hugging each other tightly. They were young and exuberant and looked as if they were playing a game. I wondered whether they had come to my room because they had no other place in which to be alone together.

Later, I saw that the smoothness of Aung San, the hardness of him, the tightness of his skin and its velvet texture as he lay there stretched out upon the bed, was opposite to the soft, spongy, slightly bloated body of his friend. The friend sat cross-legged beside Aung San, in lotus position, with his flabby flesh flowing over his body in curves that gave him breasts and folds and bulges that were almost feminine. In that divine posture, he was smiling on his friend, the pair of them the halves of that whole, that yang and yin, the male recumbent, resting, the female, upright, alert, and active. I watched the female half and saw in him a Bodhisattva, an androgynous incarnation looking out on me and on us all, the spirit of compassion surrounding him with an aura that could draw into itself all the ills of the world. He looked at me, and his eyes threw into me the feeling that I was suddenly still, that my body and mind were at rest, and that if I stayed that way for no more than a moment, I would come to the realization that I too am the world, that I am all its aspects, that I am free of all compulsion toward understanding. In the flash of an eye, this anonymous being had awakened in me an instant of repose.

Aung San and his friend were with me for hours, exhausting my mind more than my body. I tried to hold back my thoughts, afraid that I would be drugged by the hypnotic effect and power of my own meditations. At last, they took up their robes and enveloped their bodies within them. They smiled back at me as they opened the door and left. Some minutes later, I got up and washed my face in a bowl of cold water. I put on my trousers and felt my pockets empty, my money gone. There hadn't been much—five dollars in kyats—but I had been rolled, rolled by two Buddhist monks, one of whom I had dreamed to be a Bodhisattva!

*   *   *

In all those years, in all the singular, bizarre, and exceptional places I'd gone to, in all the farcical events, nothing had ever touched me physically. Not the slightest hint of dysentery, or of diarrhoea, not a single body ache came my way. I was indestructible, monks, wild men, leeches notwithstanding.

In New York, however, when pains in the region below my stomach lasted too long to be indigestion, I knew that I had cancer, in spite of having long since decided that I would be the one member of my family *not* to come down with it.

"I have cancer," I said to the doctor, when he asked what the trouble was.

"Nonsense," he said. "You seem intelligent enough not to jump to conclusions before an examination." But his eyebrows went up when I said that my mother had died of cancer, her brother had died of cancer, my father had died of cancer, my older brother had had three operations for cancer of the bowel, and my younger brother had recently been operated on for the same thing in the same place. I had no idea what my grandparents had died of; all were dead before I was born.

Naked on the table, I felt the doctor's strong, warm fingers probe my abdomen. "Oh!" I said when he touched a tender spot.

"That hurt, did it?"

"Yes."

He pressed into the same spot again. "How about this?"

"Oh!" I repeated.

"There's something there all right, and it may be nothing more than a gas pocket. We'd better see the roentgenologist for a barium enema as soon as possible."

The nurse telephoned for an appointment for the following day and gave me a list of instructions on giving myself an enema that night. In the morning, I stretched out on the roentgenologist's X-ray table and a nurse stuffed a tube past my anus into my colon. "Just breathe deeply and hold it in," she said several times as she pumped the barium into my bowel. She turned me this way, that way, took pictures.

"Keep holding it," she said and went out for the doctor. He came in and smiled and looked through the screen of the fluroroscope.

"Can you see it?" I asked.

"See what?"

"The cancer, of course."

"It's nothing," he said. "It's nothing. Don't worry."

When I had noisily evacuated the white liquid into the toilet bowl, I returned to the table and received another tube into myself.

"This is only air," said the nurse as I accepted the pain. "Hold it! Hold it!" she said, took more pictures, went out for the doctor.

"Well?" I asked as he looked through the screen again.

"Oh, I can't tell anything until I develop the film." The conspiracy of silence amused me.

Three days later, I was in the surgeon's office. He placed the negative of my bowels on a ledge and turned on a light. "Do you see this, right here?" he asked, pointing to a knoblike projection in the middle of my large intestine. "I'm going to do what is called a resection. I'm going to cut it here," he said, indicating the right side of the knob, "then cut it here," indicating the left side, "and sew the pieces back together and you'll be as good as new." He was direct and honest and I felt comfortable. I had absolute faith in him.

At Mount Sinai Hospital, my friends of Tiber Press, for which I worked, handed the admitting clerk a certified check for one thousand five hundred dollars before I was allowed upstairs to my room. In the evening, the young resident stopped at my bed on his rounds. "And how are you this evening? You're looking splendid and cheerful. Tell me, what's your problem?"

"Cancer of the bowel."

He pulled back. "What do you mean? You haven't even been in the operating room and you're saying things like that! There's nothing about it on your chart, so don't worry. You'll be all right. Believe me, you'll be all right. Just don't worry." I wasn't at all worried.

Two days later, after I had eaten nothing but Jell-O, my groin was shaved, a peculiar sensation, particularly around the testicles. Early the next afternoon, on 25 March 1970, my forty-ninth birthday, I was wheeled into the elevator. Although I was sedated, I remember saying to myself, "For heaven's sake, the worst that can happen to you is that you'll die!" That made me feel better. I think I woke up in the recovery room.

I hated the tubes that went in and out of my body after the operation but, even so, I managed to shave myself partially the next morning. It wasn't easy getting up from the bed and moving the metal stand that held the fluids feeding me or accepting the drains through various apertures.

I think it was my younger brother who paid the bill before I could leave the hospital. I stayed with him and his family in Great Neck for two weeks, sleeping in the living room on the convertible couch. Soon, I managed to walk around the block.

My recovery from then on was rapid, and I looked forward to holding to my plan of going to Indonesia as soon as my body and finances had recuperated. The operation had to be ignored and my pursuit of the wild man continued.

A friend from Asia Society had said, "Just listen to me. Nias is the place. It's off the coast of Sumatra. Not easy to get to but it's got everything you want. Absolutely no tourists. A couple of missionaries along the coast and that's it. Nothing in the interior but the primitive people you are looking for. Fire worshippers and headhunters."

His descriptions, based on reading, not personal experience, had convinced me the island was a place of excitement. Eight months after the operation, I crossed the States in a bus to Los Angeles and boarded the *Tagaytay*, a Norwegian freighter on its way to Singapore.

Among the nine passengers was a middle-aged man from Brooklyn named Herman, who had embarked in New York. He was heavy, balding, loud-mouthed, and he wore a tie and jacket at all times. During dinner on the evening we sailed to San Francisco, I overheard snatches of conversation between him and Monty, a hulk of a man who was a Life Master and who later made the lives of three passengers difficult because of their limited knowledge of bridge. When Herman mentioned Brazil and Indians, I gave him my full attention. He was saying, "Just last year I was there with my construction company. I've been in the construction business now for forty-five years and I've been all over the world. But Brazil, boy, it's hot! And boy! Those women! Like when they're only fifteen or sixteen, already it can't mean anything to them they've been doing it so long. They go at it as if they were born screwing. But how they stink! After five minutes, you can't stand it no longer. Not that they don't wash. All the time they wash, even with soap when we give it to them. No fooling,

Monty. They go into the rivers and they wash and still they stink. They can't wash off that terrible smell. They're savages, those people, and they smell like animals. They ain't human beings at all."

Herman shifted around in his chair with pleasure, preparing himself for an extended lecture. He could see that other passengers were beginning to listen.

"So if we kill them, there ain't nothing wrong with that. We're building a highway, ain't we? The Brazilian government sends in troops and the troops get killed. It was eighteen murdered the last time. So naturally they told us we could kill all we wanted. They ain't letting us work on the highway, so we have to kill them. If their houses are in the way, we help them move somewhere else, nice and peacefullike. We help them, believe you me. But some of these sonsabitches, they don't want to move. They want to stay right where they are. Dumb bastards! They don't know what's good for them. And they don't know how good the highway is, and what it means for them and the whole country."

By this time, coffee was being served and the whole table was listening.

"Let me tell you how we kill them. We take these planes over, see? The government gives us the planes and we drop these incendiaries on the villages. Burns them out and burns them up, so either they're dead or they have to go somewhere else. That's the only way we can get rid of them. We have to burn out the jungle anyway. That's hard work, let me tell you. We have to keep dropping the fire bombs so the trees get burned down to the roots. Can't have them growing again. Believe you me, it's hard work. Why do you think the Brazilians gives us so much money? Stinking savages! Cannibals, that's what they are! They ain't good for nothing! Go around naked all the time, eating and fucking and that's all. We seen them with their big clay pots like bathtubs with the painted bones and feathers in them. They don't even care about their own people. They die, they stick them out in the jungle on platforms and let the birds eat them. Those birds, they come and eat those bodies clean. That's no way to treat the dead. They ain't got no respect. So what if we kill them? We gotta build the highway. Do you know all the money that road is gonna bring in? A highway all the way from the Atlantic to the Pacific? All those hotels and restaurants and gas stations and automobiles going across it all the time? So it takes twenty years to build, and the only way to get it done is to kill them all!"

Herman was unaware that not everyone felt about the Indians as he did, and he continued, oblivious to others' thoughts. "Just to show you what murderers they are. I was going along the jungle one day, just going along minding my own business with these friends of mine, see? Not doing nothing. We had these big rifles. And I turn around and Pete is laying on the ground there dead, and I see this other guy George fall over. My two buddies dead right there. And I turn around, there's this crazy-looking animal with a blowgun pointing it straight at me. I say, *"Shema Yisroel,"* and the spirit of my dead wife must have come and I don't know what happened but all of a sudden he puts his blowgun down and disappears! So help me God, it's the truth! That's what we're up against. . . ." I listened and never said a word, and was happy the next day when Herman discovered that he had to have an eye operation and flew back to New York.

Two strangers came up the gangway in San Francisco, a man about forty-five, vaguely Oriental in eyes and cheekbones, with a scraggly beard and long unkempt hair, and his American wife, in her early twenties, flushed with the pleasures of pregnancy, also with long, unkempt hair. They both wore blue jeans, torn, patched, faded.

"No," the man said, "we're not passengers yet. We are just looking over the ship because we hope to take it next summer."

We sat and talked over tea. "You're going where?" he shouted when he heard my destination. "Nias! You must be kidding! I'm Indonesian and I thought I was the only one in this country who'd ever heard of the place. It just so happens that my sister's husband is the doctor there!" Kamaloedin Anang wrote a letter for me to take to his sister. He was a teacher of philosophy at the University of California at Berkeley.

The *Tagaytay* sailed across the Pacific, through good weather all the way. I jogged around the main deck for half an hour every morning and, after the second week, jogged in the afternoon, as well. I sunbathed and read mysteries, reread *Middlemarch,* Oblomov, most of Conrad, ate everything put in front of me, drank whiskey, studied the stars from charts in the wheelhouse, and played bridge until midnight. My body ached for whatever trials were ahead, and I rushed

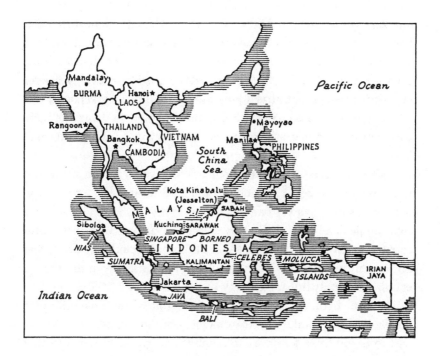

past Singapore, noticing only that it had changed in the ten years since I'd been there, and skyscrapers were replacing the area of the markets. Another three weeks of travel by boat, bus, and truck took me to Sibolga, a port on the west coast of Sumatra, where I waited several days for the *Gunung Kawi,* a small boat that took textiles and foodstuffs to Nias in the Indian Ocean and returned with copra and piles of crude rubber. The boat was sixty feet long, and its decks were loaded with baskets and crates of fruits and vegetables. On top of them, between them, and around them, ninety-eight passengers crouched and huddled with their own bundles of belongings and food.

One young man was the butt of many jokes among the other men. He was tossed from one to another like a soccer ball and handled roughly but with affection. He was also fondled with mocking gentleness, and when the captain came by, he stopped to pinch the young man's cheeks, kiss him loudly on the lips, and then explode into hysterical laughter. The young man, whose name was Peter, was pulled into piles of bodies and packaged within them, tied up with arms and legs. Shrieks of pleasure erupted and settled into soft chuckles. In the morning I learned that Peter came from Menado in northern Sulawesi. He was very good-looking, with a feminine way about him that was the obvious attraction for the other men. He had rounded cheekbones and full lips, long black well-combed hair, a body slender and lithe, controlled but yielding. He lounged on blankets and was brought bread and bowls of rice. He sometimes made money on these trips between islands, or by spending time in army barracks and small hotels.

My bed for the night was a board shelf covered with a straw mat infested with roaches. The shelf was too narrow for me to turn over on without displacing myself and was so short my legs were forced into a right angle. The deck of the tiny cabin was stacked with metal suitcases, wooden boxes, and packages of food and clothing. There was no light inside and no door to shut out the noise. From my shelf, I could look out at the gentle sway of the ocean.

The cool light of the moon, the slow roll of the boat, the easy creaking of the planks, and the chugging of the engine, with the rise on waves and sinking into troughs, moved my mind with images that appeared in the doorway's rectangle of sea. I was looking through another doorway at a rectangle of garden and the horizontal bar Moe and I had set on posts cut from a telephone pole, and I saw myself swinging in great circles, doing backward lifts, hanging from my knees and ankles, simple acrobatics easily learned. I was swinging round and round, flying off, upward into heaven—until with anguish I saw my brother passing by me with a friend. I was in the bed in which my mother slept with my father, in the room behind the kitchen in back of the store. I was looking out through the open door to the garden where Moe and I later built our telescope. I think I had the grippe and was in bed with a baby's bottle in my mouth, though I had been weaned years earlier. I was ashamed to be seen by that friend, for I was too old to be sucking on a nipple, and I wanted to sink into myself and disappear, to die right then, to kill myself. I had pulled the covers over my nose so that the bottle could not be seen. But it was in my mouth and I could feel it with my hands. My mother came into the room, pressed a hand on my forehead, and comforted me.

So did my first view of Nias comfort me, and I expected it to nourish me and give me the wild man. I could almost hold the island in my hands and mold it into the place I looked for, though my eyes could then see nothing but Gunungsitoli and its two long warehouses and a Customs building with tin roofs, small shops lining a street, and behind them the roofs of a few small houses. Coconut trees edged a beach in front of forested hills spotted with the gray patches of rubber trees. It did not look like the home of the wild man, but mystery lay beyond the hills.

Ashore, Customs and Immigration officials carefully and ceremonially examined my baggage and passport and questioned my reasons for being on so remote an island. At the mention of Dr. Abednego Hadi's name, the formality disappeared, the men shook my hand in welcome, and a policeman in gray uniform was called to attend me. He shouldered my bag, led me the short distance to the hospital, and guided me through the paths between yellow flowers to a wooden house behind hibiscus bushes. A tall, thin, smiling Indonesian in a doctor's white jacket and trousers came up and said, *"Guten Morgen! Guten Morgen!* I'm Dr. Hadi." I said, "Good morning," and followed him into the house and was introduced to his wife. Both spoke excellent English.

"I bring you greetings from Kamaloedin Anang," I said, delivering his letter to Mrs. Hadi. Her hands flew to her face with shocked surprise.

"Anang! Kamaloedin Anang!" she repeated several times while trying to open the letter. She shouted to a servant, my bag was taken to another room, orders were given to prepare food, and I was led to the bathroom for a bath and shave while Mrs. Hadi wept through several readings of the letter.

At dinner Mrs. Hadi told me about her brother. "In 1943 Anang was working on a ship. Deckhand, I think you say in English." Mrs. Hadi had spent four years in Germany with her husband while he went to medical school; her English as well as his, had a slight German accent. "The ship was in the Sea of Java when it was bombed and sunk by the Japanese. It must have been terrible for Anang. He was only seventeen at the time, but he was lucky. A few survivors were picked up by the crew of an American ship that took them to a hospital in San Francisco. After the war, he tried to get in touch with us, but we had gone away because our home and our whole village had been burned by the Japanese. I was a baby then and don't remember much, but my father told me it took a year before we were able to reach safety in the mountains near Bandung. It was very hard. We walked and crawled through the jungles and my mother had malaria. We had no quinina. She died, and I don't remember anything. We were all right, though, and we stayed there until the end of the war. It was a long time before we heard anything from Anang. We thought he was dead. So you can imagine the joy we felt when we received the first letter."

Mrs. Hadi stopped to wipe away the tears on her cheeks. "That was in 1962. He told us how he had gone to all the ships in San Francisco that came from Indonesia, always asking about us and giving the captain letters to mail. We were so happy, we couldn't believe it. He wanted to come right home for a visit, but my father told him to wait, because of Sukarno, and we didn't know what the police might do. But now he is coming. Anang is coming! He will have a baby and they are coming here to Nias!"

After several days of heavy rain, Mrs. Hadi announced that Ama Rudina was available the following day to take me across the high mountains to the district of Gomo, where he was going for a brief holiday at home. Ama Rudina came to meet me that afternoon and to warn me that no European had ever gone that way; he advised that I should consider the easier journey of going by motor launch to the southern tip of Nias to Teluk Dalam and walking in from there. Sister Dorotea, a German nurse working in the hospital, had already told me that it had been two years since anyone had visited Gomo, and the stones of La Husa were bound to be so overgrown with grass that it would take a week to hack our way through. Pastor Hahn, who had arrived in Gunungsitoli only two weeks earlier and had never been outside the town, insisted that he knew everything and that I should not trust the Catholic information. He was certain that the south was the most interesting site on the island, and that I would be well-advised to hire his launch to take me there. He would be happy to go along with me. Pastor Heering, a Catholic priest who had been living on Nias for over ten years, said that the south was certainly worth a visit but that Gomo was without question the most provocative area, though getting there would be difficult. To his knowledge, no foreigner had ever walked from Gunungsitoli to Gomo, though a couple had gone to Gomo on mules in the 1930s. All this talk, of

course, excited me, since it made Gomo seem as remote and as difficult of access as I had hoped.

Ama Rudina was exactly my own age but looked ten years older.
The skin was tightly drawn across his face, except for the deep fur-
rows on either side of his mouth. His hair was short and was always
covered with a brown cap during the day. His ears were so close
against his head that his cheekbones appeared more prominent than
they were, and his small eyes seemed unusually deep set and narrow.
He spoke no English and I spoke only a few words of Indonesian. All I
knew of Niasis was *"Yahovu,"* a word of greeting.

Ama Rudina arrived the next afternoon to say that a "motor"
would take us to Idanôgawo, twenty miles to the south, on the only
stretch of road on Nias. I took up my shoulder bag stuffed with food,
and ballpoint pens for gifts, and we went to town and sat on the ce-
ment stoop of a shop that sold cloth from Sumatra and Java. The
"motor," a truck with no fenders and an open back with a railing of
wooden slats, came lumbering down the street at six. It was so packed
that there seemed no way to squeeze into the solid lump of humanity.
The mass, however, opened when we climbed up and quickly swallowed us. The truck set off, swaying and crawling through mud-filled
holes and ditches that tilted the truck almost to the point of no return. For a while, the road curved with the coast, and I watched the
sea as the sun went down, and then ships in full sail moving toward
home while a full white moon rose behind them.

We arrived at Idanôgawo around ten, took up our gear, and started
walking through the moonlight into the forest beyond the village. We
crossed a wide river, wading through the strong, cold current, and
then heard what sounded like a choir practicing church music. We
climbed a hill to the house of the assistant *wedana*, the local government official. The house was lit by pressure lamps and was crowded
with people in ill-fitting missionary clothes. We were welcomed with
a nod of the head and a gesture toward some chairs while the assistant
wedana continued conducting hymns. A great bowl of rice appeared
after midnight.

Ama Rudina had been well briefed about me: who I was, what I
did, where I came from, that I was unmarried, was an orphan, had
two brothers and lived with neither, the number of days I'd spent in
Gunungsitoli, the name of the boat on which I had arrived, the fact

that I had met Mrs. Hadi's brother in America, and that I was staying at the hospital. In other words, he knew almost everything that
might be of interest to anyone we met. The assistant *wedana* and the
others listened with fascination and sympathized with my lack of
family. Later, Ama Rudina and I were led to a room where we slept
on boards with four young men, the youngest of whom tossed and
turned and cried out several times during the night.

At first light, Ama Rudina and I got up and prepared to leave, but
we were obliged to stay for food. We waited an hour for prayers to
end before the rice was served. When we set out, Ama Rudina said it
was eight miles to Gomo.

It was easy going, and I was excited by entering the jungle again. I
breathed in dampness and mold as if they were the purest, revitaliz-
ing oxygen. I was back in my first experience, my first thrill of forest.
There had been no Peru, no Borneo; there had been no cancer, no operation. Everything was new and fresh. I was on my way again,
driven helplessly onward into the forest, propelled as if from a can-
non, as if earlier, during my time on the *Tagaytay,* on Sumatra, on the
Gunung Kawi, in the home of the Hadis, and even that last night in
Idanôgawo, I had been deadened with sleep or drugs, and the forest
had awakened me, injecting fluids that turned my limbs to wings. We
were nowhere; we had simply begun to walk; but the past, the future,
the devils, the lamas, the wild men, were rumbling through my body.
I was unaware of anything but a primordial impulse that forced out
reasoning and rationality, forced me forward.

The trail was flat and embedded with stones, an old narrow road
once neatly paved from village to village. Beside the trail were betel
palms and coconuts, banana trees and papaya growing wild in undergrowth. Little groves of tapioca, coffee, and tea stood isolated in
the forest, and other clusters of food-bearing trees surrounded the few
houses we passed. We met no one during those first hours.

The mud soon made the trail a bog. The slickness of my sneakers
slowed me down, and Ama Rudina told me to take them off. The
muck was soft and slippery and sucked me down. Each time I lifted a
foot, a plopping sound of suction hit the air. Sometimes at the edge of
a marsh, Ama Rudina warned me not to touch the dense bushes of
lugud, a plant with poisonous leaves. With bare, tender feet stepping
softly, I waded through mud and streams, over smooth and sharp

stones, tripping over logs and vines, but going on with all my usual strength. We reached a river that rushed over rocks, and we stripped and stretched out and cooled ourselves in its waters, lying on boulders beneath the surface with only our faces above water. The sun beat down and was reflected off rocks and leaves and loose debris; it shone on pools in calm corners and sparkled in spray that showered the air like rain. I was getting close, I knew. No man was seen, no animal, but the water running over me while clouds swirled overhead concealed, like the silent forest, depths of unseen turmoil.

On the other side of the river, the trail wound upward, tiring me for the first time. Chilling rain poured down; we covered ourselves with banana leaves, a single one as good as any umbrella. Enclosed by the forest and by cloud, we could not see the mountain that rose above us, but I felt its ominous presence. We had been walking more than four hours with the only stop that cooling fifteen minutes at the river below. The time had been enough to cover the eight miles Ama Rudina had said was the distance to Gomo, and I was expecting to arrive at any moment. The trail continued upward, with mossy stones and prickly bushes to scramble over. I was becoming exhausted, but Ama Rudina walked on as if we had just left Idanôgawo. He did not notice that I was slowing down. My shirt was wet with perspiration, and my trousers absorbed the moisture from my waist and thighs. My ears got stuffed, and I stood still, panting, unable to go on. A sharp pain in my abdomen brought tears to my eyes. I felt dizzy and sat down in the wet earth.

Until that moment, I had been satisfied that my body was only slightly changed from what it had been before my operation. I had had a moment's panic on my way to Los Angeles when I stopped to visit friends in Iowa; returning from a ride on horseback in the snow, I was attacked by severe adhesion pains as I was lifting my leg over the horse's rump. My foot caught in the stirrup and I fell onto my back. I couldn't move and envisioned another immediate operation. The attack passed and I pushed all thoughts of it into the back of my mind; other spasms had shocked me on board the ship, but I had suppressed that memory as well. However, as I sat there in the mud with Ama Rudina telling me to get up, I knew that my strength was failing.

Ama Rudina looked at me in surprise. He gestured for me to get up, but I shook my head. He pulled me by the arm and said I could

rest at the house on top of the hill, only a few minutes away. My vision was blurred by the time we reached the house. Someone shook
my hand and invited me to sit on a bench in a large room. Two
women in faded sarongs entered and knelt in front of us. *"Yahovu,
tuan,"* they said. *"Yahovu."* They carried small bags of pandanus leaves
from which they took betel and its savories. From behind the dark
scrim of my fatigue, I watched one of the women pare the areca nuts,
cut them in half, and hand them to the other woman, who wrapped
them in sirrih leaves with sprinklings of spices and the lime of crushed
shells. She held the finished package between two fingers of the left
hand, worked on a second and held it, too, until the third was complete. The first was then handed to me, the second to Ama Rudina,
the third to the man of the house. My concentration on these prepa-
rations prevented me from seeing anything else that might have been
happening in the room, but I knew that Ama Rudina would be talking and answering questions. The house was crowded with women
and children, and men with long knives and spears. I was vaguely
disappointed that the men were wearing shorts and long-sleeved
shirts.

The betel had revived me, and I accepted a second offering. The
pain continued in my abdomen. Someone brought fresh coconuts,
and I drank two with a backward tilt of the head. Water poured out
of my skin, making everyone laugh. A sleeping mat and pillow were
brought out, and I tried to rest while several men and women stood
over me and stared. I fell asleep but was immediately awakened by
the rattling of tin plates. A bowl of rice was put on the floor in front of
me, and Ama Rudina and I dug into it with our fingers. When I
began to chew, I gagged and couldn't swallow. I started to pant
again. I tried to make Ama Rudina understand that I wanted to
spend the night there and rest, but he insisted that we go on. I was
vulnerable and sick, but I got up and followed him as if he were my
own Svengali.

The trail then led down the mountain, and all signs of civilization
disappeared: no houses, no coconut trees, no bananas, tea, or coffee.
My feet were sucked into slime and held there. It was painful to pull
them out, to lift them off the ground, to take even a single step. I
wanted to collapse and be enveloped by the mud. I was going into the

unknown, overcoming cancer on the way, I was Stanley in darkest Africa, I was Speke and Burton in search of the Nile. I was hearing Larry in the distance saying. "Holy Moses! I can see us now. There we are, coming up out of the trenches. *Rat-a-tat-tat-tat!* The Germans are shooting! Get down, you fuckheads! Get down! There they are! *Rat-a-tat-tat-tat! Whru-u-u-up! Clunk!* There goes Sid down the drain, blood spurting out of his head! Shit! There goes Leonard, belly ripped right open! Cocksuckers! Shitheads! There I go too, a big hole through my chest! *Clunk!* and down I go, dead as a doornail!! But you, you bastard! *Rat-a-tat-tat-tat!* The bullets come hot and strong! In one side, out the other, right through you! Holes like crazy all over your body! But you, you bastard, you go right on! No matter how much blood, how many holes! Right on as if nothing had happened!" And I get up and go on.

I am leading an expedition in the Congo. Tsetse flies attack my followers, schistosomiasis flows in their bloodstreams, their testicles swell up with filariasis, and my whole safari falls dead of convulsive diseases, leaving me to go on alone in a wilderness untouched by gods and men.

I was swimming in the forest as if in water, my arms reaching forward, my hands parting twigs and trees; I was naked, unscathed, unmarked, reaching out, carried on by the current toward the end of my journey where my goal would be the golden love of all the world. Birds would fly down with food, trees would caress my flesh with supple branches. I would float downstream in water and in mud, the sun would color me black, and muscles would grow on my slender figure so that no arrows could penetrate the toughness of my skin. Men would do my bidding, worship me. The mountains would be climbed with ease, the rivers, the forests crossed in luxury. No exertion would cause me pain, no strain would bring discomfort.

But I was panting, barely able to breathe. The real world forced my drifting mind into focus when another mountain was there, and I closed my eyes in frightened frustration, vanquished by the elements, unfit to make this simple journey. I climbed in agony, not caring what Ama Rudina thought, seeing myself only as a failure, conquered by age and illness, and trying to overcome my faults by going on, lifting one leg, then another, pushing on no matter what the pain. We came to a halt on top of the mountain, and Ama Rudina lifted his arm and swept it in a half circle, pointed into the distance, and proudly, triumphantly, announced, "Gomo!"

We were on a ridge with hills rolling down in front of us. Even through my mindless fantasy, I could see the mist in the valley below hiding the chasms into which we were about to descend. Peaks and humps, zigzags and knobs distorted the line of horizon and surged upward through the world of green, solid, shining, shadowed green. The ridges were fuzzy, the valleys filled with fog. The sky was bursting with thunderheads of black and gray, while below them dark patches of purple signaled rain.

Night fell like an avalanche as lights began to flicker in front of us. I held myself together, not seeing the village we entered, not noticing the house we were in, unaware even that I sat upon a chair. I was chewing betel, I was choking on rice and hearing roars of laughter from the people around as Ama Rudina recounted events of the day. Being their source of amusement gave me strength enough to force myself up to act out my stumbling walk. I fell onto the floor and laughed with all the others, then slept on past dawn. I awoke with pain when I moved.

I was in a huge, oval room with walls that slanted inward from eaves to floor. The thatched roof pitched up in a sharp curve. A window was a square of wood held out by a long pole. Within the room a stillness, a dimness clouded my view; I could hardly see the thick pillars and beams engraved with crocodiles and human shapes shimmering as if awakening under magical incantations and sliding along the floor up the ladder to one level, up a second to another platform, the crocodile coiling itself like a serpent up the spiraling stairway to the peaked roof, from which hung spears, shields, and garments of mail that juggled themselves into images of men wearing armor and hurling spears at one another.

My head cleared for a moment when the headman shook my hand. His body was hard and sinuous, with veins along his arms in high relief. His hair was short and his face looked carved in ivory so ancient it had turned bronze with age. His cheeks were more bone than flesh, as was his entire body, though there was a strength in him, a sturdiness that came from generations of headhunters who had lived in violence and had prepared their bodies for combat. He called out for coffee, and when I sipped it I gasped for breath. A woman pulled up a stool and sat in front of me and offered betel, which calmed my breathing and stopped the dizziness. After a while I was able to walk around.

The village was clean and well constructed. The houses were set onto the side of a hill, with stone stairways and paths leading to all its levels. Pigs wandered the streets or nestled together under houses. Coconuts grew everywhere. Women and men carried long bamboo containers of water from a stream where I showered under the spray that rushed from a bamboo aqueduct. Carvings of stick figures, abstracted crayfish and shells, and geometric patterns covered the front wall of most houses. Floor beams projected outside the buildings, curving upward and ending in the rough shape of a hand, a knob, a penis. Men paraded around for me in old armor of skins or chainmail woven of rattan and hurdled the high, square wall of smooth stones that stood by itself in the center of the village compound, a reminder of days when villages were walled against raiders and the young men were trained to vault the walls.

In the morning Ama Rudina and I set off through thick forest for the stones of La Husa. My mind was not functioning. The backs of my thighs were shaking, and I had difficulty holding myself erect. Adhesion pains came and went. My breathlessness and inability to eat had so enervated me I was easily swept on by Ama Rudina's need to return to Gunungsitoli. I could do nothing but follow along. I look back now and see those days as a dream from which I sometimes woke up and drifted on my feet.

I could not let Ama Rudina go on alone. He had captured me with his vital force, as the wild man had captured me with his virility and power, filling me with a hope that had bound us together. A bond had been created between us, and there could be no separation without my losing the potency that I absorbed from him. I saw him as myself carrying Darinimbiak through the forest in Peru, his life's juices draining off while I tried to replace them with my tenacity. He was weak and dying from an uncontrollable dysentery, and I was taking him to drugs at a mission.

The head of the mission, a priest in full senility, understood only that Darinimbiak was dying and therefore was a soul in need of saving. He demanded from that wasted body and delirious mind a confession of his sins, demanded it from one who had known no sins, had never known anything but his own village and the forest around it, which no influence had ever approached to despoil anyone's life or death. I had talked to Darinimbiak and had listened to his ravings as he lay dying, as I in Nias was raving then. I clutched at a picture of him in my mind: his head in my lap, his hair flowing onto the blanket under me, my hand caressing his forehead and cheek. I had tried to cure him with love, while Ama Rudina used his will to keep me going—not that death was near me, only a frightening debilitation. Darinimbiak had died in my arms, and I had felt a world fall away and myself sink with it.

Had he been my wild man, lost in the land of tapirs, his own heaven? No, he had never been that; he was no wild man, only what my arms had enclosed. When he died I was back in loneliness, though others were there whom I loved, too.

I don't know why, but I needed him in Nias; I needed him close as I lay in half sleep, half delirium, just as, when waking from my operation, my brain clouded then, too, I had needed his presence in me. I was fine, I knew it, and wanted no hand to hold, no tearful eyes looking down at me. But I wanted Darinimbiak to possess me in that time of pain, to let him dissolve into dreams, perhaps a wild man, but gentle, oh! so gentle. In Borneo, too, the men, those headhunters of another time, with what gentleness they came my way, with what gentleness their glances, their fingers touched my flesh!

Perhaps I needed a nostalgic smile from Ama Rudina instead of that hard laugh that forced me to my feet, forced me to climb the great mass of rock to the grassy compound with clear sky above it. I could see the tops of tall, rectangular stones and three small houses leaning sharply to one side, then a woman coming from one of them, two middle-aged men from another, three young men from the third. We were welcomed onto the porch of the largest house and sat on rough boards and chewed betel. The oldest man sent the younger ones to cut the grass.

The stones of La Husa were indistinct, but I could see they varied in size and shape. I struggled to gauge with my eyes the height of stelae that rose above my head. They were pitted and moldy with age and weather, simple, with no ornamentation but a series of concentric circles raised above the surface near the top. The stones stood like phalluses in front of circular slabs, intended for gifts, perhaps, or for the sacrifice of animals or humans. I was there myself, fading in and out of reality, too tired to focus, but seeing myself on one of those flat tables, immolated as a burnt offering in atonement for my sins and failings, stabbed, with my heart pulled out for all to see and eat. I was on the round, the female element, while behind me, standing firm, was the great male stone, waiting to enter me in death. Strange animals faced me, staring fiercely, three-headed dragons in cubist style, basilisks and Hydras, and above them all, on top of the tallest monolith, was Cerberus, watching over the compound. The brilliance of the sunlight at noon distorted the odd shapes with its shadows, and the discolorations of mold added confusion to the forms. I could not look at them without turning them into the phantasms they were meant to be. A solitary, recognizably human figure, without hair or any indication of sex, stood as if a witness, like myself, to the gods at work.

Ama Rudina prodded me, and we went on. Time and space passed as if I were walking in my sleep. I don't know where we spent the night, but I remember a bowl of soup that I could eat. We walked in the morning before it was light and arrived at midday in Idanôgawo. I collapsed in a room above a small shop. Ama Rudina brought rice, but I refused it; he brought dry biscuits that stuck in my mouth. I went to market myself and was attracted to limes, bought five dozen, ate them all, then bought two dozen more and ate them on the truck to Gunungsitoli, from which I had started out.

Dr. Hadi knew what had happened as soon as he saw me panting. I was dehydrated and needed salt and rest. He had learned that the distance from Idanôgawo to Gomo was twenty miles, not the eight mentioned by Ama Rudina. Dr. Hadi asked why we had hurried back, and Ama Rudina explained that I might have gotten sick had I stayed on in Gomo. He had been told to take me there and to bring me back; he could do nothing less.

Chapter Eight

Deserts and mountains produce spiritual religions, jungles religious spirits. No mystics come from forest depths. Buddha was born in the Himalayas; Christ, Moses, Muhammad, in Palestine, Egypt, Arabia. The reality of this swept over me one morning in a gasp of revelation while I stood on a balcony at the edge of Lake Maggiore. I was staying at Casa Eranos in the room in which Jung had lived, sleeping in the bed in which he had slept. I was deep in the mood of Oriental philosophies and had spent the previous evening reading Lao-tzu. The wind chilled me, for it was January and the sky was still dark. Clouds were slowly rising, to reveal the surrounding mountains covered with snow. The melancholy, lonely feeling brought on by the stark intensity of the mountains blended with my susceptibility to the *Book of Tao* and invested me with a sense of mystical worlds, of infinite universes, of timeless life. I thought of a friend who had said, while speeding along the Hudson in his Jaguar, that the thrill of orgasm was equaled by the thrill of landscape, and at that moment I felt the truth of it with an orgasm of enlightenment, a convulsion of my being's core, shaking me into contact with the Lord, with the Void, with the sense of all the spirits in whom I hoped to dwell. I was overwhelmed by the strength of this emotion; I felt a rush through my head of storm and turbulent air that could have carried me off into nothingness. It was the emptiness, the vastness, the Void itself that was filling me and sweeping me into mystical moods.

No deep, dark jungle permitted these sensations. I had to be on plains or mountaintops or on the sea, wherever land and sky stretched on to limitless space, where the sky at night is deep when the stars and planets shine. I had to look into distance beyond my rational mind, to think in terms of cosmos and mortality. In jungle lands the forest surrounds and envelopes; the sky is invisible. Who sits there alone to look up at the canopy of the forest? Spirits attack from those heavens, the dead revenge themselves. The enclosure of the jungle encloses the mind, allowing no opening for contemplation, no rest from being on guard.

The Doughtys, Digbys, Burtons, Stanhopes adored the desert, those barren, open spaces from which they filled themselves, enriching their awareness in the desolation. I saw and lived it myself in Libya, in that sere landscape, in the sky clear of cloud, the sun hanging like an orange globe, hovering in the immense expanse with nothing to disturb the world around it. It was weird and absolute, that emptiness, so strange that I was often floating in the heavens, standing high above the sand.

But there is more that I wish to convey, and it begins from the time I came to Sebha, center of Libya, center of the Fezzan, where I stopped at a small Italian hotel and was its only guest. The one other hotel, the Palace, normally had the richer clientel, but it too was empty then. Its owner, Hadj Moursi, an exile from the land of Egypt, spoke English perfectly and French, Italian, Spanish, and German fluently. He was of enormous girth and was always dressed in black, a flowing shirt and baggy pants tied at the ankles. He had a library of paperback books in European languages and in English. He was glad for company and invited me to tea every day. Handsome teenaged boys surrounded him, seeing to his comfort, tenderly stroking his forehead as if it always ached, trimming and polishing his fingernails, his toenails, propping up the pillows of his wicker chair, and serving delicacies directly into his mouth. He was fond of giving me advice and had a list of purchases for me to take on my journey: two dozen loaves of bread, and dozens of tins of tunafish, sardines, peaches, pears, figs, and whatever fruit was available.

The newer section of Sebha wasn't much to look at—the two

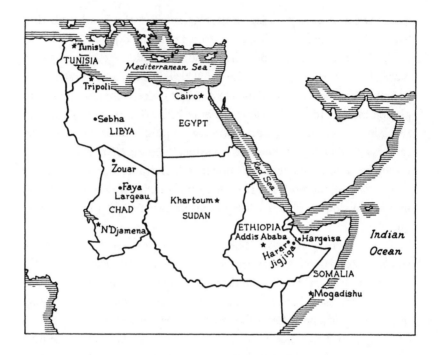

hotels, some government offices. It was hot and dry; barren, stark, and blinding, with no shade except inside the buildings. The older part of town was livelier and more pleasant, and I took my morning walk through its marketplace and streets lined with houses made of mud.

Sebha, along with the Oasis of Murzuk to the south, had been the crossroads of the great caravans from central Africa and from the west and south, going up to Egypt and the Mediterranean. Nomadic tribes controlled the trade, though in the Middle Ages some was in the hands of Jews. Millions of black slaves were brought up from below the Sahara and taken to America, to Europe, and to the Middle East, passing through that place in which I sat and awaited transportation. The sick and pregnant had been left behind, and their descendants, the people around me, retained the traces of that blood from far-off places. Barbary pirates also passed through with hundreds of thousands of whites pressed into slavery in Niger, in Nigeria, and in Chad. Even now, it is said, Arab dealers in central Africa find young girls for harems and boys who become the eunuchs and catamites of Middle Eastern sultanates, and caravans of thirty thousand camels still make their way each year from Timbuktu for the salt from the flats of Taodeni.

The days passed slowly. I read, made a few sketches, wrote letters, and came down with the flu. It was hot during the day, hotter than I've ever known, not a surprising fact since El Azizia, a town to the north, had been listed in the *National Geographic* as having had the highest recorded temperature on earth, 136° F in 1922. Sometimes while writing in my room, with perspiration dripping from my forearm onto the paper and blotching the ink, I looked out my window at a truck standing there alone in sand, its shadow always directly under it, as if the shadow were permanent and never moved with the moving sun. It was always the same, the truck outlined against its background like a child's cutout toy. Everything in that searing light had a hard-edged quality, blurred only when the wind was blowing up the sand.

Five weeks passed in this simple way before a servant from the Palace Hotel came to tell me that a truck was leaving for the south in two day's time. Hadj Moursi lent me a rough blanket, a turban of long, white cloth fringed with pink, and a barracan, long and white like a nightshirt. The driver would bring them back on his return trip north. The vehicle was heavily laden with cardboard boxes, crates, sacks, textiles of various qualities and colors, and all the material and food for the journey.

Although the language of Libya is Arabic, Mahdi, the driver, spoke enough Italian for us to talk together. He had learned it in school when the country was under Mussolini's domination. Mahdi's face was round; in its center was a wide mustache with dots of nostrils and eyes above it, and below, the mouth hidden under untrimmed hairs. His young assistant, Chari, smiled infectiously whenever our eyes met. Both wore trousers under their flowing barracans and long turbans around their heads and faces against the sun and wind. It was Sayed Mohammed, short and squat, who owned the truckload of goods going down to Faya Largeau, in the north of Chad. He had two helpers, Abdul and Ali, both in their early twenties. They were so much alike in height, shape, and dress, with their heads wrapped in turbans, that it was difficult to tell them apart unless I looked at the formation of their eyes. Sayed, always in dark glasses, even at night, sat in the cab with Mahdi and Chari, while I, wrapped in my own turban, remained on top with Abdul and Ali. We all looked ragged in our old garments, and after I had not been able to use my razor for several days, it was no longer possible to distinguish my foreignness until I opened my mouth to talk. The only available mirror was the rear-view one at the side of the truck. Abdul, Ali, and I squatted on spare tires and boxes and rugs, and when my back hurt, I stretched out and looked up at the sky.

The truck set off at four in the afternoon, and we were immediately in the wilderness. There was no road, and only occasionally did tracks appear where the wind had not blown them away or covered them with sand. We made a brief halt at sunset for the others to wash their hands with sand, turn toward Mecca, and say their prayers. Two hours later, we stopped for the night. In spite of my heavy jacket, my barracan, and the blanket, I shivered against the cold. Chari brought wood from the back of the truck, siphoned water from one of the three drums, built a fire, and began cooking spaghetti. I was not yet aware of my role with these men or of the etiquette of traveling in the desert, and I did not wish to intrude on my companions' supper. I opened a can of sardines, offered it to the others, received a refusal, and ate it alone with a piece of bread. When the spaghetti was cooked and a sauce had been prepared from fresh tomatoes, I was invited to eat. I took the whole bundle of my food then and handed it to Chari. Everyone smiled and patted me on the back, for they had expected us to eat our meals together. When we finished, Chari cleaned the utensils with sand. The bread lasted more than three weeks, though after the first week it was so hard we had to soak it in sauce before biting into it. Our drinking water was cooled in *guerbas,* the goatskins that hung on the side of the truck, the process of evaporation in the hot sun cooling it to an ideal temperature.

We stopped in soft sand that first night. Mahdi dug a shallow trough, wrapped himself in three blankets, and went to sleep. The sand on the surface was cold but it was warmer several inches down. Even so, the frigid air kept me from sleeping until Abdul, alert to my tossing and turning, came over with extra blankets, under which we huddled together. In the morning, we rubbed our hands with sand, said our salaams, made coffee, opened the canned fruit, which tasted like ambrosia, and started out in the dazzling light, the air still icy cold.

The landscape was always in change. I had thought of the Sahara as being one sand dune after another, the *erg,* as they call it, but I discovered it was quite varied; there was never any particular feature of the desert that continued for any length of time. There was the *hamada,* the area of small rocks so destructive to tires, violet in color, almost lunar in feeling; and there were valleys and cliffs and mountains. There were huge windblown, sand-carved stones with great holes in their centers, looking like Henry Moores. Puddles of mirage appeared as if after a rainstorm. The pale sky of morning turned yellow and white with the midday sun, bleaching out the ochres and umbers of the landscape, and changed to bright oranges and reds in the evening. Sometimes, in the brilliance of that vast space, the sun doubled, repeated itself in my eyes, two golden spheres side by side setting into pink and purple sand. My view of everything became distorted, for the truck was unequally loaded and we tilted slightly to one side, the horizon sloping to the right. Rarely was there anything growing around us—occasionally some scrub, some camel's-thorn. The desolate landscape was sad and forlorn, but it was also vitalizing and refreshing, building up excitement with each day of changing scene and changing color, changing texture of the air itself.

The sand was often a problem. *"Fesh,"* Mahdi called it, the soft sand we sometimes got stuck in, and *"Feshfesh,"* softer still, the sand in which we always got stuck. The first time I heard the gears grinding and saw the wheels turning to no effect, I thought we were there for good, but I quickly learned to help place the steel plates under the wheels for the needed traction to get out of a pit. These plates were long, perforated sections of steel that had once been used by the U.S. Army to build airstrips overnight and had since been abandoned. Four of them hung on the side of the truck until needed. The sand had to be dug out in front of each tire before the plate could be of use, not always an easy job. Sometimes the *feshfesh* was so bad that once the truck began to move it couldn't stop until the ground turned hard again, and we carried those heavy plates for five or ten minutes. At other times, the truck had to climb steep, two hundred-foot dunes. Mahdi prepared himself for these by stopping the truck well in advance of the dune, listening carefully to the motor, and then, keeping it in low gear, moving on without the slightest hesitation. To slow down or speed up could mean disaster.

Our third afternoon out of Sebha, there was an odd snapping sound from the bottom of the truck. We got down and crawled underneath. Chari came out, faced Mecca, and began to wail, "Allah, Allah!" The others also came out and prayed. We sat in the shade of the truck and Mahdi said, "We've broken the rear axle!" I thought about walking back to Sebha. Food might be difficult, but not as difficult as the problem of water. How many gallons were necessary for sustenance each day of walking in the desert? How much did one gallon weigh? How many days to the nearest well? What about the mysterious *foggaras* or *gogarras,* those canals under the floor of the desert—were they in this area? Gurari! that was the name of the place, the bottom of an old lake fed by waters flowing through man-made underground aqueducts. But where was it? In Libya? Algeria? Niger? And what of the huge reservoir of water scientists say is under the Sahara and has been there for hundreds of thousands of years? Could anyone ever find his way down to that?

The men were talking. They gestured and shouted. Suddenly they got up, climbed onto the truck, and began unloading. Everything came down—boxes, crates, firewood, barrels, drums, goods, tools, spare parts for the truck, water, gasoline. When it got dark, we had supper and went to sleep. In the morning, after prayers, the unloading continued. Chari let out a yell and pushed an iron bar down from the truck. It had been at the very bottom, a spare part almost forgotten. No one had thought there would be a use for it. Carefully, the rust was scraped off the bar with sand. The truck was jacked up, the broken axle removed, and I was asked to examine the serial numbers. Miraculously, they matched. That night we rejoiced when the truck again began to move, and in the morning we loaded up the mass of goods.

Mahdi drove by instinct rather than by the sun or any markers. Not that there were never indications that we were going in the right direction. There was a long-deserted Quonset put up by the French in World War II, the whole inside scribbled with the names of soldiers and passersby who could read and write or draw pictures. I added my own name. There were scraps of metal and sections of truck like skeletons of dead vehicles—fenders, doors, and other parts, sitting there abandoned in the wasteland like sculpture set in place by Chamberlain or Stankiewicz. We went along the edge of the great Sand Sea of

Murzuk and passed through the small oases of Zuila and Al Katrun, where the Tibbu live. Tall, black, elegant, with thick lips and beak noses, they are Hamitic, a race like no other in the Sahara and one of its earliest peoples.

During the day, my body was completely covered with my barracan, my head with the turban. When the *ghibli* blew and sand filled the air, the turban could be wrapped so that only a slit was left for the eyes. My hands darkened in the sun as if they'd been dipped in brown paint. Everything tasted of sand, and there was hardly a moment when there was no grit in my mouth. It never seemed exceptionally hot, though, even with the temperatures always above 115 during the day. The air was so dry I never perspired, or else the sweat evaporated so quickly I wasn't aware of it. Yet there were times when the sun beat down like a hammer. My back ached for the first several days because there was nothing to lean against on top of the truck, but I soon adjusted to that. There was an easy relationship between the men and myself, as if there were some permanent connection between us or as if we were brothers or old friends. We talked with few words and understood one another quickly, partly because conversation was simple and limited to events around us. There were no philosophical discussions, no times of anger or of the slightest discontent. Everyone helped to dig out the truck when necessary. The only complaint came from Chari, who developed a boil on his right buttock and found it unpleasant to sit. He expected me to have a salve to help him, but I had nothing and tried hot pads to no effect. He continued his work as usual, and when we got to Faya Largeau, I was able to buy some medicaments that worked.

Much of the time, I'd sit between Abdul and Ali on top, thinking about Doughty and Burton, T. E. Lawrence and Jane Digby, about *Beau Geste* and the Foreign Legion. Wilfred Thessiger had said that never for an instant was he comfortable in all the months of his crossing the Empty Quarter of Arabia, never was the journey anything but hell, with never-ending aches and pains, with freezing nights and fear of raids, and the sand, always the sand everywhere in everything; yet, never for an instant did he wish himself elsewhere, never for an instant was the journey anything but magical. The biblical Israelites, unlike Thessiger, complained of everything in Sinai—the bitter waters of Marah, the thirst, the hunger, the forty years of wandering—and they had the protection of the Lord. Maybe we did, too, for when we'd cracked that axle, another had appeared as mysteriously as water from a rock or manna in the desert.

We, of course, traveled in relative ease, even when jolting over rough spots of broken rock or grinding through the *feshfesh* or sailing over the smooth floor of the *erg*. Our experiences were in no way comparable to what they had lived through on foot and camel, in a time of violence around them; yet I, too, in my short time, like those British travelers, was taken in by that land of encircling horizon, where I often looked into distance and saw nothing but unlimited, unbounded desert, a region unconstrained and uncontrolled. It caught at my breath like a blow on my back, and I understood for a moment why the desert held them all—in its clean, virginal vastness, untouched, unfulfilled, one delved into the farthest reaches of one's soul, where one could search for answers never imagined elsewhere—and I understood in that same instant the whole astonishing need of myself to be out there in that wild and eloquent terrain, bringing pain and joy and lust, proving to no one but myself that I am a man, equal to any and all.

What is it then that always whispers with a roar that I am no normal male? What makes me run and run in desert lands and far places, demanding pain to prove my mettle, urging myself to feats of daring, reaching from despair to demonstrate a fearlessness, a strength, a potency, facing all the forces I describe as masculine? That friend who lived next door to me, who tossed me over his shoulder one day with glee—he may have proved his aptitude for judo, but did he prove his strength was mightier than mine? Does the number of his wives make him more manly than I am? Yet, I ask myself, is my drive to reach the unknown, to go farther and farther into danger a way to masculinity or nothing more than masochistic drama?

What standard did I use to measure myself against the desert? It was there for me to cross, a savage loneliness for me to conquer. Yet what was in its sand but sand? In its heat but heat? What *was* there to be conquered? The wilderness was bleak and barren, but it told me of the universe. Surrounded by the emptiness of that empty world, I breathed in life with increasing intensity, feeling exultantly a lover in the sun, in the sand, in the blank and glaring sky. I watched a sudden caravan passing down a dune a hundred yards ahead, moving like an undulating worm, separating, breaking into men and women and their camels, riding up to us in silence. I looked at them wrapped against the sun and watched them move into the distance, eighteen, twenty of them, disappearing into haze. It was a moment of passing life, a family, a village, on their way from unknown to unknown. It was no feat for them, those thousand miles of desolation; they knew the direction of their lives.

The truck crossed into Chad and arrived at the Guelta Mouri Idie, where we filled our *guerbas* with water, bitter but not as bad as the waters of Marah. We had been traveling for weeks and knew we'd crossed a border only because the mountains were there. We entered the lower canyons of the Tibesti Massif and spent the night in a narrow gorge, where small gazelle raced off at the sound of us. The next day we twisted through high gray and red walls and looked up at dead volcanoes. I helped gather camel's-thorn for firewood and saw goats climbing cliffs. When we came to the Oasis of Zouar, a blast of green with date palms, banana trees, and gardens of green vetetables, we stopped at the barracks of a fort and were lined up by a Negro in army uniform, a sergeant whose face was a mass of vertical tribal scars, a Sara from the south. We might have been his troops falling in for inspection. A white man walked up, wearing a stiffly starched khaki shirt and shorts with a knife-edged crease. His blond mustache was well trimmed and his hair was crew cut. He peered through gold-rimmed glasses at our passports and papers without so much as a "Bonjour, monsieur," whereas I had expected a "Dr. Livingstone, I presume." After parking the truck, we borrowed buckets and washed at one of the wells, and then bought fresh tomatoes and lettuce and gorged ourselves on hands of bananas. In the morning our papers were ready and were returned to us by the sergeant. We traveled on another two days and arrived at Faya Largeau in the midst of a gusting *ghibli*.

The market, an open square under the brilliant sun, was always crowded by seven in the morning with Goran, Arabs, and Saras, with French soldiers, and with camels and goats. The Goran men, like the Tibbu farther north, were tall and slender and wore white or light blue *guftans* that reached down to the sandy soil and turbans tied high on their heads. There was a purity in their bearing, in their walk and stance, heads held high, backs straight, eyes wide and staring. The women were much shorter, as if from another race, and looked drab in their faded skirts and blouses. They were lively and talkative, without the simplicity and restraint of the men. At noon, the heat emptied the square of men, but the women sat in full sun and gossiped around their baskets of millet and dates and dried fish, their piles of spices, herbs, onions, eggs, tomatoes, firewood, and charcoal. By six in the evening, the crowds had returned, and the women were buying and selling, walking around with heavy loads on their heads while the men in pairs walked hand in hand, sat in rows along the walls, or squatted in circular groups. Men were the sellers of cigarettes, blocks of sugar (the women sold the salt), candy, and soap, and they did the tailoring. Through it all walked the camels.

A truck was ready to go the six hundred miles down to Fort-Lamy. A group of drunken Sara men, on leave from the army, stood beside the old vehicle. They turned and stared as I approached. All were large and broad shouldered and wore shirts and trousers or shorts. One of them, a massive man who had the deepest rake of scars on his face, pointed to me and whispered to his friends. They burst into laughter. He bent a knee and said in a loud voice, "Vous couchez avec moi, m'sieur?" Everyone laughed again. He ran a finger down the scars on his face, took a knife from his back pocket, opened it, and walked toward me with his arm raised. No one was laughing then. I started to laugh; it was a nervous laugh, but it was laughter. The Sara with the knife began to laugh too, and then his friends laughed. The driver hooted the horn and all eight of us climbed aboard the truck. We started off at three in the afternoon, and the seven Sara men fell instantly into sleep.

When it got dark the truck slowed down and stopped for the night at a little after nine. It was not as cold as it had been in the north but it was cool. Only one of the men came down to eat, my friend of the knife. The others slept on. He was a tall man, at least six foot three, and was muscular and handsome. He lifted his left leg and showed me a small scratch. Without a word, he handed me a Band-Aid. I cleaned the wound and bandaged it. After a while, he asked why I was so silent and told me his name was Albert. He was Catholic, he said, like all Sara. He lived in Doba with his wife and three children. He invited me to eat with him and his uncle, who was the assistant to the driver. They liked the fact that I had seven loaves of bread. They did no cooking but ate out of cans—artichokes, crabmeat, vegetables, far better than my sardines and tunafish. After supper, Albert took down the sleeping mats and blankets and bade me bed down with him. "Couchez avec moi?" he whispered.

Sometimes I think I am better than others, stronger, hardier, more manly. *I* will dare where others only dream. I set up dangerous contests and force myself to win them. Perilous journeys attract me the way poison attracts a suicide, the way the edge of a precipice urges me to jump. I hear a story and run to verify its deadly truth. I hear of a shooting incident on the border of Ethiopia and Somalia and rush to confront the guns.

Two years after I crossed Libya and Chad, I am in Ethiopia. In Addis Ababa warnings posted in the American Consulate—about border clashes and the killing of three French archeologists thought to be spies from Djibouti—goad me toward the frontier. Whether the murders have been done by fanatic Copts from Ethiopia or by fanatic Muslims from Somalia is not known, a mystery that adds romance to the violence.

I stop for my exit visa in Harar, a town no longer the wild city in which Sir Richard Burton, first Christian to enter its fortified walls, had had his trying days, while outside the town Speke was savagely deprived of his testicles. But even with its modern changes Harar remains of interest. I am intrigued with the house in which Rimbaud had spent his last years, its front door holding a plaque commemorating his life.

An immigration official, beside whose office weaverbirds are nesting, cautions me against traveling farther east, but I resist advice and go on to Jigjiga and find a truck going to the frontier. Several passengers are already established on top of the load of cargo when I climb up. The cargo is *chat,* an intoxicating leaf chewed raw that is going illegally into Somalia. The passengers chomp on leaves all through the trip across the great desert of the northern Ogaden. The truck is stopped once by a policeman who appears out of nowhere and orders the passengers down to be searched for weapons. At the border itself, I am roughly handled by two uniformed men and taken to the radio shack, where an army officer has already been informed by wireless of my imminent arrival. The officer is gruff and unpleasant but he speaks excellent Italian. Without preamble, he says, "You wanted to go to Somalia. Well, there it is! Go!" He points into the black of a moonless night. I ask if I might spend the night before going on, but he is adamant. "Go!" he orders.

In front of me is the dried-up riverbed that separates the two countries. A black man, his face invisible in the black night, takes me to the edge of the frontier and directs me with his rifle. I stumble on rocks down into the wadi and turn on my flashlight. Immediately the thought comes to me, My god! What a perfect target I am with this light in my hand! I turn it off and see nothing but visions of men lined up on the far bank, all with their rifles aimed at me. I am a spy shot dead in an unknown land, my face buried in the rubble of a ravine, my corpse covered by darkness.

I keep flashing the light on briefly and step carefully, trying to be silent and not succeeding. The crackle of rock against rock sounds like explosions. Slowly, I make it to the other side, to a small village. A man comes up and I shakily ask, *"Polisi? Polisi?"* He leads me to what turns out to be the police station. A tall, black man in pajamas, sitting beneath a large photograph of Mao Tse-tung, takes my papers and examines them closely. When he is satisfied that my visa is in order, he takes me out for rice and vegetables, then back to an unlocked cell. I sleep under another photo of Mao. In the morning, the police, glad to be rid of me, put me onto a truck going to Hargeisa.

I take a bus toward Mogadishu. It is crowded with black men, tall and thin. I sit next to a friendly man with whom I speak Italian. Behind us sits a shriveled, elderly man, naked but for a twist of white cloth around his waist and a long necklace of amber beads. He carries a walking stick and a large, well-worn book I assume is the Koran. I take him to be a holy man. He leans forward and pokes the man next to me with his stick and questions him in a grating voice. My neighbor says, "He wants to know where you come from. What country you live in."

"America," I say. "New York," I add.

My neighbor translates, and the holy man begins to shout. "America is no good!" I learn he says. "Russia is good! China is good! America is bad! Bad!"

There is mumbling from the other passengers as the bus bounces along through heat waves that blur the land outside. Angry cries from one end of the bus to the other make me nervous.

"What religion are you?" asks the holy man through the interpreter.

"I have none," I say.

"None?!"

"Heathen!"

"Pig!"

"Jew!"

"Christian!"

"Unbeliever!"

Some of the passengers wave their fists at me. Tomatoes fly through the air and two of them hit me. The driver stops the bus and yells at the men. We move on.

Although no one speaks for a while, there is an undercurrent of hostility. My neighbor asks, "Are you married?"

"No."

The men who hear this smile cautiously, as if they knew the next question. "Do you know that we may have four wives? In your country you have only one, but we may have four." Everyone is smug about this superior way of living.

"And do you know *why* you may have four wives?" I ask. "Not two or three or five, but just four?" My friend turns around to the holy man and they discuss this in loud voices. Everyone listens.

"Muhammad said four is right, and four is good," he translates hesitantly, knowing this is not a full answer.

"But why the number four?" I ask again.

The holy man looks through his book and the others talk and question one another.

"I will tell you why," I say after a while. The men strain forward in their seats and everyone is alert. "Muhammad said that if a man has only one wife, she will be always quarreling with him. With two wives, they will always be quarreling with each other. If there are three, two will take sides against the third and they will always be fighting. But when a man takes four wives, there will be two taking sides against the other two and peace will reign in the house."

The men grin and laugh. The bus stops at a solitary house in the wasteland and we get out. A few of the men pat me on the back, and one of them says, "Would you like a Pepsi-Cola?"

What would have happened had that story of Muhammad not been in my mind to turn them from their anger? Would those men have pelted me with more tomatoes, or would I have disappeared into that hot land, killed like those Frenchmen taken for spies? Did I go there with that in mind, a disappearance in a far-off place, hoping thereby to become a legend? Am I wanting to be like my brother, now dead and gone, but still circling the planet, still sending signals from his Earth Resources Satellite? Or would I be content to vanish like Hassan, whose youthful spirit had been too restless to remain confined and had driven him to sail to freedom? Like me, he had wanted no ties of love or place; he too had needed the world to fly in.

His image, wings wide, soaring through clouded skies and over misty forests, had remained with me for three years before I met his friend and lover. I had sought him, that lover, on an island below the South China Sea, where lateen-rigged dhows, sampans, scows, junks, and square-rigged luggers with white, red, and orange sails crowded a harbor next to modern merchant vessels from Java and Borneo on their way to Celebes and New Guinea.

The tale of passion that had been told to me by Dr. Meyer in Bali, and I looked forward to meeting Herr Wegmüller, its protagonist, as if I'd known him for years; I could feel his presence as I sat stiffly in a pedaled trishaw going through the shop-lined streets of the Udjung Pandang. The entrance gate of his house opened into a garden shaded with large trees bending over neatly built houses. I was led through courtyards by a young man of twenty, who might have been Hassan himself, with his square face and cheekbones so wide and high the deepset black eyes seemed propped upon them. His nose was tiny, his lips thick and broad. He wore a white shirt and sarong and spoke some words of English

A faded sign reading "Vice-consul de France" was tilted over a dark porch. To the left was another gate that led to a path through a flowering garden, at the end of which was the inner courtyard of the main house. Wicker chairs and a couch puffed with pillows were immediately inside the inner gate, under a balcony that served the second floor. The patio was a garden of densely growing plants crossed by a stone walk. One whole side was the open living room and dining area, separated by embroidered silks and painted screens. There were fading photographs on molding walls or leaning on Chinese black lacquer furniture. Oil and electric lamps of ancient and modern make hung from the balcony or stood on bamboo tables. Webs of vines were draped from beams. Cheap knicknacks were mixed with old celadon and porcelain in cabinets and glass cases.

I sat in a wicker chair, drinking tea, reminiscing over these madeleines of Herr Wegmüller, conjuring up his pasts, real and unreal, journeys he'd made to distant continents with dark characters from Conrad, and voyages into the South Seas with Maugham. Visions of him in youth came easily, his body naked, muscles aquiver, handsome, blond, gracious, laughing, an arm around the shoulders of another youth, posing, hugging him, falling deeply into oceans bubbling with pearls. He had had the things I longed for—beauty, peace, strength, and masculinity. Were these enough, I wondered, or had he searched beyond his hoarded wealth, beyond the adventures he had experienced?

Those riches had been in the waters around him, in the seas of Arafura and of Banda, in the Sea of Ceram. He dove into them and brought up oysters full of pearls, and traded them for gold or sold them in the East or West. He worked long hours, hired a helper, then hired another; he bought a boat, filled it with spices as well as pearls, then bought another. He assembled a fleet and went on to New Guinea, traded for bird of paradise feathers, dealt in copra and lumber, traveled to Halmahera and Fakfak, to the Aru Islands and to Banda, gathering in money and materials, investing in land, in trade goods, and in banks. He bought half an island and built a house, from which he supervised his armada with a hand so gentle the islanders of all the islands loved and respected him. His home was furnished with Chinese antiques, often gifts, with huge porcelain bowls and gilded screens, with richly embroidered wall hangings and carved cabinets, with teakwood tables and ceramics from ancient graves. In those early years of this century, the East Indies were full of Europeans who owned and worked the plantations of nutmeg, mace, cinnamon, and cloves, and who lived in ornate houses with floors of marble imported from Italy. There were many ships then, plying between the islands and Holland, Germany, and France.

Herr Wegmüller lived a very active life, and although he was Dutch, he was appointed Vice Consul of France. He was an acknowledged homosexual and did not keep his affairs secret. He always had a young man openly attendant upon him, though he was by no means flamboyant. Each of the young men would stay with him a year or two, until he married or, as had happened only twice, until Herr Wegmüller tired of him. When there was a wedding, Herr Wegmüller paid for the ceremony and celebration and built a house on his grounds for the couple. When children arrived, he was godparent. In this way, a small village grew up around him of his former lovers and their families. Hibiscus and frangipani were always in flower, and there were banana and banyan trees, jackfruit and palms that made for lush and beautiful surroundings.

When World War II burst upon Southeast Asia, and the Japanese were certain to invade the island, Herr Wegmüller converted his million dollars' worth of cash and gold into rubies, emeralds, and sapphires. He put the jewels in the bottom of a flowerpot, replaced the plant that grew there, and went to bed with an easy mind. In the morning he lifted out the plant and found nothing but earth. He took the food and clothing he had prepared and went up into the mountains and stayed with friends until the end of the war. The jewels had disappeared and nothing was heard of them again. Herr Wegmüller suspected that a servant had seen him hide them away and could not resist temptation. When there was peace, he returned home and began to rebuild his empire.

Not long after Herr Wegmüller had resettled, he met a young man by the name of Hassan and fell deeply in love with him. He was the most desirable of all the men he had ever met. He was eighteen and reckless, handsome and full of energy. Before the war, Herr Wegmüller used to return to Holland every other year for three or four months, but when the time came again for him to leave, he hesitated, wanting to keep Hassan with him always. It was not possible to take him to Europe, and afraid that Hassan would not be there when he came back, he begged Dr. Meyer, who was living then, to watch over him. Dr. Meyer was reluctant to act as guardian, since he could not be with Hassan all the time, but he agreed to stop at Herr Wegmüller's house every day to question him and the servants, to make sure that all was well. A week after Herr Wegmüller's ship sailed, Hassan disappeared. Herr Wegmüller was furious when he returned and sent word out over the island to begin a search for Hassan. Sailors and shopkeepers were informed, and ships took the news to all the islands of the area.

Months later, when there was little hope left that there would be any word, on a night when Dr. Meyer was having dinner at Herr Wegmüller's house, a sailor arrived and asked admittance. He insisted to the servants that he knew what had happened to Hassan. The sailor was one of the crew of the *Teluk Agung,* a ship that had come into port that afternoon. The sailor had heard of the search only an hour earlier. Hassan, he said, had signed on that very ship, the *Teluk Agung,* which now lay at anchor in the bay. He had come aboard, asked for a job, and was taken on. The *Teluk Agung* had sailed that same evening and had gone to Borneo, up one of the great rivers, where it would be loaded with lumber. The ship was anchored one afternoon when Hassan and another young man were sent aloft to do some repair work on the topsail. When the work was done, the other young man returned to the main deck. Hassan stayed up there, sat down on a spar, near the top of the mast, and faced into the wind. His shipmates called up to him to come down, but he shook his head. When supper was ready, the captain ordered him down, but still he sat there, refusing to move. When the sun was low in the sky, Hassan stood up. He stood there, holding on to the mast. Then, balancing himself, he let go and waved his arms. The entire crew was on deck watching him and shouting, afraid that he would fall. Suddenly, something happened to Hassan's back—it began to sprout wings. The wings grew larger and larger, while Hassan waved his arms faster and faster. He waved and flapped his wings and let out a great bird screech. He leaned forward and sailed down over the crew. He flew above the heads of the men and circled the ship. Then, without a glance back into his past, he flew into the jungle and disappeared forever.

Herr Wegmüller, his cheeks wet with tears, thanked the sailor and gave him a packet of money. He looked at Dr. Meyer and said, "My beautiful Hassan is gone forever."

Unlike Herr Wegmüller, Dr. Meyer did not believe the story, though he said nothing to his friend. The next morning he searched out the crew of the *Teluk Agung,* and talked to everyone he could find who had been on that journey, and pieced the story together as best he could. The crew had agreed that Hassan had signed on, and they agreed that the ship had gone up a river in Borneo. But there the story changed, for while the *Teluk Agung* was laying anchor, a group of headhunters, carrying spears, *parangs,* and blowguns, attacked the ship. They demanded ransom, the life of one of the crew. Hassan, as youngest and newest member, was given in sacrifice and was taken into the jungle. Dr. Meyer did not pursue what might have happened to Hassan after he had been given into those other hands.

"Excuse me, Herr Professor," came a voice, giving me a distinction to which I was not entitled and bringing me back into the present. "Excuse me. I have been taking my bath." Herr Wegmüller came slowly down the ladder from the upper floor, steadying himself with a hand on the railing and stepping so that both feet were on each tread before he proceeded to the one below.

Not the firm, vigorous man of my vision, Herr Wegmüller was bent over as he shuffled in his felt slippers to one of the chairs. His middle was wide but the rest of his body was thin. His loose yellow-and-black batik shirt hung outside his wide trousers, which flapped around his ankles. His hair was full, still wet from the bath, and clinging tightly to his scalp. It was the color of fresh snow tinged with the warmth of sunlight and matched the color of his skin. He sat in his chair with his elbows on its arms, his hands folded in his lap. He was eighty-four or eighty-five, but there were few lines on his face; those that did appear spread like cracks in porcelain.

"An old man like me, it is good to see young people. You are very welcome here, Herr Professor. Not many people, young or old, visit me any more." He smiled and showed the gold of his eye teeth. In a voice that was soft, low, hoarse, he offered whiskey or gin instead of the tea I was sipping. "If you will have gin, I will drink with you." He reached out and showed me a pale bowl of Chinese Exportware that had come from Thailand three hundred years ago. "It is beautiful, no? Not very expensive, if some time you are interested in buying." He asked about Dr. Meyer and about where I was going. "Irian Barat? West New Guinea? You must go to Fakfak. So beautiful, with all the houses on cliffs over the sea. Aaaagh. It is different now, I know. It is changing. I have not been there for forty years, but also I know there are places still of interest. I will tell you, Herr Professor.

"You know of Asmat? You have heard of Michael Rockefeller?" Herr Wegmüller's eyes glistenedwith excitement. "Asmat is where he died. In the south of West New Guinea, in the jungle, in the rivers. I could not go there, but it is where you must go. They are naked cannibals, the people, and they would have killed me, like they killed everyone. Captain Cook and his men ran away from them. And the Dutch ran away, too. But it is all changing, and you will be all right."

Women were making cooking noises in the kitchen; there were girls laughing and sewing blouses and sarongs in the outer courtyard. Children walked casually through the garden. Samsuddin, the young man who had led me from the entrance gate, brought our drinks of gin. He looked at the old man with affection, almost reverence, and I marveled that he might enter Herr Wegmüller's bed. Herr Wegmüller smiled at him and touched him on the wrist with slipping fingers. "Yes, I am an old man and my family is here around me. Some have gone to Makassar or to Menado, some are with the good Dr. Meyer. But most are with me here in my garden. It is a pretty garden, is it not? And we are very happy." Herr Wegmüller had needed no esoteric search to bring him to his rich, full life.

Chapter Nine

In a Cessna flying over mountains on my way to the swamps of Asmat, I had a moment of panic when a vision appeared in front of me, like one I'd had in Borneo, this time of a man, ugly and beautiful, a Papuan with frizzy hair, deeply furrowed brows, his face painted red and black, his nose pierced by the tusks of wild boars, his ears stuffed with bamboo and bones. I could see only his face, wild and aboriginal. He was holding on to me, hugging me, making love to me. It was a terrifying moment, one that I had waited for and cherished, a moment that is still to come. Sometimes, I am the receiver in that relationship, sometimes I am the Papuan, a self of mine that I have reserved, one of the selves that I project, not only in dreams, but also into my living present. It is my future, as if that future existed now and I had only to arrive at the proper time and space to coincide with it; for the future is what I reach for, is what is already gone. The past is also there and I am living it; I am living it through sleights of hand and mind that blend my flesh and blood with his, the wild man's. I am waiting; I am restless; I am going on; I am still. My eyes water and clear, and I see myself down there, far below the plane, running, running, with the forest around me, my cheeks streaked with tears, the image dissolving as we land in Ewer in a thick field of mud.

New Guinea had stood out as my final hiding place. There was nowhere left for me to explore myself, to look for the wild man. I had evaded it with all my senses, not even permitting my eyes to rest on that area of the map north of the Australian continent. It was far too real to me for that. I knew that my time on other continents had been evasive, had been time that was no more than lives along the way, and that it was in New Guinea that I would find my first and final life. It was there that I would lose and fructify myself. The Muruts of Borneo, in spite of the savagery they could muster, had an amiable and ingratiating countenance, and the people of Peru were easily able to charm me. The wild man allowed no frivolities; he was ugly and in my concept of him was biologically, anthropologically, evolution-arily, paleontologically, Primitive Man. His surface was as violent as his interior was gentle, and the very looks of him were fierce. The rough features of the Papuans among whom I would live gave them an aspect that drove them back in time to primeval days when vio-lence, hunger, and sexual urges were expressed without preamble. No timid, lonely creature existed then, and in their midst I would live out a life of heightened sensations, making friends, enemies, lovers, re-pressing nothing, carrying out my instincts to their natural comple-tion. I could displace everything, rearrange my lives, replace my past with that of the wild man, instill his presence into my void, and stuff his integrity into my despair. I could reach out for him to enter me.

Yet, even when I knew that I was on my way, I refused to acknowl-edge New Guinea as my destination. Instead I confused it with Kali-mantan, Ceram, Halmahera, Celebes—other Indonesian places with magical names—and even went so far as to believe the rumor that an-thropologists already outnumbered the indigenous population to the extent that nothing of the old culture could remain. Why then go to New Guinea? Put it off! I told myself. Put it off!

Nevertheless, in Jakarta, I did not fail to get the permit from the police that allowed me to visit West New Guinea now known as Irian Jaya, the Indonesian half of the island. Nor, on the chance that the Indonesians would refuse my application, had I failed to acquire a visa from the Australian Consulate for the eastern half, Papua New Guinea. Secure as far as my papers were concerned, I set sail for the capital of West New Guinea, Jayapura, formerly called Sukarnopura, and Hollandia before that, in the time of the Dutch and of the American GIs in World War II.

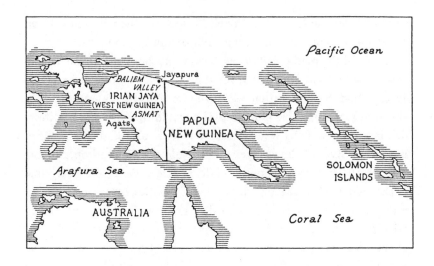

In Jayapura, information on the people and places of the interior was as obscure as it had been on Nias. Anwas Iskandar of the Cenderawasih Museum in Abepura said I would be most comfortable in Wamena, where a plane landed every day a few feet from the hotel. Father Verheijen was certain that Asmat on the south coast would be more interesting but impossible to get to. Mr. Rogers, a pilot for the Protestant mission, knew of a plane going to Asmat and suggested that Father Hendricks would tell me about it, but Father Hendricks said there was no space in the Cessna, a disappointment because it might well have been my only chance of reaching the area where Michael Rockefeller had died, an area I thought produced the most provocative carving on the island. However, there seemed no choice but to take the Dakota up to Wamena, capital of the Baliem Valley, Regency of Jayawijaya. The six passengers sat on the port side of the plane, the cargo was stacked starboard. The flight took a little more than an hour.

The Baliem Valley is hemmed in on all sides by high mountains, the highest with snow on top. The mountains burst up from the plain with a ruggedness softened by the jungle sweeping over peaks and ridges and by mist in hollows and depressions. Rivers rush down the mountains, twisting through crevices and dropping hundreds of feet in great falls to become the Baliem River, which runs through the valley and then descends to the swamps of Asmat and out to the Arafura Sea.

The Dakota landed on a strip at the edge of Wamena, a town built for traders, government officials, police, missionaries, and workmen. While the plane taxied toward the small operations building, I could see what appeared to be naked men standing on one side of the field, watching our arrival. I did not look at them as I went down the ladder and I did not look at them while waiting for my bag; my eyes barely confirmed their presence. I was not yet prepared to accept their nakedness next to so modern an artifact as an airplane. When I was ready to leave the field, I turned and faced the group of Dani men.

What had I been expecting to see? I had probed and pushed myself all my life toward a confrontation with my destiny or doom; I had waited patiently, impatiently; I had postponed and vacillated, but now, at the drop of a plane onto a strip, I was as close to the outside of the wild man as I would ever get. My breathing was uncontrolled and a pain in my chest sent spasms through me, for I was suddenly looking at untamed savages with greased, shining, ringleted hair studded with black and white feathers, with teeth of wild boar flashing white against black skin as they curved through noses, with breastplates of a thousand tiny cowries hanging on their chests like dickies, and most striking of all, their long, thin penises erect, sticking up eight, twelve, twenty inches.

The men confined themselves within a mass, as if pressed together, squeezed into the unit of a single man, with none who ventured beyond the restricted circle of their own humankind, yet ready to burst their bonds and explode into screams and violence. Outside that mass was not human life but animal life, the animal life of me, of everyone, of all but those of their own group. I stood there wanting to enter the circle, to fit into the mass, to be a molecule building the structure of their being; it was all I wanted, all I ever wanted.

The group moved toward the plane in a body, a single movement, and I could see that the erect penises were gourds, penis sheaths held up by almost invisible strings tied around the men's waists, the gourd held down by strings around their bare scrotums. The gourds leaned outward or were tied flat against the abdomen; they were straight or ended in odd loops or curls. The mouths of the men were open in wonder at the great magical force that had come down from the skies and had expelled creatures of another color, another world. I envied

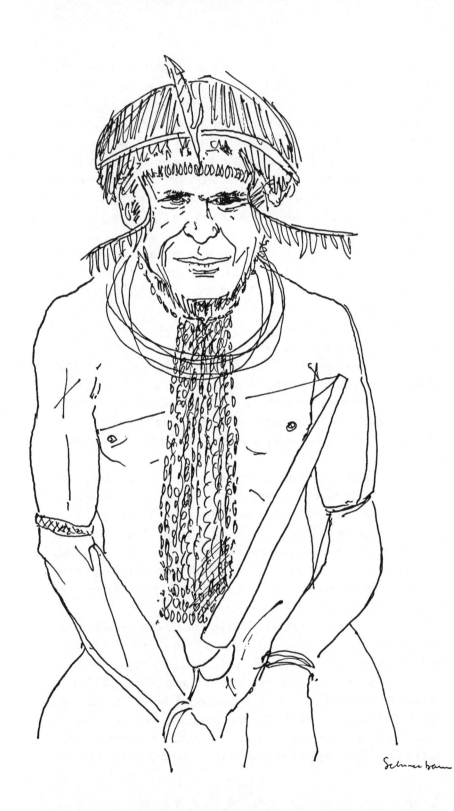

Schmerbaum '73

them their wonder. I envied them their life in wilderness. I envied even the early death, the pain of unset broken bones, the diseases that ravaged them. I envied them the spirits, the fears and apparitions that ruled their lives and made them one. I envied the power within them, the energy that was their aura, that glowed around them in flares of passion and gave them a physical presence that struck me with painful sensuosity. What else were they thinking? Were they thinking of us at all? Or were their minds only on the tobacco, matches, mirrors, the cargo the plane had brought?

I walked through flat land, walking easily, though slipping at times in mud, and on mossy logs used as bridges. The valley was forty miles long, ten miles at its widest, the mountains always close when there was neither mist nor rain. It fell at night, the rain, or in the early morning, and left the days bright, cool, and clear.

I traveled far and wide, stopping here and there a night or two, sometimes with a guide, sometimes without. Near Jiwika, I met Wasilani, son of the village chief. He took me past his fields of yams, led me to banana trees and a small wood where four pigs, guarded by two young boys, grunted and nosed through piles of twigs and leaves; he took me to a wooden gate that opened into a compound of seven huts, six of them circular, the seventh long and rectangular, the kitchen of the women. The men's hut was opposite the gate, those of the women and children extending around it. The walls were wooden slats tied with vines; roofs were domed, made of grass. The compound we entered was clear of debris, empty of people.

Wasilani bent down in front of a square hole that was the doorway into the men's house and crawled slowly through on hands and knees. I was barely able to squeeze through the opening, then stopped in front of another wall and a small second hole, a double doorway slowing down the visitor and making surprise by an enemy almost impossible. I entered the darkness beyond as if reentering a dusky womb, swathed in an obscure placenta of comfort. The ceiling of the warm room was so low I could only crouch, crawl, or sit there cross-legged.

Smoke burned my eyes, and minutes passed before I could see five men sitting by a hearth of ash and embers. Sweet potatoes were roasting in coals that gave off heat and faint light. I sat there in ease without a word of language but my hands and body. I wanted to make immediate human contact to close the gap between myself and the physical dynamism of these men. I took hold of the end of Wasilani's penis sheath and shook it and laughed, a joke, a gesture of closeness, I thought, but Wasilani's laugh was not free or rich, and I could see that he was not amused. He pushed the long gourd, which had been standing vertically from his groin, to one side with a swift, almost angry movement of his hand, and I recognized that I had unwittingly entered an area of taboo. I quickly brought out spiced tobacco, and Wasilani accepted it eagerly, with no resentment of my blunder. He took dried leaves from a small bag and put them into his mouth one at a time and soaked them thoroughly with saliva. He rubbed them on his left thigh with the palm of his right hand, pressing until each was soft and pliant enough to roll the tobacco in. He made several cigarettes, dipped them into the embers to light them, and handed one to each of the men.

Wasilani, like the others, wore black paint made of soot mixed with pig fat smeared across his forehead, a line of it across his cheeks and the bridge of his nose, and a thin coat on his shoulders and chest down to his nipples. Long black feathers were stuck into the seed headband above his ears. He took my hand and rubbed it against the short bristly hair on his chest and belly and shook his head as if to say how ugly it was. I opened my shirt and showed the hair on my chest, and he ran his hand over it. He compared its softness to the stiffness of his own. Most of his body hair had been plucked out. He ran his palm along an area of skin on my thigh, touched my nose and cheeks with a finger and said in Indonesian, *"Indah! Indah!"* Beautiful!

When it was dark outside and the men had laughed and gossiped and smoked, and we had eaten our fill of sweet potatoes, we went up through a narrow hole in the ceiling to the sleeping floor. It was too dark to see anything, but I crawled along the soft grass that covered the bamboo of the floor. I turned my flashlight on and saw the men lie down with their heads to the outer edge of the hut, their feet to the center, lying there like spokes of a wheel. I removed my clothes and stretched out, but the grass irritated my skin and I put my shirt back on. There were eleven of us, close to one another. I felt the roof arch above my head, and I was tranquilized again by the womblike quality of the space, enclosed in my own sensuality, feeling the heat of the

fire below, thinking back to the cold room of the small hotel in Wamena where three blankets had not been enough to keep me from
shivering and where mosquitoes had buzzed my ears all night long.
Here, I might have been in bed with my brothers, the three of us
under one blanket, my uncle and my aunt behind us on another bed.

A few of the men removed their *holim,* their penis sheaths, and were
naked in the dark; others, more modest, slept with them in place.
Someone moved up against my back and put his arm on my chest, a
hand under my shirt, clasping my armpit. The smell of pig grease and
body odor was strong, a fragrance, they said, attractive to women. I
reached behind me and put my hand on the buttocks of the man
there. He moved up closer, held me more tightly. His penis sheath felt
strange pressing along my back. At that moment, I was another spoke
of the wheel.

Being that spoke should have satisfied me then, satisfied ideas and
images and thoughts. I was even coupled with a wild man in a way
that might have made us one; I might have dissolved and been absorbed by him, might have absorbed him into myself. But I was
wanting then a different closeness, an emotional intimacy, not sex,
though that too, not love, though that too, but an absolution from
past living, a dissolution of him *through* me that would filter out absurdities, stupidities, my humiliations. I rent my soul and guts, pulled
them to pieces. I, a spoke of the wheel, was thinking back to my father, my pain of him, never, almost never, thinking of my mother's
love, thinking only of the pain he brought and I accepted.

I was there, part of that wheel of life, thinking back to a single
agony, one that tears into me at times and that came over me with
terror in that hut in New Guinea. Why there? Why then? What connection could there be? For I was in school in Brooklyn graduating
from P.S. 102. I was in a hut filled with naked black men, in an auditorium in a school filled with white gentiles, Scandinavians mostly,
some Irish, some Italian, some anti-Semitic. I was in the last row of
students, since my name begins with S. Parents were already seated
behind me when the leader of the school band lifted his baton and everyone stood up. The auditorium was crowded and all began to sing,
"Oh-oh, say can you see . . ." Within seconds, one voice sounded out
above the others, a loud, foreign, Jewish voice, an intonation that
could come only from my father. "Dai dee dai, dai, dai, dai," he sang.

No words in English, only an articulation of Hebrew modes, as if he were candling eggs in back of the store and chanting from the Torah. I burned with humiliation and wanted to hide where no one could ever find me.

My father is gone, the hut is gone, and I am out walking in the valley again, seeing everything from a distance, smaller than life. I walk farther into the valley, wanting to be there, knowing it is a place for me, though something in me refuses acceptance of the world in which I move. I can go no deeper than the surface. I can go nowhere and am bored. In Asmat later, I think back to this time, seeking explanations, finding none. In the swamp, in the jungle, the thrill is immediate and intense, inescapable everywhere around me. I cannot avoid the forest; it is my womb, more real than any hut, any warmth, any comfort, the tendrils, branches, arms, wrapping themselves around me, embracing me, enveloping me. It is a womb from which I will soon emerge to be born anew.

The valley is open land and level, with hardly a hummock to hide behind, so open I thought the gaping sky had taken the mystery from the land. The land was clean and bare and glaring, no place for spirits to find cover. If in other times and places I sought a mystical component to my life, in virgin wilderness I preferred the hedonistic trees, the sensual, forceful, tempestuous quality of the people.

Once, on a walk with Suleiman, a Moluccan who sometimes accompanied me, a slight breeze carried strange sounds. A transistor radio, perhaps? We had crossed a low hill and were going through a grassy plain, on the edge of which were gardens where women were bent over weeding with their digging sticks. I stopped and put a hand to my ear and questioned Suleiman with my eyes. *"Orang-orang* Aikima," he said. The men of Aikima. Soon we could hear the chant more clearly, and the men came over the hill, jumping up and down with high spirits. The sun was behind them and nothing was clear but their silhouettes. They screamed and waved their arms when they saw us. They ran with their sticks held high. Their running was like nothing I'd seen before, their *holim,* the penis gourds, jutting forward like prowheads heralding their approach, bouncing up and down, swaying to the right and left. They charged as if in attack, and Suleiman cowered behind me, afraid to look at them. The men were coming, racing down a slope, their sticks and spears in readiness, their penis

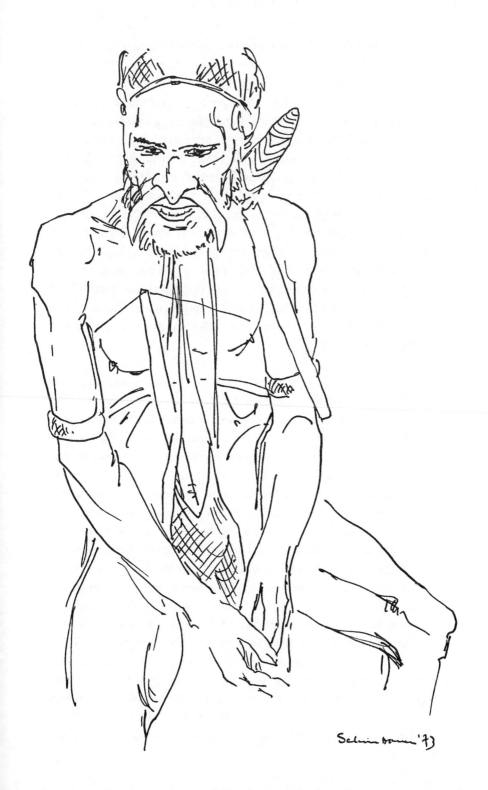

Schindbau '73

sheaths brandished like their lances, their screeches getting louder and turning into a great wail, coming closer. Suleiman uttered noises of terror, and I, unthinking, watched their advance as if with a camera's eye. They sprinted in a burst of speed to assault and rush over us, but stopped short, suddenly laughing at the shock and fear on Suleiman's face, and surprised that I too wasn't cowed, hadn't run off.

There were seventeen of them, each one then slowly, one by one, coming up to clasp my wrist as I clasped his, saying, *"Naghe'ak, naghe'ak"* ("Man"), the single word of greeting to other men. I was a stranger, not an acquaintance to be held by the hips in greeting as I had seen men do, standing with hands on one another's hips, chatting happily; and certainly I was not close enough in friendship with anyone to reach out and hold his testicles in salutation, the greeting of friends who would kill for each other. A few of the men raced ahead of us, and I watched their hard buttocks and muscular thighs tighten up in strain. The others walked with Suleiman and me and sang all the way to Wamena.

Whatever sense of attachment I had for the valley and its people lasted but a short time—a month, six weeks. In that open land I felt empty, except inside the huts. I wanted the dark forest, the fantasies and phantoms that filled me there. I brooded on life in the wild slough of Asmat where stories of headhunting and cannibalism were rife, where Captain Cook had left twenty men dead, where savages had killed Michael Rockefeller, it was said, where each ship that entered a harbor had been welcomed with violence and cruelty.

A plane at last was going there and had space available. It left at dawn and flew directly south, above banks of cloud where mountaintops materialized like islands on a sea of mist. Farther south, the mountains fell away, leaving nothing below but the vast swamp of dense jungle from which I had formed my vision of the wild man running, his face painted and pierced, his body pressed into mine.

The Cessna landed in Ewer on a strip cut into the forest, a field of mud so thick the plane could not taxi but stopped and sank up to the top of its wheels. One other passenger was on board, Yani Yunus, agent of the Government Tourist Office, going to Agats to arrange local color for the arrival of the *Lindblad Explorer,* the first tourist ship to visit Asmat. Mrs. Yunus was a woman of great vitality. "Everyone calls me Ibu," she said. "I help the people and they call me Mother, Mother Yani."

The Indonesian doctor of Agats was in Ewer waiting for the flight to Jayapura. He would be away from Agats several months, he said, and offered a bedroom in his house. I do not remember much about Ewer. A man in shirt and shorts, an American missionary, directed the unloading of the plane's cargo by several young men in shorts, and there were other people around; yet, nothing and no one made any impression on me because again I was holding my emotions still, allowing nothing to excite me at first.

But I could not control myself in the boat that took me and Mrs. Yunus down the Pek River toward Agats, the jungle right there, the noisy motor scaring from it flocks of parrots and herons and pairs of pelicans. Twice the steersman pointed to crocodiles that I could not see until they moved and slid from logs into the water. The Pek narrowed to bring the forest close, widened, narrowed again. There was no land to be seen; the tide was high and the trees stood on roots that seemed to grow from the water. Curving plank roots twisted into mangrove, straight roots flared from pandanus, and roots dropped like vines from branches of banyan. We were moving through a tidal forest of rhizophores and strangler figs, and of sago palm, the primary food of Asmat. We passed a woman seated in the center of a canoe and an old man standing naked in the rear, both paddling silently. They watched us go by, then twisted and held their paddles firmly as their canoe was caught in the waves of the motorboat's wake. We reached Flamingo Bay, crossed it, entered the Asewetsj River, and soon arrived in Agats on the coast.

My first sight of the town was a disappointment, because Ibu Yani had led me to believe that naked men walked the streets. I had not known that it was not an Asmat village but, like Wamena in the mountains, had been settled by outsiders. A Dutch official in colonial times had settled there briefly and had found the land and climate too difficult for him to stay. Father Zegwaard, a missionary of the Sacred Heart, established the first permanent settlement in 1953, living with and recording the life of the Asmat, headhunters and cannibals who had a reputation of being the fiercest group on the island.

Twenty years later, Agats was a town of four hundred. The people, foreigners all, looked like those of any eastern Indonesian village and were mostly immigrants from Kai, a group of islands off the eastern Moluccas in the Arafura Sea, the great body of water that separates Asmat and West New Guinea from Australia. Most Kai Islanders are black, or darker than Indonesians from islands farther west, but like the others, they have small features set in round faces. (The Papuans of Asmat and New Guinea are a race apart, black, broad nosed, with wide mouths, frizzy hair, and prominent brows.) A group of American missionaries and Indonesians from other islands made up the rest of the population of Agats.

Ibu Yani, more openly excited at being there than I was, led me along a wooden walkway above the mud to a compound where the Catholic Sisters lived, where she would stay and I would eat. The Mother Superior, a Kai Islander like the other Sisters, had a grim look about her in her starched white cap and blue habit. She ordered one of the sisters to bring out mosquito netting, sheets, and blankets, and sent her with me to the doctor's house to make up the bed. The wooden house was old, simply built in the days of the Dutch, with three large rooms onto which was attached the shoddy, covered structure of the cooking area and bath. The floor of the bath was made of thin slabs of wood unevenly put together, while the toilet was a hole in the boards, under which hungry pigs roamed and grunted. A month later, one of the boards broke while I was squatting there in the middle of the night, and I started to fall through. Fortunately, I was able to catch myself by my elbows before falling all the way. I had dreams for several nights of myself in the muck surrounded by pigs eating excrement and taking bites at my arms and legs. In the living room a pressure lamp hung from a beam and was the only light in the house. Mr. Bontuyu, a merchant supervising the reconstruction of the walkways, slept in one bedroom with his pregnant, unmarried daughter. Two teenaged assistants of Bontuyu slept on mats of pandanus leaves on the living room floor.

When I had arranged my small wardrobe on the single chair in my dark bedroom and was going out to buy candles, a middle-aged man in uniform approached and introduced himself as Renwarin, the chief of police. He welcomed me and said he had come to save me the trouble of taking my papers to his office. He was a Kaiese, about fifty, very friendly. He invited me to a wedding in the church that after-

noon and to the party afterward. We went out together and he
pointed to a shop where candles might be found.

The buildings of Agats are raised on stilts, seven or eight feet above
the mud at low tide, and are connected to each other by wooden
walkways. Clumps of coconut trees, planted by the Catholic fathers,
give it a lush, romantic look. The salt water of the sea moves inland
every day with the tide, affecting the rivers as far as sixty miles inland
and covering the floor of the forest, making the planting of vegetables
and other foods not indigenous to the swamp almost impossible. The
wooden street, covered by the sea at times of highest tides, runs along
for several hundred yards, with buildings off both sides. The hospital
and the mission with its high school are set back from the sea. The
connecting walkways circle the whole of Agats, with narrow board-
walks leading from the walkways to the houses, opening out the village and giving it a feeling of great space. Three or four shops sell rice
and tobacco, clothes and canned goods. From almost anywhere along
the walkway, the Asewetsj River and Flamingo Bay can be seen.

I walked on and people nodded. A group of young Papuans from
the Catholic high school were playing soccer in mud so deep they
looked as if they moved in slow motion, it took so long to pull their
legs up from the mire. A friend once reminisced about his army days
on the north coast of New Guinea, about playing baseball with his
squad while a group of Papuans stood around watching. Someone
was throwing a ball; someone was swinging a bat. Some men were
running; others were standing still. The Papuans watched and shook
their heads uncomprehendingly. Now, here in Agats, some were kick-
ing a soccer ball.

A young woman called out in English, "Mister! Mister!" She came
out of a shop and held tightly on to my forearm with both hands. She
had large black eyes, coffee-colored skin, a small nose, wet lips, and
hair cut in a modern, windblown style. She was short and wore a tight
dress that barely reached her knees. "I am Nani, Mister. You will help
me, please. I need your help. There is money for you when you help. I
will show you my house and you will come tonight." She pointed to a
house in which she said she was staying. I tried to back away from
her, but she held on to my arm. "The police are bad here. They steal
my things. There is much money in my things. I am from the Sura-

baya University. You will come tonight and I will show you." She would explain later, she said, when we met at the wedding party.

The church was a large, well-designed, well-constructed A-shaped building. The wedding was a double one; the brides were sisters and the grooms were the best of friends. The men wore black suits and white gloves, white shirts and black bow ties. The brides wore elaborate lace gowns. It was startling to see this Western custom out there. The bishop of Agats, in richly decorated vestments that would not have been out of place in a cathedral in Europe, conducted the service in Indonesian and gave a short sermon, and the ceremony ended with two softly sung hymns.

At seven-thirty, I went to the SOSKA, the social hall built by the Catholic fathers, a barnlike space with folding chairs arranged in rows facing a stage. The brides and grooms were receiving on the platform, and gifts were piled up beside each couple. When I offered my congratulations, I was asked to remain on the dais with the honored guests: the closest members of the families, the bishop, the head of the army, the superintendent of schools, the mayor, and Renwarin, the chief of police. Plates of rice and meats, strong coffee, tea, and cookies were served to the more than two hundred people in the hall. By nine o'clock the chairs had been moved to one side, and a six-piece band, led by one of Bontuyu's assistants, was playing music of the Moluccas on handmade ukuleles and guitars and a bass made from a large wooden box, a broom handle, and a cord. The music sounded Hawaiian.

Renwarin pulled me onto the dance floor and led me into the men's circle that surrounded a circle of women. The bishop entered the men's circle a few minutes later. Each of us held onto the shoulders of the man in front. The step was simple. Renwarin called out instructions to move forward, backward, about face, stand still. Later, a rock and roll band took over. I danced with Ibu Yani, setting off howls of laughter when we tried the twist or Charleston. The band changed again, and Renwarin and the school superintendent took me into the Kai Island dances and taught me the complicated hand and leg movements.

Nani appeared and grabbed my wrist. She was splendidly dressed in a long red gown. "Mister, my dear! I hope you will dance with me." The band was playing a foxtrot, the only slow dance of the evening. She pulled me close, but I moved back and held her at a distance. She frightened me. "My dear. I have been traveling around Indonesia now for two years, collecting artifacts for museums. I have many Asmat things here in Agats, and you must help me take them out to Jayapura or Merauke." By then I knew that it was illegal to take more than two carvings out of the area without government permission, and I did not want to get involved with her in any way. She tried to pull me close again. "My dear! My body is hot for you! You will come to my house later, at four o'clock, yes?" I apologized and said that I had been up since three-thirty that morning, almost twenty-four hours and had to go to bed. "But you must help me, Mister. I have no money and soon there will be a boat to Merauke. You must come to my house. My body wants you."

When the music stopped, I sat with the bishop, Alphonse Sowada, a Crosier, born in Minnesota. I liked him immediately. He had a round, cherubic face, was in his forties, had a degree in anthropology, and was fluent in one of the five Asmat dialects and could understand some of the others. He'd been in Asmat thirteen years and had traveled with Michael Rockefeller shortly before his disappearance. They had been friends.

At midnight, Renwarin brought whiskey and we danced furiously together, the bishop, Renwarin, the superintendent, and me. The superintendent was a big man, tall and heavy, with a light skin, lighter than that of most Kai Islanders. I liked learning the delicate movements from him because of his decorous manner and because of his patience and the delight he showed when I moved correctly, with restraint and with a certain amount of grace. When I returned to Asmat eighteen months later, he was gone, having been sent back to Kai for having stolen twenty-five thousand dollars of the school's money. A son of his had gone into the ministry and was in training in Agats, a fragile youngster of nineteen, shy, intelligent, atoning for his father's sins.

Nani got up to dance with an attractive man in uniform and held him tightly, cuddling up to him, pushing her hips and groin into his groin in a provocative way that made the crowd gasp and scream with pleasure. Renwarin, shocked, separated them, and Nani sat alone and sulked. The bishop said, "She's been around for a couple of months now. When she first arrived, she claimed she was collecting for the University in Abepura and for the museum in Jakarta. Renwarin was good enough to put her up in his house until she began making embarrassing passes at him in front of his new wife, who was jealous. He put a bed into a small, empty government house and told her to move there. She went upriver and brought back shields and other carvings. After a while, I don't know why, Renwarin got suspicious and asked to see the papers from the museums. She didn't have anything at all, not even a letter with the name of a museum on it. She broke down and cried and admitted she wanted to sell the carvings to foreigners in Jakarta. Renwarin confiscated everything, about two hundred pieces. Now, he says he's going to put her on the first boat that comes along."

At four-thirty in the morning, I went back to my room, got up three hours later, had breakfast, went out for a walk, and ran into Nani, who seemed to have been looking for me. She asked me to her house for tea. There, she led me to a dark, back room where she opened a sack of rice and lifted out six human skulls decorated with white cockatoo feathers, red and white seeds, and loops of sago fronds. There were also three simple stone axes, the handles made of bamboo. They were beautiful. But I wanted nothing to do with Nani.

"Look," I said, "you have to know that I am not interested in buying anything."

"No, you must not buy. You must talk with Renwarin and tell him there is money here and that I must have the carvings back. He can make money and you can make money from me." Suddenly, she threw her arms around me and said, "Kiss me! Kiss me, my dear! You must help me." It took most of my strength to pull away from her. "I have big carvings, too. Big ancestor figures and spears and shields. There is much money, you know." I tried to explain that I had just arrived and did not want to involve myself. I was not interested in making money this way. When I left, she was still crying out, "Help me, Mister! Help me!"

Later, at lunch with Ibu Yani at the sisters', a woman rushed up and shouted, "Renwarin is sick! Very bad! Very bad!"

We hurried to Renwarin's house and met the bishop coming out. "He's dead, I'm sorry to say. No way to help him without a doctor. It must have been a heart attack, but we'll never know. Too much dancing last night, I suppose."

Inside the house, the sounds and smell of death were immediate. Mrs. Renwarin was screaming, "Papa! Papa! Why did you leave me?"—words that instantly took me back to my father's voice crying, "Rifcha! Rifcha! Why did you leave me?" as if he'd loved her deeply. Mrs. Renwarin was standing over her husband's body, sobbing, "What will I do? Who will take care of me?" as my father had stood over the enshrouded body of my mother, saying "What will I do? Who will take care of the children?"

Mrs. Renwarin was short and chubby. Her hair, wet with perspiration, was streaming down her damp face. Thirty people hovered around her and the body laid out on their bed in the center of the living room. Men and women went up and put their hands on his forehead and stood there and wept. Ritual mourners, all women, wailed behind the bed. By evening, most of the people of Agats had gathered there, the women inside, the men outside, squatting on the veranda, sitting on the walkway. In the morning, a man came to my room and asked me to take photographs of Renwarin and the funeral. Ibu Yani was in the house comforting Mrs. Renwarin when I walked in. A uniformed guard stood at attention beside the bed, holding a rifle on his shoulder. Renwarin's face was uncovered, but an Indonesian flag was spread over the rest of him. Wads of cotton batting covered his nose and mouth to absorb the body fluids that flowed in the intense humidity of Asmat. The cotton was removed and Mrs. Renwarin stopped crying, combed her hair, and posed calmly behind the body. Several mourners pushed their way into the line of the camera's eye, and the wailing stopped. The guard inched his way into the photo. As soon as I put the camera back in its case, the keening began again. It was like a visit once to my mother's grave, chatting with close relatives in a car going to Queens, and everyone cheerful and pleasant walking along the cemetery paths until the gravestone came into sight, and the wails began, loud and plaintive, as if my mother had died the week before. A rabbi said a prayer and the ritual was over. We were laughing before the tears could be wiped away, and we gossiped light-heartedly as we returned to the car.

The head and humidity of Asmat forced immediate burial. By ten that morning, a small seaplane had landed on the Asewetsj. The body had been washed, tied in a white cloth, and put into a coffin, which was slowly carried along the walkway with a military honor guard.

Because the coffin would not fit through the door of the plane, the body was taken out, laid on the floor and covered with the flag. Two army men escorted Renwarin to Merauke.

That same morning, a small boat arrived in Agats, also on its way to Merauke. In the confusion of Renwarin's death, Nani managed to get a letter from the mayor's young assistant stating that she could take out her carvings. The policeman on guard at the storeroom where the artifacts were kept looked at the official stamp and, unable to read, took her word for what the paper said. The carvings were wrapped in burlap and put on board the boat. Mr. Sombo, head of the army, heard about the letter, went to the ship, and ordered everything returned to the storeroom. He told Nani that had she been a man she would have been put in jail months ago. But he let her take five pieces along. She visited me twice before the boat left, still hoping to convince me to help her, and even gave me her address in Jakarta. When I was leaving Asmat a few months afterward, the mayor gave me a list of the carvings in storage and asked me to try and sell them in New York. However, by the time I had questioned dealers and had written to Agats with the information, the carvings had disappeared.

Every day, I talked to Bishop Sowada about Asmat. He was generous with his time and was open and honest. He was not at all sure of the good the Crosier Fathers were doing there and once even questioned the purpose of teaching the Asmat to read and write. He mentioned Carleton Gajdusek, later a Nobel Prize winner for isolating kuru, a deadly virus among the Fore people of Papua New Guinea, whose women sometimes contracted the disease through eating human brains. Gajdusek had been in Asmat in 1960 for the first time and had written in his journal that the Crosiers were destroying the social structure of the Asmat because of their lack of understanding of local culture. When the Fathers read this, they examined themselves and their work and felt there was some truth in what he said. I admired them for admitting this, and Gajdusek became a great friend of the mission. The Crosiers who later went to Asmat took degrees or courses in anthropology and sociology before leaving the States.

They were not perfect, these missionaries, but I liked them and made friends with all but one. Before going to Asmat I had a prejudice against missionaries, feeling they must have extraordinary arrogance to go into a foreign country and tell the people how to live their lives, tell them that everything that they had been doing in the past was wrong and that only the missionaries knew the right way. Yet, I found myself liking these men from our first meeting and had to change my attitude. It was partly because of this new attitude that I returned to Asmat two years later for a year and a half and stayed at the mission when in Agats.

I went back to catalog the artifacts in the museum the Crosiers had built with financial help from the JDR 3rd Fund and other, smaller organizations. The museum had not been open during my first visit there, but I had seen the carvings the missionaries had collected and was taken by their strength and originality. When I learned that no one would catalog them, I offered to train myself and do the work for the museum as a volunteer, if they would permit it. Bishop Sowada, whose diocese owned the museum, and Father Trenkenschuh, Advisor to the Museum, seemed delighted, and in New York I took instruction at the Museum of Primitive Art and the American Museum of Natural History. When I returned to Asmat, I got to know the Crosiers well and made permanent friends among them. Only Father Ed, the parish priest of Agats and Sjuru, its neighboring village, disturbed me.

Ed and I did not get along from the day we met, though I don't know why. It might well have been my own fault. He was tall and attractive, in his late thirties, maybe forty, from the Middle West— Minnesota or Wyoming—like the other Crosiers, had a deep voice that projected long distances even when he whispered. He insisted on using a microphone in church, even though without it he could easily be heard outside the building. At the mission, he was always humming, singing, or making noises of some kind, as if he wanted everyone to know he was there. He was a good gardener and kept his younger parishioners busy bringing soil or the mulch of wild hen's nests from upstream so he could plant bougainvillea or lemon trees. He was the only one to put beautifully flowering plants in pots in front of his room. He had great energy and was always talking about or listening to school or personal problems in his office or out in Agats.

I slept at the mission and ate with the fathers and brothers when I was in Agats. Before meals, they took turns saying a short prayer. One day, Brother Clarence asked me to give the prayer, and I said that the only ones I knew were in Hebrew. "Fine," they said. I mumbled the prayer, *"Baruch ataw adonoi elohenu melech ha'olum boray p'ri ha'adama,"* which, according to my *Book of Daily Prayers,* translates into, "Blessed art thou, Lord our God, King of the universe, who createst the fruit of the earth." There were six of us that night; five sat down immediately. Father Ed remained standing until he had said his own prayer aloud in English. The others at table were embarrassed and would not look at me. Dinner conversation was at a minimum. Later, Brother Clarence apologized.

But back to my first visit, when I had not yet been outside Agats, except to visit Sjuru, which was connected to Agats by a mile-long dangerously deteriorating walkway. It was the bishop who suggested that the captain of the *Lindblad Explorer* might let me go down to Biwar Laut with the ship; I could stay on by myself and return to Agats by canoe. The *Lindblad* was touring out-of-the-way islands of Indonesia and included Agats as one of its two stops on the south coast of Irian Jaya. When the *Lindblad* arrived, it anchored out in Flamingo Bay, and the visitors were brought ashore in small rubber boats called zodiacs. When the ship sailed that evening, I was given the luxury of a cabin with a shower and toilet.

The next morning at six, some miles offshore, rain was coming down heavily and the sea was rough when the small boats were lowered from the deck of the *Lindblad.* The passengers were middle-aged and older, retired insurance salesmen and their wives, doctors, teachers, and other professional people. The zodiacs bounced as the waves washed over them, soaking those who were unprotected. One elderly woman cursed loudly that her hundred-and-twenty-dollar Gucci raincoat leaked as soon as it got wet. The rain was warm at first but colder as we went on. Four hours later, with the shore line still in the distance, we came to water so shallow the boats went aground. We stopped and had sandwiches of pork and chicken, pickles, beer, apples, Coke, and various sweet cakes and candies. Everyone was in good spirits. Several of us pushed the boats into deeper water, where the motor cleared the bottom.

Two canoes appeared with ten paddlers standing in each one, decorated with streaks of paint and feathers, and rowing with long pad-

Schmerbaum '73

dles trimmed with a line of white feathers along the shaft. Soon, twenty painted canoes were around us. The men tossed up clouds of magical lime, chanting war songs, ululating, screeching, and blowing bamboo horns. They moved in unison and knocked their paddles against the boards of the canoes with a clacking sound. At the end of the song, a series of grunts was followed by high-pitched yelps that lasted several seconds. The faces of the men were red and black and white; on their heads were headbands of cuscus fur dangling with Job's-tears seeds and shells; white cockatoo or black cassowary feathers were stuck in their hair. They wore necklaces of dogs' teeth and arm bands of plaited rattan that held ceremonial knives made of cassowary bones or human thigh bones. Bits of mother of pearl hung on their foreheads or around their necks. They were the wild man as I had always envisioned him.

I wasn't aware of having moved from the sea into a river until the men of the canoes were swarming over the zodiacs, overwhelming everyone with their physical presence, their smells, and their curiosity. Each zodiac was circled by five or six canoes, the men no longer paddling but holding on to the boat and being carried along by its motor. As the river narrowed, we went on in single file. One man, with small white circles painted on his face, was almost in my lap, feeling the texture of my hair with his long thin fingers, then touching the hair of a woman next to me.

We began to hear drums and then could see dancers ankle-deep in mud on the shore. The pathway through Biwar Laut was lined with strips of sago leaf. The men, the women, and the children were painted and feathered. The women danced in a large open circle to the right of the men's house. The men danced to the left of it, dancing a simple wiggling movement of the knees, and a shaking, wiggling movement of the hands in front of the groin. Some of the men were in shorts but most were naked; the women wore simple skirts with woven waistbands and strands of sago fiber pulled together between the legs and tied up in back. A masked dancer hidden in a casing of woven sago fibers, fronds, and leaves twirled and swayed among the men. He ran through the village, swishing the fronds on his arms and waist, chasing children, who laughed with pleasure or screamed with terror. The hand of the spirit inside reached out from the dangling strips of sago leaves, pulled the penises of the boys, pinched the nipples of the girls, and gave them potency and fecundity.

One of the dancers followed wherever I went. He had red ochre around his eyes and a thick line of white around his face; there was a bone through his nose, and bird of paradise and white cockatoo feathers in his hair. I made a drawing of him and wrote his name, Bimanum, at the bottom. I asked in pantomime if I could buy the bone carving in his nose and he nodded his head. He slipped the *otsj* from his septum and wiped some of the mucus on his arm. It was still wet when he gave it to me in exchange for tobacco. A few seconds later, I noticed tears in his eye; then he began to cry. I took the *otsj* from my pocket and tried to give it back to him, but he refused it and continued crying. It was some time before I understood that the tears were his way of saying good-bye to the *otsj.* He had carved it himself and had named it for an elder brother who had been killed.

At this time, I understood nothing of Asmat culture. I had talked to the bishop, but I had not prepared myself with reading and had looked at only one of the mission library books. The need to go out of Agats as quickly as possible was too strong for me to sit and read, though I knew I would regret it later. I had arrived at Biwar Laut as part of a group of tourists, but I knew that they would leave and I would remain by myself. Their excitement and fascination, of course, was no less intense than mine, though they accepted and reveled in it in a different way. The experience was unique for all of us. It had been set up in advance by Ibu Yani, but the Asmat themselves were unaware of the concept of being on show; they were as tantalized by the outsiders as the outsiders were by them, and they were so engrossed in their own dancing and feasting that they were putting on no act.

The tourists left Biwar Laut at three o'clock, but the dancing continued throughout the night. Before dark, the men moved into the men's house, a long, open hut facing the river. The women were no longer to be seen. One of the men wore a watch; others smoked Kools or Lucky Strikes, spoils of the visit. Emptied beer cans were used as cups for water, the tabs dangling as decorations from ears or foreheads. The men were dancing to drums and the wail of songs. It was hot inside the hut and everyone dripped with perspiration. Some wore a triton shell around the waist, symbol of the fiercest headhunters. With the visitors gone, except for me, there was a new, wild, and convulsive force to the dancing. The men's knees moved in and out erotically, pumping hips and groins back and forth, penises flopping and sometimes touching and rubbing one another, in sensual preparation for contact to come. I was dancing and perspiring, too, my white body looking sickly in the light of the fires, their bodies invisible but for the sparkling sweat, the paint, the reflection of eyes and teeth.

Bimanum was there, a new *otsj* through his nose. Red ochre was freshly painted around his eyes, the red eyes of the black king cockatoo when enraged, the red of menstrual blood of evil spirits, the red of the sun. His shoulders were streaked with red; a tassel was knotted around his neck. We danced facing one another, and he wiped the sweat of my body with his hands and rubbed it on his face, wiped it from my chest, my back, my buttocks, my thighs, and smeared it over his naked self. Older men came and wiped away my sweat, too, using my excretion as magical ointment.

Bimanum's head was haloed with white feathers. A woman stood on either side of him, the only women in the hut, his wives Ushira and Yavu. Ushira's face was old and worn but full of strength and passion. Her long nose was cut with a line of white, broadened by a white shell spiraling through her septum. Her hair was a mass of brown cassowary feathers, with seeds hanging from the headband; her arms were circled with white and red. Yavu was smaller, thinner, had no recognizable face, for it was ravaged by yaws. There was a hole where her nose had been, and parts of her lips and ears were gone, leaving scars of dried up sores. There were no lids to her round, shining eyes. Her facial skin was deeply pitted and covered with white paint. They both carried strips of sago leaves, and with them they wove and looped long tassels in my hair, tied one around my neck, others around my arms and thighs.

Yavu's face opened into a smile as she offered her empty, wrinkled breasts for me to suckle. I looked at her wasted face and shivered and wondered whether yaws was infectious. I took hold of her breast and sucked the nipples, which offered no milk and tasted like cardboard. Around us, men screamed and yelped as the dancing continued. I moved to suckle at the breasts of Ushira, also dry and tough. The two women spread their legs apart and I, a baby being born, crawled through while they yelled and groaned in pain, their bodies twitching and quaking as they gave birth to me. Bimanum brought cracked crabs and sago and tasted each piece of food before passing it on to me. He was my father now, Bimanum, with his score of headhunted victims tallied by the skulls at his doorway, with his naked body painted and feathered before me, my own naked body pale and weak before him, filled with sudden strength and glory, my mothers there, too, Ushira and Yavu, all three committed to defend and feed me for the rest of my life. No wonder I dreamed illusive dreams that night; no wonder I delved anew into my family roots, finding myself in Olduvai a million years ago, in Altamira painting bison on the walls of caves, in Asmat carving ancestral figures and avenging the deaths of murdered relatives.

Late the next afternoon, before I'd begun to see anything of the village; a party of thirty-two, including Bimanum, Ushira, and myself, left Biwar Laut in four canoes loaded with sago and carvings to be traded in Agats for tobacco, clothes, aluminum pots. Ushira stood behind Bimanum and paddled like a man. I sat like a woman but did not paddle. Instead, I bailed with a sponge of sago fiber. We moved down the Jiwe River, with the jungle enclosing us. It was thick with mangrove, nipa palm, pandanus, nibung, and stands of sago. There were gigantic ironwood trees, firewood, canoe, and bark trees, all tied and looped together with rattan vines and the bare lianas that drooped with huge clusters of scarlet flames of the forest. Clouds of mosquitoes came in waves to attack us. The headman chanted of the white man among them. The paddlers in front of me were naked and I watched their muscles ripple as they moved. They stood with right leg forward, paddle to the left of the canoe, the heel of the right foot stamping, the paddle entering the water to the rhythm of the chant. The men grunted at the end of a phrase and then were silent while the paddles dipped noiselessly into the water. We passed into the wider Ow River, which opened near the mouth of the Siretsj and emptied into the Arafura Sea. We beached at a muddy bank amid the debris of the forest, where a hut on pilings stood against the wall of trees, a place of bivouac. It had been roughly put together with pandanus thatching and sago bark on floor and walls.

I sat on a log on the wet beach, watching the sea swallow the sun until a horde of tiny flies began biting fiercely. I went back into the hut, where someone was chanting. Ushira unfolded a pandanus sleeping mat for me. She sat before the fire roasting balls of sago, turning them with bamboo tongs until the outer layer was black, crisp, chewy. The inside was bland and tasteless, like a handful of Gold Medal flour stuffed into the mouth. In the canoe, Ushira had given me sago in tubular form, mixed with sago worms, which was easier to eat than the ball and might have tasted even better had it been mixed with human flesh in the old manner of Asmat. Ushira handed me several large shrimp, tender and satisfying.

Bimanum, my father, placed his mat next to mine, close to one of the fires. He talked to me, squinted at me, telling me it was time to sleep. I slept and awakened to see Ushira adding wood to the fire. Men were laughing in a far corner, their faces and chests flickering in the light of their own fire. I woke again later to mumbled chants. I huddled up to my father, closer to his warmth. I huddled up to my father in Brooklyn and he moved away. My mother had just died, relatives slept in my bed with my brothers, and I was left alone. I put my hand on my father's hip and he turned away. Bimanum pushed himself back into me, clasped my hand and held it against the muscles of his chest.

In the morning, we broke open roasted crabs with hard clam shells, ate chunks of sago, and were in the canoes by dawn. The phalanx of our canoes crossed the Siretsj and reformed into single file at the mouth of the Jet, where the water was lined with nipa and mangrove. Large gray birds sailed over the surface of the river, and hundreds of small red birds flew up into shapes of pulsing paramecia, then divided into Vs and disappeared into the forest. Rain came down and soaked the clothes I was wearing to return to the mission, leaving me chilled and messy. Rain bounced off the hair of the men and slithered down their bodies as if they were oiled. They were dry as soon as the rain stopped, while my hair dripped, my wet clothes clung to me, and drops of water stood on my skin until I brushed them away. A fire was burning in the back of the canoe on a layer of mud. The men paddled on, stopping at times to paint themselves and to roll tobacco and light their cigarettes from coals passed along on the blades of paddles. In the swamps of the Famborep River, we eased through papyruslike plants and other reeds, and we arrived in Agats at dusk.

Chapter Ten

One day I asked the bishop about Michael Rockefeller and what had happened in 1961. We sat in comfort on the couches of his living room with ice and a bottle of Johnnie Walker.

"You know he was a trustee of the Museum of Primitive Art in New York. He had been here a couple of months earlier on a collecting trip, but he came back in October and we went to my village of Saowa-Erma in his catamaran. He liked his boat because he could load a lot of stuff into the pontoons. He was happy about the whole expedition, and when we came back to Agats, he spent the last day cataloging the artifacts in the storeroom and preparing to return to New York. He was going south in the morning on a two-day trip, and I offered my motorboat because it was faster and more stable than the catamaran. My boat had twice the horsepower. He was going out to sea, but that didn't bother him. He had gone everywhere in his catamaran and wanted to use it on his last trip, too. I said good-bye to him at dawn the next morning.

"There was Michael, René Wassing, the anthropologist with him, and two men from Sjuru who knew the village of Otsjenep, where they were going. The sea was rough. You know how shallow the sea is here. Well, the Betsj is a big river and a deep one. It comes pouring down and hits the sea with a bang. It was rough and the waves were washing over the boat, filling the pontoons with water. The pontoons had been loaded with metal axes and knives for trading, and of course all that weight would have made the boat sink. So they dumped everything overboard. But the waves got bigger and bigger and the catamaran finally turned over. The two men from Sjuru swam ashore for help. The Asmat are damned good swimmers; they have to be in these waters. When the two men jumped in, they were three miles from shore. But good swimmers or not, they had their problems. Fortunately, they made it to land all right by helping each other.

"They stopped somewhere along the coast, borrowed a *prao,* and came back to Agats about four in the morning. They woke Father Miller and the father superior, but we had no plane and there was no way to send a message on the radio to Merauke until after six. When the message got through, planes were sent to look for Michael and Wassing. In the meantime, they were holding on to the upside-down catamaran, which was drifting farther and farther out. When there was no sign of help that morning, Michael assumed the two men had drowned. He decided to swim ashore himself, leaving Wassing, who couldn't swim, with the boat. By then, the tide had carried them ten miles out and they could see nothing but water. The sea was calmer, but there were still waves. Wassing was all right and was found later that afternoon. But Michael tied two empty jerry cans onto his back to keep himself afloat and jumped into the sea. They say he was an exceptional swimmer, but nothing was ever found of him, no body, no clothes, no anything, although the jerry cans turned up down the coast some weeks later."

Alphonse, as I called the bishop, fingered the open collar of his batik shirt and cleared his throat. "Of course, anything is possible, since there is no proof either way. You can make up whatever story you like. He could have made it to shore and been picked up by the people of Otsjenep. He could have been killed and eaten by them. Some people do believe it. But it's hardly likely, what with the waves, the sea crocodiles, and the sharks. Oh, I know the crocks and sharks aren't as numerous or as dangerous as we're led to believe, but don't forget that when Michael jumped in, he couldn't even see the shoreline. For myself, I think there is one other possibility, that he did make it to shore and was in such a state of exhaustion that he would have died then or the next day. If the people of Otsjenep found him, they would have buried him and never said a word. No one would ever find a grave in the jungle. They would have figured that if the Dutch found out about his death, they would have been certain that they had killed and cannibalized him.

"Anyway, it is pretty difficult for me to believe that any Asmat can keep a secret as important as that. It's against their whole concept of masculinity. If the people of Otsjenep had killed him, someone would have talked within weeks. Boasting and exaggeration are part of their culture. Of course, you realize that at that time, Omandesep was fighting with Otsjenep, and it was the people of Omandesep who told the story of Otsjenep killing him. It was a perfect way of getting back at their traditional enemy."

When I was at the Museum of Primitive Art in New York, I was able to read Michael's journal. He must have been a fine and sensitive man. I was especially struck by his concern about his visit to Aman-amkai, a village famous for its carvers. A Dutch anthropologist, Adrian Gerbrands, had been working there for some months when Michael arrived to stay with him. Gerbrands had not been lucky enough to see any feasts there, and when Michael arrived with his vast amount of trade goods, the people went all out and put on a great display. Michael wrote that night about the resentment Gerbrands must have felt about the rich young man who just walked into the village and was able to buy and do everything he wanted. However, Gerbrands not only did not resent him, he was of great help and treated him with affection and understanding.

Bontuyu, my housemate, was going to Basiem in his motorized canoe and took me along. He had studied the tidal charts and had timed our departure at nine-thirty to arrive at the mouth of the Fajit River when the water was high. We moved out from the small pier in Agats into the Asewetsj and then into the Arafura Sea. A breeze came up and Bon frowned. He pointed to the dark clouds coming from the south, the direction in which we were heading. It wasn't long before we were bouncing on waves that washed over us. The shoreline was hidden in fog. The wind got stronger and we made little headway. Bon had said that if the day was good, we would reach Basiem within four hours, but we had already been traveling six without gaining much distance. At three in the afternoon, Bon turned toward the

Schwachtmann '73

coast and landed at a muddy beach with a bivouac. Five people from Sjuru were there. They had been in the forest chopping sago and were on their way home. Although we had food with us, we traded tobacco for fresh crabs, nipa fruit, and fish. The fruit was bitter. The tobacco I had brought along comes in *lempeng,* thin wads of pressed tobacco mixed with spices. The Asmat are addicted to it.

The three men and two women in the bivouac had ringworm over their entire bodies. They stayed close to us and watched our every move. In the evening, I sat on the beach and looked up at a sky washed with yellows and purples, a horizon full of black patches of rain. When I turned, I saw the men sitting silently behind me. In the hut, we slept on crackling pandanus leaves around two fires.

The next morning the sea was so choppy at the mouth of the Siretsj that we were almost swamped. The wind carried us back to the north, and we were forced to pull in to Per, a small village we had passed the day before. In the men's hut, drums were brought out and chanting began within a few minutes of our arrival. Men painted themselves and came to see us. I tried to sketch but couldn't draw because my hands were stiff from holding on to the sides of the canoe.

Rain drenched us at dawn, then stopped. The surface of the sea rippled in an easy wind. Shorebirds sailed and circled above us. At the mouth of the Betsj, the canoe began to pitch and roll. Bon said, "This is where Michael Rockefeller's boat turned over," and no sooner were the words out of his mouth than our motor sputtered and died. Without its driving force, we were swept by the wind and tide into a whirlpool, where spirits dwelt to whom I was about to pray for help. In the meantime, I paddled to keep us from spinning too rapidly. Bon worked on the motor for ten minutes before it caught and we were off to the south, cruising along the coast to the Fajit River, where we turned in toward the village of Basiem

From the canoe, we watched pairs of women in waist-deep water at the river's edge moving slowly upstream with ovoid fishing nets, children digging in the mud for crabs and snails, and men paddling home after a day of fishing with spears and bows and arrows. I was feeling back to a time when man's relationship with his surroundings was vital to his being, when he absorbed his life and blood from the land and the spirits with whom he lived.

Men were yelping on the river bank, *"Ow-ow-ow-ow-ow!"* Behind them, coconut, papaya, and banana trees hid the houses of Basiem. Sago palms grew farther upstream. Canoes with carved prowheads were beached above the mud. A man naked but for the triton shell at his waist greeted us, and others followed where we walked. Children with small bows and arrows of bamboo and nipa leaf touched us and ran away in pleasurable fear. Older youngsters, male and female, happily displayed festering wounds on their arms, double rows of them, from shoulder to wrist, where hot coals had been pressed into the arm, searing out a quarter of an inch of flesh. Some had burns that extended in a V across the breast. Close to the bank of the river were the small, roughly shaped, bottomless canoes with their prowheads shaped into turtles, ceremonial guides on the way from childhood to adulthood. Scarification and initiation rites had taken place two days earlier.

The whole of the village compound was layered with mud, crossed by thin logs as walkways. Like all Asmat villages, it was divided by a narrow waterway into upstream and downstream halves. On the downstream side, we went up the notched log of a ladder into the *yeu,* the men's hut. One of the men who came and sat next to me held a signal horn in his armpit like a beloved object; it was a magical instrument that would sound its sepulchral voice to frighten enemies or announce the victorious return of men from a raid with enemy bodies bound and decapitated. The horn was cut from a section of bamboo now black from the oils of the hands that held it. Its penis shape was incised with figures and scrollwork, symbols of the headhunter. Next to the man with the horn sat a young man with his hair covered with woven strands of sago fiber, hair-lengthenings tied in loops and fringes, other strands tied around his neck. He wore several wide bands of rattan on his upper arms, wrists, and legs, evidence of his recent adoption by a family of the village. Other men and women wore smaller arm bands as decoration or magical charms.

Drumming had begun as soon as we entered the hut. It was dark inside, mysterious and evocative. Small fires were burning, a long row of them. Above each fireplace was a rack of shelves on which meat was laid out to dry, and *an* bowls, for sago, and other receptacles were kept. Beams held spears, bows and arrows, paddles, and folded sleeping mats. Sago ribs and fronds braced and thatched the walls; sago leaves covered the peaked roof. We sat on nipa leaves overlaid with bark. I gave out tobacco, and men brought crabs, fish, sago, and a small pale fruit that looked like an apple and was deliciously tart. Someone chanted and others joined in; several men danced. Two men with wooden carvings within the folds of their legs sat and worked, using as chisel a hammered nail instead of bone and shell, the mallet still an old stone ax. Boys, when not distracted by our presence, watched them work.

Fumeripitsj had been the first carver, long ago, long before people walked the land. He could talk to no one, for there was no one to talk to, and he was lonely. He was at the Siretsj River one day and fell in and drowned. War, the great eagle, flew down and pulled him out and saved his life. Then Fumeripitsj was cold and wanted shelter. He built a *yeu* for himself, a huge ceremonial house in which he sat alone, for there was no one else around. He cut down trees and from the wood began to carve figures of men and women. He filled the *yeu* with the figures, but they had no life, none moved or talked, and still he was lonely. He carved a drum, hollowing out the log with fire, shaping it to suit his mood, covering the top with the skin of a lizard, and sealing it in place with his own blood. He beat the drum and the wooden figures began to move. They walked and danced and were the ancestors of all Asmat, the ancestors of all the people around me then.

Early the next morning, men listened to Bon and nodded in agreement as he made arrangements for them to cut ironwood and take the logs to Agats. He breakfasted on rice and canned sardines, got into his canoe, and started on his way. I stayed on until paddlers and canoe were ready to take me farther up the Fajit to Buepis. When we got there, a group of men and women lined the river bank, receiving me with spears for sale, shields, bowls, ancestor figures, decorated human skulls, bunches of sago worms, and chunks of sago wrapped in leaves. The spears were carved with arabesques a foot or more from the pointed end, a five-inch blade that seemed to have no use. Shields were laboriously carved and painted with animals and birds, flying foxes, cuscus, the black king cockatoo, the hornbill, all representing the headhunter. Roasted sago worms—black and crisp larvae of capricorn beetles that had laid their eggs in holes in felled sago trees—were spiked on splits of bamboo. The worms, two or three inches long, matured in six or seven weeks and were eaten raw or were wrapped in leaves and carried back to the house to be roasted.

In the dimness of the *yeu,* it was easy to imagine the spirits of the dead everywhere, hovering in corners, in the roof, in the forest outside, within every object around. Each object was named for a recently dead ancestor and was a constant reminder of the need for the maker to seek revenge for the murder. No one here dies of natural causes; no malaria in itself brings pain, no cholera dehydrates, old age brings no waste, no stillbirth comes from internal defects; death and illness occur only through the ritual magic of enemies. The spirits in the carvings to be sold had already been appeased, their deaths avenged. I held up an *an* bowl filled with sago worms squirming like the shimmering human brains the bowl had often held.

In other villages, men crowded into the *yeu* day and night to look at me. In Baous, an old man was sitting on the floor, a teenager settled between his thighs, the boy leaning back against his chest. The man's hand moved across the boy's abdomen, then cupped his testicles and fondled them. I saw no more than this, but I knew of ritual *imu mu,* of old men being offered youngsters as wives until the boys married, a ritual that I had hoped would extend to me. I knew of bond friendships established by parents between their children, sometimes between adult men as well. The friends were playmates in youth, their rapport usually including the deepest sexual intimacy. It was a permanent relationship, terminated only by death. The men defended one another in all disputes and after marriage exchanged their wives for a night or two at times of unusual and supernatural events, deaths, storms, appearances of spirits, sickness, ceremonial cycles. For me, it seemed an ideal progression: masculine allegiance in youth, marriage with wife exchange in adulthood, and finally, in older age, an affair with a young boy for well-being.

I had long ago discarded my mosquito net to decrease the distance between myself and the others at night, but I made no intimate friends. I knew that my own man was living and breathing around me and I was consciously aware of his presence, though distance and separation continued. It was not only physical closeness that I wanted, not only recognition and communication of my desires, not only deeper knowledge and insights, but also emanations the men would quickly sense, silences they would understand, vacancies they could enter and make use of as they pleased. I moved from village to village, but I moved in space, not time; I moved from daylight to daylight, but I lived in time, not space. In the evenings, I watched swarms of bats flying across the river, though the river was different each night; in the nighttime, I was enveloped within identical groups of men, though I slept in different villages. I could choose a face to examine and describe, but the faces were one, and I did not know how to make the simple contact I craved. I sought to relax my body, to slacken my tensions, but my energies did not come to rest and my perceptions remained in another time. I strained to focus them into the present, into the space around me, wanting myself to be acceptable to everyone. But I was outside myself and was self-conscious. In the canoe, my tensions softened, and I allowed the landscape, the forest, the birds to enter me. But no man entered and I entered no man. I listened in quietude to the changing character of the life, while underlying all was the physical need that kept me in the suspense of never knowing whether contact would or could be made. I went on to Otsjenep, to Jow, and up the Betsj to Atsj, along dreamlike rivers, every turn bringing new colors and shapes.

Atsj, at the confluence of the Betsj and As rivers, with its huge population of over a thousand, was the residence of the assistant district officer, Simón. He was from Merauke, capital of southeastern Irian Jaya, and was the heaviest Papuan I'd seen. His face was bloated, and his small eyes were always closed. His kinky hair was cut short. He wore a khaki shirt, long trousers, and the only pair of shoes I'd seen outside Agats. His feet were too wide for them, and the laces could never be tied. He was soft and gentle and talked a lot about himself, never asking about my own background. He had been to Holland to study for the priesthood, but he'd had no vocation for it and was sent back home. He spoke Dutch and French as well as English.

I stayed at the house of the Dullahs, a Toradja family from central Celebes who were cutting ironwood and sending it once or twice a year to Merauke for shipment to Surabaya or directly to Japan. I slept with six workmen on a long platform with seven mattresses and seven mosquito nets. The platform almost filled the room, leaving barely space along one side to squeeze through. Above the mosquito nets, a bundle of crocodile penises hung from a beam, drying until ready to be put into containers and covered with alcohol. The first yield would be thrown away and fresh alcohol poured over them. The penises would dissolve and become a potent aphrodisiac. The Dullahs bottled and sold it to Chinese and Indonesians in other parts of the country, where powdered rhinoceros horn was also in demand for sexual stimulation.

The family took me in as soon as I landed with my paddlers. Husband and wife were light-skinned, handsome, and genial. They paid little attention to me, except to be certain I had enough food and enough water for my bath. They traded with the people of Atsj for crocodile skins, feathers, and food, and hired men to cut down the ironwood trees.

Simón, the assistant district officer, went with me to Amanamkai, the village well-known for its carvers, where Michael Rockefeller had spent time with the Dutch anthropologist. Amanamkai was up the As River, less than an hour from Atsj. Simón ordered his paddlers around in a quiet way that at first I thought was gentleness of manner but later decided was indifference and sluggishness of character. He showed no interest in anyone but me, and his interest in me was only to demonstrate his own importance and to parade his knowledge of languages. "He never pays his paddlers," Mr. Dullah had said. "And then he complains that no one wants to work for him." In Amanamkai, I had hoped to take advantage of having a translator, but we did not even walk around the village. Instead we sat on the veranda with the headman while Simón talked about himself.

"They thought I was a spy when I came back from Holland and didn't trust me. It was right after Independence and Sukarno was president, so everything Dutch was bad. It was not easy for me. I was trying to go to the university in Sukarnapura, as Jayapura was called then, but I had no money. They finally gave me permission and a scholarship and then, just because I marched in some demonstration about making the whole island of New Guinea into one nation, they put me in jail. I was in prison for a whole year. A year for being in a few demonstrations. What kind of government is that? It was a terrible time."

The headman could not understand Simón's English, but he smiled at me and nodded. He wore ragged shorts and a ragged shirt, slipped on in honor of the visitors. The hole in his septum drooped to his upper lip and the deep scars on his back welted up like the burns of fire. Simón picked at his dirty fingernails. He easily slipped the shoes off his feet, stretched, and arched his back. A man brought

chunks of sago, and Simón asked if I would buy them for the paddlers. More sago came and I bought each piece with tobacco.

"When I got out of prison, I went back to the university and graduated. But they all hate me. They hate me in Jayapura and they hate me in Merauke because I went to Holland and because I believe in a Papuan nation. Why else would they give me a job way out here? What is there for me to do? I am wasting my life. The people have nothing and there is nothing for me to do. There isn't even a cinema and I have no friends. My wife got tired of being here and went back to Merauke. Even the Father hardly ever visits me." When Simón had talked himself out, we left for Atsj.

In the canoe, the paddlers were suddenly jumping up and down and hooting, "Yuh! Yuh! Yuh!" They lifted their paddles and jabbed the air at two crocodiles sunning on logs that lay along the river bank. The men jabbed the air as if the paddles were spears, but the crocodiles did not move, as if aware there was no danger. I had not seen those crocodiles, just as I rarely saw anything in the forest until the men drew my attention to it. Someone would point to a turtle, a bird of paradise, a catfish skimming the surface of the water, and I would look and try to focus my eyes, but more often than not the creature would be gone before I could see it. There was more life than I would ever see, and there were depths beyond me. If I arrived at a place, if I stepped into a canoe, if I turned my back and waved, I said *"Der momo,"* the Asmat phrase of courtesy, hello, good-bye, thank you. When someone takes my hand to help me over a slippery log, I say, *"Der momo,"* and his face lights up. He answers, in the very same words, "I love you."

In the canoe, on the way back to Atsj, the paddlers again were jumping up and down. One began to chant. "Oh," said Simón, "a silly story. They had a friend who drowned. He fell in love with a girl who wouldn't have him. He stabbed himself and jumped into the river. They found his body between the roots of those mangrove trees, and they sing about him whenever they pass this spot."

The canoe stopped at a bank and the paddlers went into the forest. "They're just going to defecate," said Simón. "Defecation is done in secret, and everyone hides himself when he goes. Not like pissing over the side of the canoe." We were traveling on the As River. The Asmat word for defecate is *as;* we were therefore on the River of Shit.

In Atsj, Simón had the sago I had bought for the paddlers taken to his own house and ignored their payment. I gave them tobacco, then sat at the river's edge and watched the long lines of egrets flying over the river. At dusk, I sat on the boards of the walkway, facing downstream, where the double line of huts was becoming hazy as the smoke of stoked fires seeped through roofs to cloud the village and forest. In the black of the moonless night, the tree opposite me flickered in the light of fires from the house beside it. I watched the tree and saw that the light did not flicker so much as it pulsated. It glowed and stopped, and I looked more carefully. The light went on and off like the lights of a Christmas tree. I looked again and saw that the tiny flashing specks were fireflies! Synchronous fireflies that could turn on and off! All at the same time, a whole tree of them!

It did not take long to understand that the narrowest rivers and streams gave me more of the wild man than did my time in the villages with the men. The Bajir River brought reason and dream together when I traveled it. The birds appeared in flocks and pairs, in swarms and single flights that made my skin flush with anticipation. Birds of paradise flew high, barely recognizable; shrieking parrots banded red and purple flew up and settled back down; black and white ducks camouflaged themselves by their motionless presence in still trees; large gray and brown spoonbills flapped in the foliage or soared above us in pairs; in the evening, flying foxes glided through space on furry wings. I saw wild hens, white cockatoos, and even the rare black king cockatoo raising its spiked crest. Orange butterflies fluttered like blinking lights, and snakes slipped under the water and shimmered in refractions of sunlight. The canoe moved upriver through shadows and lights that changed each instant, paddled by bodies shining, sparkling, black. The men chanted of spirits that lived in the plankroots of mangrove, and of spirits that took the shape of crocodiles, fireflies, mice, rats, parrots, and opossums. The chant was carried on the tranquil air until it faded into the forest. A paddler balanced himself on the rim of the canoe, walking to the rear as if on solid ground. I looked up and realized that I could name birds and trees, not many, but enough to please me.

The canoe was moving through dark night when a spasm of chills shook me. The Great Spiral of Andromeda was high above, but I could touch it all, all the unseen, unknown galaxies; I could touch everything within my reach; the leaves, the water, the birds, the men. I could fall into the sky, into the angle of Vega, Deneb, and Altair, dropping through the great emptiness within me, dizzying myself with flight as air rushes by. I breathed in the millennia of primeval life. I was cold and shivering.

In Damen, the dancing is erotic, the movements the same as elsewhere, but there is a looseness of limbs, a sensuality. I wind myself up, I let myself go, I spin around and touch the men nearby. We walk into night with bundles of wooden strips as torches, and we dance around a fire. The shadow of the jungle is low and stark, no longer the vast depth of the daytime forest. There is no moon; the Milky Way crosses the sky like jostled sparks, the Southern Cross leans as if falling onto the horizon, and I search for Cassiopeia and the Pleiades, only to find the sky so full of bright stars that I cannot discern the ones I am looking for. I remember that I am in another hemisphere where constellations change. I stand by the fire absorbing the universe; it wells up inside me, not with tears or pride, but with the burst of orgasm, a frenzied paroxysm.

One morning I am in one of four crowded canoes. The men are decorated in spectacular fashion, bones or shells through their noses, faces painted, feathers in their hair. They chant and knock their paddles against the sides of the canoes. The weather deteriorates out at sea, and the wind comes up with rain. The canoes bounce and slap onto the waves. The shoreline disappears in haze. The canoe in which I sit lurches, and three men fly out. I see them floundering and waving their arms, and I think, Damn! There'll be another Michael Rockefeller incident when I too fly out! But the tide is low, and I see the men standing in mud, not splashing in deep water.

The weather remains poor, and we beach for the night at a bivouac, with the rain still falling steadily. It is cold, and we huddle close to the fires for warmth. The bivouac leaks, and water sizzles and splatters as it drops from the roof onto the fires. There is no sleep for anyone. We pile ourselves on top of one another, covering ourselves with pandanus mats. The tide comes in and the sea enters the hut. It is the time of the year's highest tide. No dry place exists inside. The wind crackles the leaves, lifting them off and carrying them away. The rain pours in.

In the morning, the air is still. The rain has stopped, but the waves are uncomfortably persistent. I trust my companions to know the sea and the canoes. At eight, they decide to leave. By the time we are out to sea, the rain has begun again. We shiver with cold. It is two hours before the rain stops and the sea calms. The sun comes out. It has been cold, but suddenly it is hot, the quick change from cold making the heat more intense. The men paddle slowly for hours, not bursting with song but silent with strain. I watch the perspiration dripping down their backs and along their thin thighs and calves. We all are parched.

At three in the afternoon, by my reckoning of the sun's position, we come upon a bank of mud, and the men chatter and chant again. They point to rolling mounds of mud rising from the sea like low hills from a plain. They beach the canoes, strip off the bits of clothing they wear, and jump headlong into the mud. They wave me in and I follow. Oh! delicious mud! Oh! cooling, sensuous mud! We roll around and rub our bodies with the viscous slime. We hoot and howl and swim in muck with luscious delight. We wallow in orgasmic pleasure, I in my own sense of moving deeper into my life.

Close by Agats, in the village of Sjuru, at the mouth of the Asewetsj River, I am in the *yeu*. A drum is beating and a group of men surround me. I am seated on the *gargar* floor made of palm leaves. Someone enters with branches of *fum*, the paper mulberry tree. He hands pieces to other men and sits down beside me. The men strip the bark and separate it into two layers, keeping the softer, cleaner fiber, and discarding the rest. They pull the fibers into threads. They are sitting with the foot of one leg on the thigh of the other. Within a few seconds, the fibers are rolled on the heel of the foot into cord. Holes are pushed through the cord with thorns and threads are forced through to create a tassel. Other men strip rattan and weave it into arm bands, to which the tassels are tied. Dotsjemen, headman of Sjuru, watches and supervises the work.

Two naked men come in and stand to my right. An old man, also naked, sits in front of me, our knees touching. The two standing men are rubbed with red ochre by other men, spreading the color over their entire bodies. Though it is barely noon, the light in the *yeu* is dim. The old man, whose name I never learn, sees clearly. He speaks, points, directs the decoration of the men. White paint is smeared over the red with fingers or small pieces of wood, making a circle around the face, circles around the nipples and knees, a circle around the navel. The men stand stiffly, as if bewitched, not moving even their eyes. The old man is chanting his instructions. A twig is taken up and a zigzag line is scratched through the still-wet white on the faces, leaving a thin red line. Feathers and furs are brought out from hidden places. Dotsjemen takes an arm band and ties to it an old sheaf of cockatoo and cassowary feathers. The feathers are held together by a knob of beeswax set with red seeds and tiny white cowries. The band is slipped over my left arm as he chants, "Sembét, Sembét, Sembét." An old bamboo bag, cascading with feathers, is hung around my neck so it covers my chest. In the background, I hear the men in a long drawn out, *"E-é-é-é-é-é-é-é."* A cuscus headband is put on my head, and sticks of white feathers are arranged within it. White streaks are painted on my face. The old man sings, "Sembét, Sembét, Sembét," and then he talks to me, looking into my eyes. He is looking into me, beyond me. He is looking at Sembét, dead father of Dotsjemen. It is *his* feathers and fur cap I am wearing; his breastplate is upon my chest to assure everyone of my full manhood. He is whispering to Sembét, the great warrior who has taken a hundred heads from Per, from Amanamkai, from Atsj, and from villages whose men and women he helped wipe out. His eyes move to a corner of the *yeu,* to the decorated men, who are dancing. His eyes move back to me. He is giving me Sembét, making me Sembét, and I am listening, for Sembét is talking, telling me, reminding me of our past, of our initiation, of how we hunted heads. Desoipitsj and his brother Biwiripitsj, our ancestors, have taught us our ways, and we have followed them.

Old Chief Warsekomen described it all to Father Zegwaard and Sembét told Dotsjemen. Desoipitsj said, "We need a head; take mine." Biwiripitsj refused at first and then agreed. He cut off the head of Desoipitsj and pinned it to the floor with his dagger of cassowary bone. The head of Desoipitsj spoke from the floor, telling Biwiripitsj to take up his body, cut it from anus to armpit, armpit to collarbone and neck; from neck to collarbone, armpit, and down to anus again. The chest came out; the legs and arms removed. The upper body was ready to eat; the lower part, mixed with sago and rolled into long sticks, would be eaten at ceremonial cycles.

Desoipitsj instructed further. Biwiripitsj roasted the head and put it in the rafters for the night. In the morning, he scalped it, cut off the nose skin, removed the jaws. With a shell, he cut from the root of the nose to the nape of the neck, then peeled back the skin. He held the skull over the fire, broke a hole in the temple, shook the mucus and brains out into an *an* bowl of sago leaves, and gave it to the old men, who dipped their hands into it and eagerly gobbled it up. He painted the skull with ash and ochre and covered it with netting and Job's-tear seeds and cassowary feathers.

"In this way," Sembét said inside me, "we learned to cut the flesh, the flesh of men and women and children. In this way we learned to cut the flesh of pig and crocodile. Now. Do you remember the great *bisj*, the poles of our ancestors, being carved here in the *yeu?* My father had gone out. My mother's brothers had gone out. They had gone to seek the mangrove tree. They uprooted the tree and cut it down with their stone axes. They trimmed it, leaving one root erect, a penis like my penis, your penis. They tied it up with strips of sago leaf and it floated down the river and they blew their bamboo horns. All the women were waiting. They shot their arrows at the tree and screamed and danced as if it were a captured enemy. The carvers worked then. They worked on the penis, big and hard, carving it with tails of cuscus, tusks of pigs, hornbills, heads of enemies."

The voice stopped and I was unaware of my own existence. I was the chant itself, its very vision. If I looked around, I saw painted men dancing; if I looked at myself, I saw my body painted, too. The old man was going on, Sembét was going on, "The penis, all carved, burst out, and the men sought vengeance for our dead. Into the forest they ran, into the village of Amborep they ran. Early, early in the darkness it was, the men of Amborep asleep. My father and my mother's brothers took a man, Sembét was his name, and put him into the canoe. Other men took men and put them into their canoes. One only was in my father's canoe. He was tied there, and when the canoe came to the whirlpool, they cut off his head and blew their horns. They were blowing their horns when they came here, and the women shot their arrows and screamed and danced. Many canoes came, and the *bisj* were standing in front of the *yeu,* as high as the *yeu* they were, and the blood from the heads was thrown over them, the blood of our head, the head of Sembét, flowing over our ancestors, Sawari, Jaka-pir, Jimit, Jitatim, Dayoh.

"We were inside the *yeu,* here in Sjuru, and my mother's brothers decorated me. They covered me with burnt earth, painted me with strips of lime and soot. They put an *otsj* through my nose and a triton shell around my belly. They put the bamboo breastplate on my chest. I was becoming a man, and the head my father had taken was put between my legs, into my groin, against my penis. The head would make my penis grow quickly, would fill me with manhood. My name became Sembét, the name of him whose head lay in my groin. I was smeared with his blood and with the ash of his burnt hair. The head was in my groin, and I sat there in shame, staring at the skull for two days, unable to move, eating only in secret, letting the head send into me, through my penis, all the power it contained. I went into the canoe with my relatives, with my mother's brothers, and I stood there with the head resting at my feet. Like an old man, I was leaning on a stick. Like an old man, I got weak. Like an old man, I got weaker, and I collapsed and fell to the bottom of the canoe. I got old and I died. They lifted me up, my mother's brothers, they put me into the sea, my mother's brothers, and when they took me out, I was an infant, a curled-up new-born babe, unable to stand or walk. I crawled on the floor of the canoe, and I could not reach a paddle. Slowly, I was able to stand. Slowly, I was able to talk and see things that I could name. I spoke the names of all the rivers and all the streams. I named all the birds of the forest and all the trees. I came back to the *yeu* and I was a man. In one day, I became old and died and was born again and grew to be a man. In one day it was.

"The canoe took me toward the setting sun and death. It took me toward Safan, where the spirits dwell, beyond the sea. I went into the sea and I came out of the sea. The canoe turned and went to where the sun would be born and I too was born. I was growing and I was grown. I had grown to my manhood. In this way were we men."

Sembét was telling me this, reminding me of my rebirth. He was telling me that I had come to my own manhood. With his breastplate on my chest, I have come to be a man; with his name replacing mine, I have taken on his duties, and he need no longer return to the land of the living. He will go on to Safan. I have his powers now, his masculinity, his strength. I too can take a hundred heads, for I have gone through my rite of passage.

The old man in the *yeu* is still in his trance, though my mind is clear and refreshed. Was it he who entered me or was it Sembét? Where is he now, in his rapture, the old man? The sun had been shining, but now it is black night outside. Hours, hours, have passed through unknowable time. Did I eat the stinging nettle leaves? Did I taste the ginger root? If I dreamed, if I visioned, it is gone, and I am aware only of my rebirth, that I have come to life again, that I am Sembét. And I have entered the wild man as he entered me.

LIVING OUT
Gay and Lesbian Autobiographies

Joan Larkin and David Bergman
GENERAL EDITORS

The Other Mother: A Lesbian's Fight for Her Daughter
Nancy Abrams

An Underground Life: Memoirs of a Gay Jew in Nazi Berlin
Gad Beck

Surviving Madness: A Therapist's Own Story
Betty Berzon

You're Not from Around Here, Are You? A Lesbian in Small-Town America
Louise A. Blum

Just Married: Gay Marriage and the Expansion of Civil Rights
Kevin Bourassa and Joe Varnell

Two Novels: Development *and* Two Selves
Bryher

The Hurry-Up Song: A Memoir of Losing My Brother
Clifford Chase

In My Father's Arms: A True Story of Incest
Walter A. de Milly III

Midlife Queer: Autobiography of a Decade, 1971–1981
Martin Duberman

Body, Remember: A Memoir
Kenny Fries

Widescreen Dreams: Growing Up Gay at the Movies
Patrick E. Horrigan